Jane Austen, Feminism and Fiction

First published in Great Britain in 1983 by
THE HARVESTER PRESS LIMITED
Publisher: John Spiers
16 Ship Street, Brighton, Sussex
and in the USA by
BARNES & NOBLE BOOKS
81 Adams Drive, Totowa, New Jersey 07512

British Library Cataloguing in Publication Data

Kirkham, Margaret
   Jane Austen, feminism and fiction.
   1. Austen, Jane   2. Feminism in literature
   I. Title
   823'.7   PR4038.F/

   ISBN 0-7108-0468-7

Library of Congress Catgaloging in Publication Data

Kirkham, Margaret.
   Jane Austen, feminism and fiction.

   1. Austen, Jane, 1775–1817 – Political and social
views.   2. Feminism and literature.   3. Women in
literature.   I. Title.
PR4038.F44K57   1983   823'.7   82-13937
ISBN 0-389-20336-X

Photoset in 10/11½pt Linotron Bembo by
Rowland Phototypesetting Ltd
Bury St Edmunds, Suffolk
Printed in Great Britain by
The Thetford Press Ltd, Thetford, Norfolk

Jane Austen, Feminism and Fiction

Margaret Kirkham
Senior Lecturer, Bristol Polytechnic

THE HARVESTER PRESS · SUSSEX

BARNES & NOBLE BOOKS · NEW JERSEY

To Robert

Contents

Part Four: Feminist Criticism of Society and Literature in the Later Novels

Acknowledgements

The portrait of Jane Austen by her sister Cassandra Austen which features on the frontispiece of this book appears by kind permission of the National Portrait Gallery, London.

I am grateful to *Women and Literature* for permission to make use of two articles of mine 'The Austen Portraits and the Received Biography' and 'Feminist Irony and the Priceless Heroine of *Mansfield Park*' which are to appear in the 1982 Jane Austen issue. I am grateful to the Research Committee of Bristol Polytechnic for assistance during the final stages of writing this book and to Mrs Anne Merriman for typing it. I owe thanks to Dr Anne Smith for her interest and advice and to friends, including my daughter and sons, who have listened, argued and made fun. To Alice and Ronald Gaskell, Magdalen Goffin and Peggy Mowat, who read early drafts and discussed them with me, I am especially grateful. To Robert Kirkham I am indebted for encouragement, useful puzzlement and patient interest over a long period. Lastly I must thank Helen Taylor, without whose kind and persistent encouragement and criticism, this book would never have taken shape.

C.M.K.
Bristol,
August 1982

Introduction

'a lady has the skill to strike out a New Path . . .'[1]

Jane Austen is the first major woman novelist in English. Credited with having made important advances in narrative technique and with demonstrating an acute intelligence about morals, she has been thought to present a difficult critical problem on account of the slightness of her subject-matter and her restricted attitude towards it. In this study I have tried to show that what Ian Watt called 'the enduring problem of Jane Austen criticism: scale versus stature; the slightness of the matter and the authority of the manner'[2] can be resolved if we change our historical perspective on the Austen novels and consider them in the context of eighteenth-century feminist ideas and of the Feminist Controversy of the turn of the eighteenth century. Given such a perspective, we can see that Austen's subject-matter is the central subject-matter of rational, or Enlightenment, feminism and that her viewpoint on the moral nature and status of women, female education, marriage, authority and the family, and the representation of women in literature is strikingly similar to that shown by Mary Wollstonecraft in *A Vindication of the Rights of Woman*. How important or valid the ideas of eighteenth-century English feminists were must remain a separate issue, but at least we can be rid of the assumption that Jane Austen's moral interest is of a purely personal nature, unconnected with any general changes in the awareness of her time.

The received images of Wollstonecraft and Austen are so different that it may still seem far-fetched to suggest that they were both feminist moralists of the same school. It is certainly true that the different contexts in which their work has been discussed has tended to hide the important ways in which they thought alike, and all but obliterate the common line of feminist concern and interest, stretching back to Mary Astell at the very end of the seventeenth century, in which their ideas were founded.

From the publication of *Pamela* onwards, fiction itself played a major part in drawing the attention of the public to the 'Woman Question', *Sir Charles Grandison* having a place of particular importance in relation to it. For this reason Part One examines both the development of feminist ideas outside fiction and the beginnings of Feminist/anti-feminist Controversy in the mid-eighteenth century disagreement about Richardson and Fielding. Jane Austen had the good fortune to be born at a time when the moral interest 'compelled upon her by life', as F. R. Leavis put it, was also the concern of other enlightened women and when it had begun to make an impact on the new kind of literature. Further, she was fortunate in coming of age as a novelist at a time when women had already established themselves as reputable authors. Part One therefore also deals with the importance of female authorship as, in itself, challenging accepted beliefs about the exclusion of women from all forms of public life. It ends with a discussion of the Wollstonecraft Scandal of 1798 and its effects upon the development of feminism in fiction and outside it.

Part Two is about the publication and early reception of the Austen novels in the light of the contemporary Feminist Controversy, and the effects of Scott's emergence as the major male novelist of English Romanticism upon the feminist tradition of fiction in general, and Jane Austen in particular.

Part Three is concerned with Jane Austen's ironic use of literary and theatrical allusion, especially in her two late novels, *Mansfield Park* and *Emma*. In it a theory about allusive irony in the later work, as revealing an underlying continuity of feminist moral concern, stretching from *Sense and Sensibility* to *Sanditon*, and becoming more clearly associated with Mary Wollstonecraft's criticism of the anti-feminist streak in Romanticism, is put forward. In particular, I have tried to show that Austen's criticism of Kotzebue in *Mansfield Park* is a feminist, rather than an anti-Jacobin criticism; and that critical allusion to Kotzebue also plays an important part in the ironic structure of *Emma*.

Through treating the Feminist Controversy of her time as the most important historical context of the Austen novels, I come to very different conclusions about their political import from those reached by Dr Marilyn Butler in *Jane Austen and the War of Ideas*. She regards Austen's stance as a moralist, in the eighteenth-century sense of the word, as indicative of strongly conservative, if not downright reactionary political commitment. I regard it as indicative of her sympathy with the rational feminism of the Enlightenment. The disagreement turns on how one sees Jane Austen's insistence upon Reason as the supreme guide to conduct, from which follow her criticism of Romanticism and her belief that sexual passion ought to be subjected to rational restraint. Dr Butler argues that, in Jane

Austen's time, the central question for the novelist was, 'What was the moral nature of the individual and what was *his* role in society?'[3] (my italics). So far as Austen goes *his* is misleading, for her central moral interest is in the moral nature of woman and *her* role in society. This makes a great deal of difference to the way in which her stance as rational moralist should be seen. As Dr Butler herself notes:

In sexual matters the jacobins thought and as a group behaved (whatever their opponents claimed) like forerunners of the Evangelicals. Their advocacy of reason and restraint often makes them read like their opponents, the conservative moralists.[4]

If this is true, Jane Austen's tendency to argue like 'the conservative moralists' about sexual conduct cannot be taken as a mark of her anti-Jacobinism. Rather, it suggests that she was in agreement with the rational feminist point of view, which was shared to some extent by women of widely different backgrounds, who disagreed on other matters. Because Mary Wollstonecraft and Mary Hays were among the English Jacobins, we tend to think of feminism as restricted to that group, but this is misleading; the feminist interest cut across other political divisions to a considerable extent. If the moral and (by implication) political question which concerned Jane Austen most was the feminist one, her stance as rational moralist does not carry the reactionary implications which it might otherwise appear to do. And, I should argue, the novels themselves tell us that this was so. Take, for example, the title-page of the first novel to be published.

If we know nothing of contemporary controversy about feminism, nor about the attacks made upon women authors who failed to make a show of modesty in presenting their work to the public, we may see this title-page as innocuous; but is it? The Sense/Sensibility question was the crucial one for the 'female philosophers' of the eighteenth century since, like other 'moralists', they thought Sense, or Reason, a better guide to moral principles than Sensibility, or Feeling, and wished to show that women were no less capable of rational judgement than men. In so far as Rousseau, through *Emile*, was associated with a different point of view, he was the *bête noir* of English Enlightenment feminism.[5] In so far as poets and novelists of Romantic tendency followed him in making Man rational and Woman emotional, the enlightened women were anti-Romantic. What does the title-page of *Sense and Sensibility* tell us in this context?

As Gilbert Ryle noted, the title of Austen's first novel to appear in public declares an interest in a general philosophical question and, as he says,

SENSE

AND

SENSIBILITY:

A NOVEL.

IN THREE VOLUMES.

BY A LADY.

VOL. I.

London:

PRINTED FOR THE AUTHOR,

By C. Roworth, Bell-yard, Temple-bar,

AND PUBLISHED BY T. EGERTON, WHITEHALL.

1811.

Sense and Sensibility really is about the relations between Sense and Sensibility or, as we might put it, between Head and Heart, Thought and Feeling, Judgement and Emotion, or Sensibleness and Sensitiveness.[6]

But the author's 'deep interest in some perfectly general, even theoretical questions about human nature and human conduct' has a specific context. The work is 'A Novel', that is, it belongs within the still (comparatively) 'new species of writing' in which the Head/Heart question was also the Man/Woman question. And it is 'By A Lady'. The author wishes her sex to be known, and is not inhibited by the many pejorative references in contemporary reviews to 'lady novelists'. It has sometimes been thought that, in using this phrase, Austen wished to stress her gentility, but perhaps she wished to state her sex, in the expectation that her point of view on the Head/Heart question would be understood as a female one. Had she adopted, as was sometimes done, a pseudonym – 'Sophia', or 'Eugenia', or something of that sort – female authorship would not have been so plainly asserted, for men, especially in satirical works, often adopted female pseudonyms. 'By A Lady' was the best means of declaring a female viewpoint. 'Woman' could not be used, since it would, in the usage of the time, have sounded odd and perhaps scurrilous by association with such expressions as 'a woman of pleasure', the ascription used by Cleland for *Fanny Hill*. It should be noted that the word 'author' not 'authoress' occurs at the bottom of the page, and that later works appeared as 'By the Author of . . .' (works already published). This title-page not only tells us to take note of female authorship, but also reveals that the author has had to publish at her own expense, no publisher willing to risk his money on it having been found.

Sense and Sensibility is about the need for women to have strong heads as well as good hearts, and it opens with the dispossession of a widow and her daughters, following the death of Mr Dashwood. The title-page implies that the author has a specific interest in the Head/Heart question and this is borne out by the stories of Elinor and Marianne which are unfolded.

Gina Luria dates the Feminist Controversy as at its height from 1788 to 1810.[7] *Sense and Sensibility* appeared just outside these limits, but there is no doubt that Austen's mind was formed earlier. She grew up in the 1790s and made her first, unsuccessful, attempt at publication within a few months of Mary Wollstonecraft's death, when Godwin's *Memoirs of the Author of A Vindication of the Rights of Woman* was about to ensure that feminist ideas, however moderately put, were liable to provoke violent hostility and abusive personal attack. Polwhele, in the prefatory remarks to his satire on women authors, *The UnSex'd Females* (1798), thought it a sign of the corruption of the age that works by women should be judged 'on their merits, with the same impartiality as it seems right to exercise towards men'. He sees 'the sparkle of confident intelligence'[8] in women authors as, *in itself*, a sign of 'that independence of spirit' which, as Sir Thomas Bertram says, is, especially in young women, 'offensive and disgusting beyond all common offence' (*Mansfield Park*, p. 318).

Such an attitude, whether it be found in Polwhele or the patriarch of Mansfield Park, strikes most modern readers as absurd, but we have not recognised that it also struck the best novelist of the age, who 'happened' to be a woman, as ludicrous. We know, on the evidence of the works published in Austen's lifetime, that she had an incorrigible habit of laughing at pomposity of all kinds, but we have not quite seen the feminist viewpoint which directs much of her satire. We laugh at Mr Collins as an asinine clergyman who is to inherit the Longbourn estate because Mr Bennet lacks a proper (male) heir, but do not see that, by inventing such a fiction, Austen mocks sexist pride and prejudice as it is enshrined in legal customs. We notice, in a learned footnote, that Mr Collins admires Dr Fordyce, whose *Sermons to Young Women* were lampooned by Wollstonecraft,[9] but do not connect Austen, as *feminist* moralist, with the 'hyena in petticoats', whose position, *vis à vis* Fordyce, she plainly endorses. We see that Austen was an anti-Romantic, in an age which, so far as literature is concerned, we characterise as 'Romantic', and do not ask why Austen follows Wollstonecraft in pointed hostility to the new impulse. We see that Sir Thomas Bertram is wrong about nearly everything, whereas Fanny Price is right about nearly everything, yet do not connect Austen's affirmation of Fanny's rationality with her feminist purposes in her most ambitious and, as Lionel Trilling saw, most offensive novel.[10] We see that, as Trilling also said, Emma Woodhouse 'has a moral life as a man has a moral life',[11] but that does not lead us to question accounts of *Emma* in which Mr Knightley is held to be a wholly 'reliable' narrator and in which the heroine's progress towards self-knowledge is seen as entirely under his guardianship, rather than dependent upon her own evaluation of personal experience as she grows up. We see that Anne Elliot is both more sensible and more sensitive than anyone else in *Persuasion*, but do not connect her superiority of mind with contemporary argument about the moral nature and capacity of the two sexes.

If we miss Austen's engagement with fiction and morals as a distinctively feminist engagement, we find it difficult to give a coherent account of the development of her art. In particular, her achievement in the development of the 'indirect free style' through which she was increasingly able to show the rational mental powers of her individual heroines, may seem disconnected from her central moral purpose. This study sets out to relate Austen as literary artist and innovator to her declared position as feminist moralist and critic of fictional tradition; to relate 'the sparkle of confident intelligence', which no one can miss in her work, to the feminist insistence, in her day, upon women as 'rational creatures', and to their artistic competence in the new literary form, which was both a new art and a new form of moral discourse.

I Feminism and Fiction: 1694–1798

1 Introduction

English fiction in the eighteenth century achieved, among other things, an enlargement of the scope of moral discourse, allowing new topics to be considered in new ways, encouraging authors who would not have entered into such discourse otherwise and reaching an extended audience. Among the new topics, the moral nature and status of women was one of the most important. Among the new authors were women. Among the new readers women were numerous and influential, both as purchasers of books and as subscribers to circulating libraries. In these circumstances it is not surprising that the first major woman novelist to make her mark on English literature in a powerful way was a moralist, acutely interested in moral discourse as it affected the status of women in society and bore on their representation in literature. Jane Austen became a publishing novelist in 1811, but her novels are the culmination of a line of development in thought and fiction which goes back to the start of the eighteenth century, and which deserves to be called *feminist* since it was concerned with establishing the moral equality of men and women and the proper status of individual women as accountable beings.

The terms feminism and feminist are modern, not being recorded in any of their present-day meanings until the late nineteenth century,[1] yet we apply them retrospectively to Mary Wollstonecraft and her writings, and it is becoming common for literary critics to notice feminist elements in the Austen novels. What I shall attempt here is to show how Wollstonecraft and Austen drew on the ideas of feminist moralists going back to Mary Astell, how the Richardson/Fielding dispute was connected with feminism and fear of female emancipation, how the advent of women as authors of fictional works encouraged further both feminism and fear of it, and finally how Mary Wollstonecraft's writings and the scandal which followed her death affected the Feminist Controversy at the turn of the eighteenth century.

Contrary to widespread belief, eighteenth-century feminism did

not begin with Mary Wollstonecraft, nor was it, in general, specifi
cally concerned with the political equality of women, though it is
true that, from the start, it carried political implications, first
brought out into the open by Catherine Macaulay and Wollstonecraft in the early 1790s. The feminist impulse showed itself first
in objection to the assignment of women to an inferior status as
spiritual and moral beings. The first well-articulated female claim to
equality was not directed towards enfranchisement via the ballot-
box, but to delivery from the restrictions which it had pleased male
theologians, moral philosophers and poets (rather than Providence)
to impose upon them. The essential claim of Enlightenment feminism was that women, *not* having been denied powers of reason, must
have the moral status appropriate to 'rational beings', formed in the
image of a rational God. Perhaps this claim was always tempered
with a streak of irony, for feminist moralists, even in the Age of
Reason and Enlightenment, were generally rather more aware of the
irrationality of human nature and human society than men. Poking
fun at such reverend godlings as Mr Sprint, Dr Fordyce and Mr
Collins was one important way in which women made this awareness felt. Yet they were in general confident that an improvement in
the status of women would be brought about through increasing
their powers of rational understanding and reflection. The demand
for an adequate education, the main practical concern of Enlightenment feminism, arose directly from this. The claim that women of
the middle and upper classes should be taught to think may not now
seem particularly revolutionary, but, as those who opposed it rightly
saw, it opened the possibility of social change far beyond the
schoolroom of the country house, and the drawing-rooms of the
well-to-do. If it were true that natural endowment with powers of
mind in women constituted a proper claim to the right to think and
to judge, what was to be said of the basis of authority in marriage and
the family? In an age that made Reason a God, and turned God into
The Rational Being, it was widely accepted that authority rested on
rational judgement. The feminist demand for a rigorous intellectual
education for women could not but carry a threat to the patriarchal
basis of authority in the most fundamental of human institutions, the
family. It took no great wit to see that eventually it must undermine
the patriarchal basis of authority in the government of Church and
State as well. Moreover, the arguments used by the feminists could
be seen to have a much wider implication so far as class relations were
concerned. Women had, in orthodox moral discourse, been commonly consigned to a special consideration with slaves, the unlet-

tered and lunatics. The Enlightenment feminists were what Virginia Woolf called 'the daughters of gentlemen' but, even though they might restrict their claims to women of the middle class, it did not escape their opponents that the arguments they used had equal validity for the labouring classes in England, and for the unhappy Africans enslaved in America whose plight, by the end of the century, had smitten the conscience of almost everyone who had a conscience.

Enlightenment feminism, with its emphasis on Reason and its preoccupation with the middle class, may not strike contemporary feminists as having much to do with liberation, but this is mistaken. The most orthodox beliefs, when applied to a class of persons previously excluded from serious moral and political discourse, may take on a new aspect.

2 Mary Astell to Catherine Macaulay: Women, Morals and Education

Mary Astell (1688–1731) published her first feminist treatise in 1694. It was called *A Serious Proposal to the Ladies for the Advancement of their True and Greatest Interest*³ and in it women were adjured, much as Wollstonecraft was later to adjure them, to reject an inferior role of passive obedience and to claim, by demonstrating their moral equality, that they must be allowed and expected, like men, to form opinions on the basis of rational reflection and to make independent moral judgements. Astell was a High Church Anglican who grounded her argument in religious principle, claiming that 'a truly Christian life requires a clear understanding as well as regular affections', and that, if women are to be fit for the life to come, they must aim at a beauty 'which Nature with all the help of Art cannot secure', being placed 'out of the reach of Sickness and Old Age', by transference from 'a corruptible Body to an immortal Mind'. Mary Wollstonecraft says it is her purpose to make her sex 'more respectable'; Astell says she would not allow women any longer 'to be cheap and contemptible'. 'How can you be content to be in the World like Tulips in a Garden, to make a fine *shew* and be good for nothing?'

In the *Serious Proposal* Astell advocates the setting up of a monastic college for women in which they may receive a serious education. In 1706 she wrote *Reflections on Marriage*, setting out an ideal of Christian marriage in which women are to have the status of rational beings, with immortal souls as well as domestic duties to attend to. In 1715 she wrote *The Christian Religion as Profess'd by a True Daughter of the Church of England*. In it many of the same questions are discussed, but Astell also shows herself a strong critic of male-domination in art, history and literature. She has a good passage on what we should now speak of as the promotion of exceptional women to the status of 'honorary men':

some Men say that Heraldry is a pretty Study for a Woman, for this reason, I suppose, That she may know how to Blazon her Lord and Master's great Achievements! They allow us Poetry, Plays, and Romances, to Divert us and themselves; and when they would express a particular Esteem for a

Woman's Sense, they recommend History; tho' with Submission, History can only serve us for Amusement and a Subject of Discourse. It cannot help our Conduct or excite in us a generous Emulation . . . the Men being the Historians, they seldom condescend to record the great and good Actions of Women; and when they take notice of them, 'tis with this wise Remark, That such Women *acted above their Sex.* By which one must suppose they would have their Readers understand, That they were not Women who did those Great Actions, but that they were Men in Petticoats. (*The Christian Religion*, 1715, pp. 292–3)

Mary Astell was a keen admirer of Lady Mary Wortley Montagu and, in the Preface which she wrote in 1724 to *The Travels of an English Lady in Europe, Asia and Affrica*, she shows herself engaged with the same questions as those which have occupied feminist criticism in our day. She prefaces her address to the reader with the following sisterly lines:

> Let the *Male-Authors* with an envious eye
> Praise coldly, that they may the more decry:
> *Women* (at least I speak the Sense of some)
> This little Spirit of Rivalship o'ercome.
> I read with transport, and with Joy I greet
> A Genius so Sublime and so Complete,
> And gladly lay my Laurels at her Feet.

She claims that the work she praises has an originality not to be found in the writings of men, 'the World . . . is surfeited with Male Travels, all in the same Tone and stuft with the same Trifles, a *Lady* has the skill to strike out a New Path and to embellish a worn-out Subject with variety of fresh and elegant Entertainment.'

Astell is of great importance to the history of eighteenth-century feminism for a variety of reasons. First, she outlined what were to remain the central questions for more than a century; secondly, she was a dedicated High Churchwoman, against whose personal character nothing worse could be said than that she wrote *Reflections on Marriage* after a disappointment in love – a suggestion Doris Stenton dismisses as unfounded. Thirdly, in her friendships with other women and her respect for their work, she helped to create a climate of opinion in which women gave increased support and encouragement to one another. Astell corresponded with Damaris Masham (1658–1705), the daughter of Ralph Cudworth and the friend of Locke, and she encouraged Elizabeth Elbstob, the much respected Anglo-Saxon scholar. Elizabeth Elstob became the friend of some of the literary ladies of Richardson's and Johnson's circle, Mrs Chapone and Mrs Delaney among them. It was Elizabeth Elstob who gave

George Ballard an account of Mary Astell's life and work, for his *Memoirs of several Ladies of Great Britain who have been celebrated for their writings, or skill in the learned languages or art and sciences* (Oxford, 1752). Thus Astell's influence continued into the mid-century, and perhaps beyond. It will be remembered that it was Mrs Delaney who became the friend and encourager of Fanny Burney.

Mary Astell was the most outspoken feminist of her time, and the one who did most to develop a feminist point of view about religious and moral questions, education, marriage and the value of women as authors. She was not, however, alone in her advocacy of greater respect for the intellectual abilities of women. Catherine Cockburn (1679–1749), who wrote in defence of Locke's *Essay of Human Understanding*, replied thus to a friend who doubted whether Damaris Masham could have written a work attributed to her:

It is not to be doubted that women are as capable of penetrating into the grounds of things, and reasoning justly, as men are, who certainly have no advantage of us, but in their opportunities of knowledge. And as Lady Masham is allowed by everybody to have great natural endowments, she has taken pains to improve them; and no doubt profited much by a long intimate society with so extraordinary a man as Mr. Locke. So I see no reason to suspect a woman of her character would pretend to write anything that was not entirely her own. I pray be more equitable to her sex than the generality of yours are; who, when anything is written by a woman, that they cannot deny their approbation to, are sure to rob us of the glory of it, by concluding 'tis not her own; or, at least, that she has some assistance, which has been said in many instances to my knowledge unjustly.

This letter appears in Thomas Birch's *Works of Mrs. Catherine Cockburn, with an account of the life of the author* (published in 1751), for which there was a long subscription list, including an unusually high proportion of women.[4]

Lady Mary Chudleigh (1656–1710) was provoked into feminist authorship by the Rev. John Sprint who, in 1700, published a wedding sermon on the text 'But she that is married careth for the things of this world, how she may please her husband'. In doing so, he touched on a sensitive nerve of emergent feminist awareness, for he implied that, if women had souls, these were not such as required the same preparation for eternity as those of men – not at any rate if they married. Chudleigh, under the pseudonym 'Eugenia', wrote first a tract, *The Female Advocate; or A plea for the just Liberty of the Tender Sex, and particularly of Married Women. Being Reflections on a late Rude and Disingenuous Discourse delivered by Mr. John Sprint*, which she dedicated to Lady Mary Wortley Montagu, and then a poetical dialogue, *The Ladies' Defence*. They appeared in 1700. In

both, Chudleigh attacks the belief that women are to make gods of
their husbands and questions the assumption that they are to assume
an inferior moral and spiritual status to men. Satirising Sprint, she
writes:

> Like Mutes she Signs alone must make,
> And never any Freedom take:
> But still be govern'd by a Nod,
> And fear her Husband as her God:
> Him still must serve, Him still obey,
> And nothing act and nothing say,
> But what her haughty Lord thinks fit,
> Who with the Pow'r has all the Wit.
> Then shun, oh! shun that wretched State,
> And all the fawning Flatt'rers hate:
> Value yourselves, and Men despise,
> You must be proud, if you'll be wise.

Ninety years before *Vindication*, Chudleigh makes an objection to
the practice of homilists and self-appointed advisers to the fair sex in
assigning to women the moral status of slaves or children. Her work
continued to be known and the extract quoted here was anthologised
as late as 1848 by Frederic Rowton in his *Female Poets of Great Britain*.

The intellectual women of the mid-eighteenth century were neither as racy in their language nor as clear in their criticism of male
prejudice as Mary Astell and Lady Chudleigh but, by acquiring a
reputation for learning, and becoming accepted as the associates of
men who valued them for their conversation, such women as
Elizabeth Carter, Catherine Talbot and the ladies of the 'blue-
stocking' salons made an implied claim to intellectual equality. Miss
(or Mrs) Carter[5] and Miss Talbot both came of clerical families, and
Catherine Talbot, whose grandfather had been Bishop of Durham,
introduced Elizabeth Carter to Bishop Butler, whose beliefs about
morals, and the way in which they are learnt, exerted a strong
influence on feminist thinking, and to Thomas Secker, who became
Archbishop of Canterbury. Secker made the widowed Mrs Talbot a
member of his household, and supervised Catherine's education.
Their names appear as subscribers to the works of Catherine Cockburn, and they were keen readers of Lady Mary Wortley Montagu's
letters. It was Catherine Talbot who urged Elizabeth Carter to
undertake the translation of Epictetus that made her famous, and it is
amusing, as well as indicative of continuing feminist concern with
the authority of the Scriptures about the status of women, to find
that Mrs Carter argued with Secker about the accepted translation of
St Paul, saying that, for the evident purpose of supporting the

superiority of the husband, English scholars had translated the same verb in different ways: *put away* as applied the husband, and as applied to the wife *leave*: 'Let him not put her away' and 'Let her not leave him'. (1 Corinthians VII, 12 and 13.) They had to go to the Archbishop's study and look up the passage before Secker acknowledged, 'No, Madam Carter, 'tis I that must be confuted, and you are in the right.'[6]

According to the nephew who wrote her biography, Elizabeth Carter 'detested the principles displayed in Mrs Wollstonecraft's wild theory concerning the "Rights of Women"', but his *Memoir* was published in 1807 when, as will be seen later, it was almost obligatory, in writing of a respected woman author of any pretension to learning, to assure readers that she had no sympathy for Mary Wollstonecraft. The admission that she made no effort to cultivate the society of men of letters because she had 'an extreme partiality for writers of her own sex', and that 'she was much inclined to believe that women had not their proper station in society, and that their mental powers were not rated sufficiently high',[7] shows that Mrs Carter was far from unsympathetic to the central tenets of Enlightenment feminism. Mrs Carter and Miss Talbot both made some interesting criticisms of Richardson and Fielding, discussed below.[8]

Mary Wollstonecraft's entry into the public world of authorship came about through her interest in female education. She had, with her sisters Eliza and Everina, and her friend Fanny Blood, set up a school for girls in Newington Green, at that time, under the influence of Richard Price, a centre of intellectual Dissent. By 1786 this school had failed financially, but Wollstonecraft had not only learnt a good deal about the education of girls and the moral questions which such education raised, but she had also become acquainted with some influential Dissenters and one of their most important publishers, Joseph Johnson, of whom Claire Tomalin speaks as 'the most important man' in Wollstonecraft's life.[9] Johnson published Wollstonecraft's *Thoughts on the Education of Daughters: with Reflections on Female Conduct, in the More Important Duties of Life* in 1786. It has a good deal in common with Hannah More's 1799 *Strictures of the Modern System of Female Education*, for in both are apparent a strong concern with religion and morals, and a wish to foster high moral principles and conduct in female Christians, which might be seen as characteristic of the Evangelicals.

Hannah More, through the eminence she enjoyed as a literary woman, as well as a philanthropist and a friend of Wilberforce, helped to make respectable the idea of a public role for women, even though she dissociated herself from any feminist intention. As Ray Strachey says:

It may seem strange to maintain that Miss Hannah More and Mrs. Trimmer and the other good ladies who started the Sunday School and cottage-visiting fashions were the founders of a movement which would have shocked them so profoundly; but it is clearly true.[10]

Hannah More's slighting reference to Wollstonecraft in a letter to Horace Walpole is well known, but there is reason to think that she did read *Vindication* later on, and that it influenced her own work on female education.[11] Hannah More was acquainted with Catherine Macaulay (1731–91), through whom the line of direct, polemical feminist commitment is rediscovered in the late years of the eighteenth century.

Catherine Macaulay was an historian who made such a respected reputation for herself as to inspire the Rector of St Stephen's Walbrook, Bath, to organise a birthday party for her, in 1777, at which six odes in her praise were read aloud, the day being 'ushered in by the ringing of bells and other public demonstrations of joy'.[12] Thus did she benefit from the respect which some members of the Established Church were then prepared to pay to learned ladies. But Macaulay later offended public opinion in two ways: she made a second marriage with a man very much younger than herself, and she wrote a controversial, feminist work – *Letters on Education: with observations on religious and metaphysical subjects* (1790). Her feminist point of view had a great deal in common with that of Mary Astell but whereas Astell remained 'a true daughter of the Church of England', and did not write in days when the French Revolution had made every expression of radical opinion dangerous, Macaulay did. She knew Burke, and in his period of sympathy with the American colonists she was among his friends but, like Wollstonecraft, she objected to his *Reflections on the French Revolution*. Macaulay, in the first volume of her *History of England*, declared that 'Whosoever attempts to remove the limitations necessary to render monarchy consistent with liberty . . . are rebels in the worst sense; rebels to the laws of their country, the law of reason, and the law of God.'[13] Applying the same principles to domestic government, and making observations on 'religious and metaphysical subjects' to support her argument, Macaulay brought out into the open the connection between the belief that women had no serious duties (other than first to captivate and then to please and obey their husbands) and their exclusion from political rights. Both were founded, in her view, on false assumptions about the moral nature and status of women; the fact that so many of them did, in practice, show themselves incapable of self-government, and thus unequal to other kinds of authority, derived from the inadequate and positively damaging education which they received.

Macaulay's *Letters on Education* is a pedagogical and political work by a political historian who made no secret of her love of liberty under the law of rational principle. It was, as Wollstonecraft acknowledged, to provide the foundation of the *Vindication*. Macaulay did not deny that, for most women, distinction in learning or literature was impossible, but she thought that their knowledge, if they were allowed to acquire any, would 'come out in conduct'. She, like Chudleigh and Astell before her, and Wollstonecraft, who was yet to make her feminist mark, was a feminist moralist, anchoring her arguments in rational beliefs about ethics and taking female education as the most important field of practical feminist endeavour. Catherine Macaulay is of particular interest because she connects the disparate groupings of the Enlightenment feminist women: she first came to public notice in the pre-revolutionary period, when learned ladies were, in civilised quarters, found acceptable. She visited Hannah More in the company of Burke, and she was acknowledged by Mary Wollstonecraft as her admired predecessor. She lacked but one claim to a central position in the development of Enlightenment feminism: she was not a novelist.

3 'A New Species of Writing'

In the eighteenth century the novel was new, and was seen to engage
with the contemporary world and problems about conduct in it in
quite a new way. The controversy over *Pamela* and later *Tom Jones*,
in which Dr Johnson played an important part, was sharpened by
fears about the effect of novels upon impressionable readers. Johnson, in *Rambler 4*, sees that the novel, or 'familiar history' as he calls
it, invites readers to apply what they learn from it to themselves, as
the romances of former times did not, being 'so remote from all that
passes among men'. Further, the novel was read, without tutorship,
by readers whom Johnson did not feel could be trusted to draw
correct moral inferences from it:

These books are written chiefly to the young, the ignorant and the idle, to
whom they serve as lectures of conduct, and introductions into life. They are
the entertainment of minds unfurnished with ideas, and therefore easily
susceptible of impressions; not fixed by principles, and therefore easily
following the current of fancy; not informed by experience, and consequently open to every false and partial account.

He does not mention women specifically, but we may take it that he
had them in mind, for the satirist's nightmare of romantic girls and
their giddy governesses shut up together with a cache of novels from
the circulating library, was already familiar. Ignorant young women
were not the only readers likely to be unhinged by fiction of doubtful
moral import, but it was widely believed that they were peculiarly
vulnerable. Johnson's well-known rebuke to Hannah More, on
hearing her speak with levity of 'some witty passage in *Tom Jones*',
shows that he believed even rather learned and highly respectable
ladies, no longer so very young, to be in special danger: 'I am
shocked to hear you have read it; a confession which no modest lady
should ever make. I scarcely know a more corrupt work.'[14]
   Johnson's apprehensions were well founded, for the new genre
was to enlarge the scope of moral discourse in ways which undermined established authority. Through the detailed examination of
sexual and familial relationships, the novel exposed the dubious

moral assumptions by which they were governed. The moral nature of Woman, and the rights and duties of individual women, were not subjects much attended to in the philosophic treatise, but they could not be avoided in the novel. Moreover, women were admitted as participants in the moral debate which developed from the novel. Their importance as readers was always clear; soon they were important also as critics and authors. Johnson would have liked to see the novel used to teach morals as learned authority had already defined them. Would novelists but make their fictions exemplify received wisdom, all would be well, for 'these familiar histories' might then be of greater use 'than the solemnities of professed morality, and convey the knowledge of vice and virtue with more efficacy than axioms and definitions'. The danger was, however, that the subject-matter and the readership of the new species of writing, taken together, would call into question the whole basis of authority in morals and literature.

'Other writings', he says, 'are safe, except from the malice of learning, but these are in danger from every common reader.' True, he illustrates his point by reference to the shoemaker, 'who happened to stop in his way at the Venus of Apelles' and censured an ill-executed slipper, but this example, like his abstract language, conceals what the context of the controversy makes plain: the general objection to the entry into moral discourse of the ignorant disguises the particular objection to the entry of women. Were shoemakers to do no more than make objections to the footwear of a goddess little serious harm would come of it, and were ladies to confine their criticism of novels to the details of a gown, or the decoration of a tea-cup, that too would simply be laughable, but the threat to established authority was much greater than this, as the earnestness and vehemence of Johnson's language reveals. Women of the middle class might be excluded from the major schools, the universities and the Church, and most of them received a trivial education, but they were avid readers to whom the circulating library had provided something equivalent to an eighteenth-century Open University. They were likely to criticise much more important errors than the misrepresentation of a slipper. The idea of a woman preaching might still remind one of a dog walking on its hind legs, but through participation in the new fiction women were to acquire a public voice, and the authority of moral teachers. The 'female philosopher', who was never anything but a joke while she attempted the kinds of discourse from which her education disqualified her, was to become a powerful and respected influence through the novel. It was to be more than a century before George Eliot set the seal upon this development, but Johnson recognised the possibility as early as 1750, and it led him towards a narrow, defensive critical position about prose fiction.

Johnson was to praise Shakespeare's drama as 'the mirrour of life . . . from which a hermit may estimate the transactions of the world, and a confessor predict the progress of the passions'. But novels were read by those more likely than the 'confessor' or the 'hermit' to be influenced in their judgement by them, and their virtue needed protection by ignorance. Thus, in *Rambler 4* the image of literature as a mirror, used in the Preface to Johnson's *Shakespeare*, is specifically rejected so far as the 'familiar history' goes:

If the world is promiscuously described, I cannot see of what use it may be to read the account: or why it may not be as safe to turn the eye immediately upon mankind as upon a mirror which shows all that presents itself without discrimination.

Promiscuously recalls a famous passage in the *Areopagitica*, where Milton claims that 'the true wayfaring Christian' must 'apprehend and consider vice with all her baits and seeming pleasures, and yet abstain, and yet distinguish, and yet prefer what is truly better'. He argues that the 'knowledge and survey of vice' is 'necessary to the constitution of human virtue', and that such knowledge 'is the benefit which may be had of books *promiscuously* read'. Milton, of course, would not have thought this argument applied to women who were not designed to judge for themselves. It was because Johnson knew that women must now be included among those whose ideas about morals might be formed by independent reading that he advocated, in 1750, that the novel be regarded as a form of conduct-book literature. Johnson's anti-feminism had been clearly shown in the 1740s in his 'A Dissertation on the Amazons' (1741) and his *Life of Savage* (1744). John A. Dussinger says that

Johnson's 'A Dissertation' plays out in fantasy the horror of rebellion against the patriarchal order, with marriage and primogeniture depending on a hierarchy of male over female, husband over wife and property, and father over son. The revolt of the Amazons against the male warrior is an evil analogous with the Christian myth of the fall, resulting in constant division and strife through generation after generation.[15]

He also stresses the same 'horror of rebellion' against patriarchy in the *Life of Savage*, which 'underscores the "uniformity" of evil in the psychopathology of the woman's envy and hatred of the male'. Savage's rebellion 'like the Amazons', is self-defeating because it is illusory: the "uniformity" of life is ever in favour of patriarchal order'.[16] Johnson's praise of Richardson, in whose works a clear differentiation of the roles and duties of men and women is always made, and where the patriarchal order, including primogeniture, property rights and submission to paternal authority are upheld, should be understood in the light of his fear of female rebellion. His antipathy to Fielding and the Foundling should likewise be seen as deriving from an objection to seeing patriarchal institutions and ideas undermined. To be fair, one must say that Johnson, although he never forgave Fielding for *Tom Jones*, became increasingly enlightened about the moral status and education of women. By 1779, in his *Life* of Milton, he wrote in a manner that must have endeared him to all those women who had smarted under the relegation by the great poet of liberty of Eve to the role of serving Adam rather than God. Johnson says of Milton's own domestic practice:

It has been observed that they who most loudly clamour for liberty do not most liberally grant it . . . there appears in his books something like a Turkish contempt of females as subordinate and inferior beings . . . He suffered them [his daughters] to be depressed by a mean and penurious education. He thought woman made only for obedience, and man for rebellion.[17]

But, by 1779, Johnson had himself benefited from the moral debate engendered by the novel, and the point of view he had heard put among the circle of learned and literary ladies who formed an important influence upon his admired Richardson. In 1750 his stance on the novel was indicative of his mistrust of female 'common readers' and his objection to 'mixed characters' the particular focus of that mistrust.

The mid-eighteenth-century argument about 'mixed characters' was expressed in quite general terms, not apparently related to specific considerations about women, yet it touched on the feminist claim to moral and educational equality in important ways. The general argument, as propounded by Johnson, was that characters in whom good and bad qualities were confused should not, in familiar histories, be sympathetically represented, nor should they be allowed to be seen to prosper. The terms in which he expresses this view make it clear that what he specifically objects to is the representation of sexual misconduct in characters who otherwise show a variety of admirable qualities. 'Vice' is understood specifically as sexual misconduct, 'Virtue' as chastity. What he is really saying, therefore, is that, in the familiar history, the morals of readers must be safeguarded by a refusal, on the part of novelists, to show sexual conduct as it is – rather than as the moralist would like it to be.

Johnson was not prepared to condone the double standard of sexual conduct, whereby chastity in man was a relative virtue, while in woman it was supposed to be absolute. He wished to see chastity represented in the new kind of writing as an absolute virtue in both sexes, for only so could confidence in its value be maintained. The fear that a truthful representation of how differently sexual irregularity in men was actually judged in contemporary society, from sexual misconduct in women, gives a sharp edge to an apparently general argument. Were women, especially young women, to be fully apprised, as Fielding was busy apprising them, of the hypocrisy associated with 'the solemnities of professed morality', could it be supposed that their powers of mind were sufficient to enable them to judge aright? It was because he doubted this that he preferred Richardson's portraits of male and female virtue (Pamela, Clarissa and Sir Charles Grandison) to Fielding's portrait of the indubitably 'mixed' Tom Jones. Yet we have only to name the titular heroes and heroines of these novelists to see a major difficulty: only heroines could, with any degree of credibility, be represented as Virtuous, in this sense. To attempt to create a hero to whom an absolute, literal standard of sexual virtue was applied, was to court failure. If the 'mixed character' embargo were to be observed in the familiar history then men had to become anti-heroes, and the women had either to be rewarded by 'happy' marriages which looked specious (as in *Pamela*), or turned into tragic victims whose chastity spelt death (as in *Clarissa*).

No wonder Jane Austen declared that 'pictures of perfection' made her 'sick and wicked', for the new species of writing, of its very nature, required, if it were to be a truth-telling form of literary art, a breaking with 'the solemnities of professed morality' in favour of an examination of what was natural and probable in sexual and familial, as in other kinds of social relationships. Austen's opposition to the distortion of human nature required by the rejection of 'mixed characters' is clear in everything she wrote, and as late as *Sanditon* she takes up the cudgels against it, dismissing her comic anti-hero, Sir Edward Denham, as having been misled by too much reading of sentimental fiction. The tables are well and truly turned, for the heroine has enough rationality to judge aright of what she reads; it is 'Sir Edw:' whose understanding has been unhinged by Richardson. By making the anti-hero the victim of romantic fiction, Austen mocks those who feared that women could not be trusted as readers, and she makes sure that critics, as well as novelists, are included in her attack. Though Sir Edward 'owed many of his ideas' to Richardson *et al*, he had a 'more general Knowledge of modern Literature':

He read all the Essays, Letters, Tours & Criticisms of the day – & with the same ill-luck which made him derive only false Principles from Lessons of Morality, & incentives to Vice from the History of its Overthrow, he gathered only hard words and involved sentences from the style of our most approved Writers.' (ch. 8)

Here Austen comments ironically on both Johnson's argument and the hidden fear about the sound judgement of women readers which lay behind it. Her language recalls *Rambler 4*, where it had been laid down that

Vice . . . should always disgust; nor should the graces of gaiety, or the dignity of courage, be so united with it as to reconcile the mind.

She stands the 'mixed character' argument on its head, for it is not such a harmless (and life-like) 'mixed' hero as Tom Jones who misleads, but the unmistakable Lovelace-like villain. The weak-brained reader whose conduct is modelled on a false fictional example is not a romantic, ill-educated girl, but a silly baronet, whose advantages of education must have been much the same as those of Mr Collins.

Jane Austen's rejection of the critical position taken up by Johnson in *Rambler 4* is of great importance to her development as a novelist and there can be no doubt, on the evidence of her own work, that she saw plainly the close connection between the 'mixed character' question and the 'familiar history' as a form of moral discourse about the 'Man and Woman Question'. Through her own practice as a novelist she criticises Johnson as well as Richardson and Fielding, giving her heroines sound heads as well as warm, susceptible hearts, and generally discerning taste in literature. In order to appreciate fully how clear and consistent her criticism was, it is necessary to trace further feminist involvement in the Richardson/Fielding controversy, beginning with *Pamela* and ending with *Sir Charles Grandison*, Richardson's major failure, and a novel of particular importance to any account of feminism and fiction in the eighteenth century.

Pamela, or Virtue Rewarded, tells the story of a young servant girl whose master sets out to ruin her. Having, largely through the contrivance of her author, succeeded in evading the snares set for her, Pamela is rewarded by an 'honourable' proposal of marriage, which is accepted without scruple. Richardson, as his sub-title tells us, intended to exemplify the view of contemporary moralists that virtue is rewarded in this world, as well as the next, and is therefore compatible with self-interest. No doubt this was why Dr Slocock recommended it from his pulpit,[18] but plenty of less reverend readers thought it cynical as well as absurd – Fielding's *Shamela* being the best known of the many parodies the novel provoked. The trouble with Pamela's virtue was that it consisted in little more than the preservation of her chastity in trying circumstances, and appeared to be actuated by too calculating a prudence. *Pamela* might be seen as exposing one of the greatest weaknesses of Bishop Butler's ethics, which formed the basis of 'the professed solemnities' of orthodox moralists throughout the eighteenth century: namely that the rational calculation of self-interest in this world, taken as the beginning of virtue, led in practice not to goodness but to hypocrisy. This is the basis of Fielding's objection to *Pamela* and, as Bernard Harrison shows, *Tom Jones* may be read as a comprehensive criticism of 'the purpose and likely effects of Butler's arguments',[19] exposing, through delineation of human nature in its many varieties, the fallacy of supposing that virtue can, in practice, be reconciled with the calculations of self-interest.

Whatever view one may take of this, the general moral question is complicated by a specific issue to which neither Butler nor Fielding gave serious consideration; that is, whether 'virtue' was to be thought of in the same way for both sexes, or as different in kind and quality for men and for women. Richardson, on the other hand, did give serious attention to it, largely because he listened to what his circle of women friends and critics had to say about his novels. Fielding attacked Butlerian confidence that virtue is, in this world, rewarded and vice punished, and he attacked the belief that a man could actually be in a virtuous state of mind while being guided in his conduct by motives of self-interest; but he did not face squarely the question of whether or not this applied equally to virtuous women.

It was easy to mock Pamela's virtue if one applied her standards of conduct to a man, in whom it simply looked absurd. This is the method Fielding chooses to ridicule Richardson in *Joseph Andrews*, where Pamela is given a virtuous brother who spends the early chapters of the novel evading the improper advances of his employer's sleazy wife, Lady B. The joke is a good one and the method works very well, provided one does not take the role-reversal of the two sexes so far as to be obliged to ask: 'Can women be treated as subject to the same general moral code as men? their "virtue" becoming a matter of the general and habitual "goodness" of their attitudes and actions in every sphere of life, not specifically and well-nigh exclusively associated with chastity?' Fielding does not press his joke to this point; in fact, he abandons interest in it quite early, has done with mocking Joseph, once he gets away from Lady B., and provides for him, in the docile Fanny, a heroine of spotless and restricted virtue, quite in the sentimental mould. Later, when he came to write *Amelia*, he moved further towards the sentimental school for, whatever he might show about virtue in a hero as consisting in a multiplicity of good qualities, such as bravery, generosity, warm affections, selflessness or benevolence, he confined his heroine to a rather weak amiability, dependence and impeccable chastity.

In *Tom Jones* Fielding does show a more critical awareness of the hypocrisy implicit in the sentimental attitude to heroines. The mother of the Foundling is Miss Allworthy-as-was, before her error in entangling with Tom's father and the worse error of marrying Captain Blifel. Some of the 'bad' women, like Jenny Jones and Molly Seagrim, are treated sympathetically, and the heroine, Sophia, although chaste, is given a certain amount of courage, warm affections and a hot temper. Her chastity is guarded by the hero's extreme scrupulousness about virgins and is mocked by the antics of her comic maid, 'Honour', and her own carelessness-cum-obsessive-attachment to her 'muff'. Thus, in *Tom Jones*, Fielding implies that the sentimental ideal of spotlessly chaste womanhood is unrealistic, but he is not prepared openly to defend a 'mixed' heroine as he defends his 'mixed' hero. Indeed, in Nancy Miller, who is treated without mockery, he creates a conventionally 'virtuous' sub-heroine. Nancy is technically a 'fallen woman', having been seduced by the man she loves and wishes to marry. Tom prevails upon Nightingale to make an honest woman of her by arguing that she has no more disgraced herself than he has. Here, certainly, Fielding applies the same moral standard to both sexes, but Nancy's 'virtue' is the virtue of the sentimental heroine – she is loving, amiable and dependent even, if you look at it aright, 'really' chaste – but she is assigned the 'relative' female role to which virtue in its fullest human sense is not appropriate. Her function in the moral scheme of things is to afford Tom a means of showing his own delicate feelings towards women, without himself being guilty of seducing a 'pure' one. Thus, even in his great novel, Fielding stops short of complete realism about sexual morality, making his hero truly virtuous, despite his sexual peccadillos, but requiring in his heroine compliance with the strictest standard of chastity.

Women readers were supposed to be shocked by *Tom Jones* and sometimes kept quiet about having enjoyed or admired it, though there is plenty of evidence that many of them did. When Clara Reeve wrote her *Progress of Romance*, which was cast in the form of a dialogue between two women and a man, she declared that *Tom Jones* was not a woman's book, but put some judicious praise of it into the mouth of 'Hortensius' who, being male, is allowed, though sensible, to admire it. When Catherine Talbot wrote to Elizabeth Carter about her detestation of *Tom Jones*, Mrs Carter replied:

I am sorry to find you so outrageous about poor Tom Jones; he is no doubt an imperfect, but not a detestable character, with all that honesty, good nature and generosity of temper. Though nobody can admire Clarissa more than I do; yet with all our partiality, I am afraid it must be confessed, that Fielding's book is the most natural representation of what passes in the world, and the bizarreries which arise from the mixture of good and bad which makes up the composition of most folks.[20]

Lady Bradshaigh, another friend and admirer of Richardson, agreed with Richardson and Johnson that *Tom Jones* was immoral, but admitted to laughing at Fielding. There is little doubt that, among the well educated women of the Richardson circle and the blue-stocking salons, *Tom Jones* was admired, read and widely discussed, by no means without approbation. Astrea and Minerva Hill, the daughters of Richardson's friend Aaron Hill, when asked for their opinion of the novel, reported that they found 'much [masqu'd] merit' in it, and said that 'in every part it has Humanity for its Intention'.[21] This brought down a severe rebuke upon them from Richardson, but it seems they expressed a common viewpoint, for Lady Bradshaigh told him:

The girls are certainly fond of Tom Jones, as I told you before, and they do not scruple declaring it in the company of your incognita; for, alas! I am no awful body to them; they just say the same before me as if I were but twenty.[22]

That was in 1749, and women had to learn more discretion about *Tom Jones* as they suffered reprimand for admitting to thinking well of it, or being amused by it. Indeed, it became *de rigueur* for male biographers to show the purity of their subjects' minds by assuring readers that the aunt or sister of whom they wrote had not much cared for Fielding. Henry Austen's assertion that his sister preferred Richardson should be read with this in mind. What she and Cassandra might have said, in the privacy of their dressing room at around the age of twenty, is quite another matter.

Tom Jones did precisely what Johnson feared it would do; it encouraged respectable women to discuss fairly openly 'what passed in the world', to laugh at its absurdity and, when the laughter had subsided, to question 'the solemnities of professed morality' because it made plain that they were not well-founded in knowledge of human nature. Fielding did not show a virtuous heroine with that quality of experiential virtue which he revealed in the Foundling, but some women readers, Mrs Carter clearly among them, judged of Tom's virtue as though it were the virtue of generic Man, not just the male sex. Her use, in a letter to another woman, of a generalised moral language, which applies to 'most folks', makes it clear that she is thinking of Tom's moral composition as representative not of one sex, but of humankind. Once women readers had begun to think in that way they were not to be content with villainous heroes and 'picture-of-perfection' heroines. As Mary Wollstonecraft was to put it, in 1792, even, 'if women are by nature inferior to men, their virtues must be the same in quality, if not in degree, or virtue is a relative idea; consequently their conduct should be founded on the same principles, and have the same aim'.[23] The novel, which was obliged to show human nature in both men and women, did as much as, or more than, any other form of writing to expose the necessity of reassessing what 'virtue' ought to mean in both sexes. Fielding, perhaps as unlikely a feminist as one could hope to find, contributed to the opening up of this new moral question, although he tried to dodge it. Richardson, who found it a far more interesting and central problem, did even more.

Richardson's view of morals was essentially the same as Butler's and, since feminists generally accepted Butlerian ethics, or at least used his arguments to support their case, it may be as well to summarise them here. Butler's purpose in *The Analogy of Religion* (1736) was to show that human nature and the natural ordering of life in this world had been designed by God in such a way as to teach man moral principles. If this could be shown to be true, and if it could also be shown that the principles learnt through secular experience were those shown by revealed religion as divinely commanded, there need be no opposition between religion and Reason. Thus the rational Christian of the eighteenth-century could be satisfied that religion need not be 'a subject of ridicule, unless that of nature be so too'. The rational man, learning morals only from the operation of rational reflection upon experience, must come to accept the same principles of conduct as were commanded by Scripture. Following Hobbes and Locke in the belief that 'fear and hope' were the chief springs of virtue, Butler set out to show that self-love is not incompatible with Christian morals, but a means of learning how we ought to act:

Self-love, considered merely as an active principle leading us to pursue our chief interest, cannot but he uniformly coincident with the principle of obedience to God's commands, our interest being rightly understood.[24]

This position is maintained by arguing that, in this world (somewhat imperfectly) good actions are rewarded and bad ones punished, and that these rewards and punishments prepare us for the life to come, where the system is perfected. The emphasis on 'our interest being rightly understood' means that we are to recognise that our true interest requires a quiet conscience and a knowledge of having acted aright. Thus, while it is a common criticism of Butler that his moral philosophy was used to support the middle-class Christian's duty to make himself prosperous, his intention was to show that such qualities as benevolence and generosity brought rewards, not necessarily of a material kind, to those who practised them.

So far as feminist thinking in the Age of Reason is concerned, Butler may be seen as having marked attractions. For a start, although he was a bishop of the Established Church, his object was to show that sound morals did not depend upon faith in revealed religion. Thus, although Butler did not wish to encourage them, Deists or Atheists, as well as Dissenters, might make use of his arguments, and feminists who were 'true daughters of the Church of England' (like Jane Austen) could hold common ground on morals with less orthodox ones like Mary Wollstonecraft. Then Butler's insistence on the value of self-love, as a guide to virtue, although not, certainly, intended to encourage women to assert themselves as autonomous individuals, could be seen as doing so. Just as, in a later age, quite different ideas about self-hood led to Nora Helmer's departure from the imprisonment of doll's house play-acting, and to Edna Pontellier's awakening, so Butlerian emphasis on the merits of enlightened self-interest encouraged women to think that they might be acting virtuously if they sometimes put their own interests first. But, of course, a great deal depended on 'our interest being rightly understood'. Astell had argued that women were not to be content to be like 'tulips in a garden', making a fine show and being good for nothing else. They had immortal souls to cultivate by the exercise of immortal powers of reason. Wollstonecraft was to say angrily:

How women are to exist in that state where there is neither to be marrying nor giving in marriage, we are not told. For though moralists have agreed that the tenor of life seems to prove that *man* is prepared by various circumstances for a future state, they constantly concur in advising *woman* to prepare only for the present. (*Vindication*, p. 108)

Women took up the Butlerian view of morals and religion partly because they were, like their brothers, children of the Age of Reason and Improvement who found it possible, without cynicism, to make reason and self-interest the joint guardians of Christian virtue, and partly because the application of Butlerian ethics to the second sex was a way of advocating female emancipation from male domination. Enlightenment feminists were loud in acknowledging their obedience to rational principle, but their obligation to Reason entailed the possibility of principled disobedience to lesser authority. In this way a paradox, which has misled a good many readers unfamiliar with the character of Enlightenment feminist argument, was created. A woman might argue about ethics, using the most orthodox Butlerian language, but, if she applied it impartially to both sexes, she was an advocate of the moral emancipation of women and, by implication, a critic of the established order of patriarchal domination.

All of which may seem a far cry from *Pamela*, but Richardson had, in this novel, inadvertently opened up to a wider audience than Mary Astell ever reached precisely the question of whether women were to pursue as their chief interest the attainment of such a virtue as qualified them for the life to come, or merely such as qualified them as brides of reformed rakes like Mr B. *Pamela* is intended to exemplify Butlerian ethics, and Richardson, at the time he wrote it, was not bothered by doubts as to whether it might in fact expose the fatal weakness of the 'rewards-and-punishments' view of this world, by showing how close it came to identifying a crude, materialistic self-interest with unaffected virtue. This possibility did not worry him because he thought of virtue in women as consisting almost wholly in chastity. That chastity in the literal sense was a wholly secular virtue, having no place in a sexless heaven, did not give rise to doubts about its being accorded such a high place in the evaluation of female character. Pamela is chaste and, after her marriage, obedient, and that is all that is required of her. This was the common theme of moralists and divines in their instruction of the fair sex, but Richardson, in thus setting it down, raised misgivings about its honesty.

In writing *Clarissa* he gave female chastity a moral dimension which went beyond the literal meaning of the term. Clarissa, although she is raped, and thereby loses her 'honour' in this world, retains a mental and spiritual purity which unfits her to be the wife of a reformed rake, and makes her something pretty close to a 'bride of Christ'. In *Clarissa*, Richardson endowed his heroine with an immortal soul and showed her virtue to be rewarded where there is neither marrying nor giving in marriage. The novel was received by many readers as a deeply religious work, exemplifying Butlerianism in its least materialistic form. Edward Young expressed a common opinion when he said that *Clarissa* contained 'the whole duty of Woman', and that 'the Bench of Bishops might go to school to the Writer of a Romance.'[25] Fielding was deeply moved by it, saying in a letter to Richardson: 'God forbid that the Man who reads this with dry Eyes should be alone with my Daughter when she hath no assistance within call.'[26] Richardson's ethics could no longer be laughed at by men of true sense and sensibility, but there were a few dissentient voices among the women, and even those who admired Richardson most sometimes admitted to opinions which could not gratify such moralists as Dr Slocock. Lady Bradshaigh, one of the women of whom Richardson spoke as his literary 'daughters', laughed at Lovelace for all his wickedness, for 'never anything equall'd the Humour of that Man'.[27] Some of the women, it seems, were incapable of taking the great rake's wickedness quite as seriously as the men did. Mrs Carter thought Richardson's vicious characters had 'a strange awkwardness and extravagance': 'To be sure, poor man, he had read in a book, or heard someone say, there was such a thing in the world as wickedness'[28] – but he did not know how to make a truthful representation of it. Clearly, Mrs Carter thought that Richardson's portrayal of Man as Devil and Woman as Angel did less than justice to the humanity of either.

Among Richardson's 'daughters', however, the most serious objection made to *Clarissa* was the notion of obedience which it fostered. Frances Grainger, who argued at length with Richardson about the cultivation of the female mind, disagreed with him about the duty of daughters to submit to parents.[29] Mrs Delaney was outraged by the 'tyrannical Usage of the Harlowe's to the excellent Clarissa'.[30] Sarah Chapone found Clarissa at fault in being too submissive to her father and maintained that she ought not to have let him keep the estate left to her by her grandfather. 'Richardson seemed to her to have promulgated the harsh idea that women should never be independent and thus to have denied that they are members of society and free agents.'[31] Hester Mulso wrote at great length to Richardson, disputing with him on the subject of parental authority and a daughter's duty of obedience.[32] Such women as these, members of the blue-stocking circle, who established themselves as readers and conversationalists, were not feminists in any political sense, nor did they put their views on morals, education and literature into works intended for publication, but they have their place in the development of feminist ideas, for the point of view they represent has something in common with that of Mary Astell, though for the most part they lacked her courage and clear conviction. It was such 'daughters' who played a curious part in the composition of *Sir Charles Grandison*.

4 Sir Charles Grandison

Richardson's last novel has been widely and long held to be a failure as a work of literary imagination, but it has held a high place in the interest and affections of women, including two major novelists, Jane Austen and George Eliot, who cannot be supposed indifferent to its literary qualities. It is pretty clear that they were well aware of them, and yet, as late as 1800 or thereabouts, Austen appears to have written, or revised, a satirical skit called 'Sir Charles Grandison', and George Eliot, when she discovered the novel in 1847, said 'I had no idea that Richardson was worth so much . . . the morality is perfect – there is nothing for the new lights to correct.'[33] Later she wrote of *Grandison*: 'I should be sorry to be the heathen that did not like that book. I don't like Harriet Byron much, she is too proper and insipid. Lady G. [Charlotte Grandison] is the gem, with her marmoset.'[34] Why did Austen and Eliot respond strongly to this novel? How far did they agree or disagree in their attitude towards it? The answers to these questions throw an important light on the continuity of a female tradition of fiction, and on the curious estrangement of Austen from some of her successors in the mid-nineteenth century. I shall return to them at the end of this discussion of *Grandison* and its important place in the development of feminist and anti-feminist ideas in the eighteenth century. We must start with the composition of *Sir Charles Grandison* and the part women played in it.

Richardson had been impelled towards becoming a novelist by his writing of letters for servant girls. As he became famous and respected, he acquired an extensive circle of well-educated and well-born female friends whose advice on his novels was solicited, and with whom he corresponded at length on moral and literary questions. As we have seen, some of them had been critical of certain aspects of both *Pamela* and *Clarissa*, including their tendency to perpetuate a double standard of sexual morality by the representation of *characteristically* 'good' women and 'vicious' men. He reported in 1750 that he had been 'teazed by a dozen ladies of note and of virtue, to give them a good man'.[35] Thus, the conception of Sir

Charles reversed what is held to be common in literary reproduction. The seed was sown by the women upon the man who was to embody their ideas in a new novel. What was in due course delivered was a curious child, for Richardson's own idealised view of the Good Man as virtuous Patriarch and, as C. Griffin-Wolff calls him, 'secular saint', predominated in a work which upheld the established order of things as firmly as Dr Johnson could have wished. And yet the only character with any life in her is Charlotte Grandison, the hero's sister, who is as important to this novel as Allworthy's sister, the mother of Tom and the unspeakable Blifel, is to *Tom Jones*, and Charlotte is a shrew and a rebel of whose taming we remain unconvinced. Moreover, the novel takes up some issues in which women were particularly interested and puts their point of view: among these were an objection to duelling as an 'honourable' means of settling disputes or avenging insults; the marriage of respectable women to reformed rakes; and the respect due to old maids.

Richardson's attitude to women remained a curious mixture of sympathy, admiration and patronage, though in Charlotte Grandison we can see that, for the first time, his imaginative sympathy had been caught by a woman who rebelled against patriarchal government. This, perhaps, was the most important and beneficial result of his extraordinary attempt to become to his blue-stocking friends what he had once been to young women in service, who needed him to voice their feelings in private letters. Richardson consulted, among others, Lady Bradshaigh, Hester Mulso, Susanna Highmore, Mrs Delaney, Elizabeth Carter and Catherine Talbot about the composition of *Sir Charles Grandison*. There is evidence that he took their advice seriously, sometimes writing in accordance with their directives, sometimes altering a draft to meet their wishes. In 1754 he went so far as to canvass the idea of writing a continuation of *Grandison* in which his 'daughters' would collaborate. Lady Bradshaigh was to write letters in the character of Charlotte Grandison, or Lady G. as she had become, Hester Mulso was to take on Clementina, Susanna Highmore Harriet Byron (Lady Grandison) and Elizabeth Carter was to attempt Harriet's sagacious grandmother, Mrs Shirley, or even Sir Charles himself. Most of them refused and it all came to nothing, but it shows that Richardson's circle of female friends had some justification for regarding *Grandison* as, in a curious sense, partly their work. Catherine Talbot was proud to write to Elizabeth Carter of the role which the two of them had played in the creation of the Good Man:

did you ever call Pigmalion a fool, for making an image and falling in love with it – and do you know that you and I are two Pigmalionesses? Did not Mr. Richardson ask us for some traits of his good man's character? And did we not give him some? And has not he gone and put these and his own charming ideas into a book and formed a Sir Charles Grandison?[36]

Mrs Carter was never, as a matter of fact, so enthusiastic about either *Sir Charles Grandison* or Richardson's writings in general. As we have seen, she did not approve of the creation of 'unmixed characters' and admired *Tom Jones*. She made a characteristically feminist criticism of the essay Richardson contributed to *The Rambler* in 1751, saying that he was like 'a Mahometan' in supposing 'that Providence designed one half of the human species for idiots and slaves'.[37] This was the same essay that Jane Austen was to mock in *Northanger Abbey* (p. 30).

The boldest and least reverential of the learned ladies found the idea of the Good Man as unsatisfactory as she had found the Heroines of Virtue, but others, like Catherine Talbot, admired Richardson for attempting to show that the same ideal standard of conduct ought to apply to both sexes, and were prepared to overlook the difficulties of trying to make it apply to either. It is possible that some women who saw pretty clearly that *Grandison* was inferior to *Pamela* and *Clarissa* as a work of imagination, were inclined to think that its superiority as a work of morality made up for this. And it is true to say that Richardson's failure with an 'unmixed' hero deserved honour amongst the second sex. Even Jane Austen seems to have felt this, though she could not help laughing at its many absurdities as well.

Brian Southam, in his Introduction to Austen's '*Sir Charles Grandison*', says:

Richardson designed *Grandison* as a kind of conduct-book, a didactic entertainment, from which young people could take an enjoyable and instructive lesson in manners, in behaviour correct for polite society.[38]

This is true, but it leaves out the controversial nature of conduct-book manners and morals which Richardson defended overtly, and about which some women were deeply sceptical. As Jocelyn Harris says, *Grandison* is about 'the relationship of power between a man and his wife':[39] or, as C. Griffin-Wolff says, about 'the pattern of moral order that is normally associated with family government'.[40] Richardson wishes to show that patriarchal government within the family is in accordance with the principles of natural morality, as well as with revealed religion. He does so by making his Good Man an exemplary patriarch. To quote Griffin-Wolff again:

Richardson begins his solution to the woman's problem by depicting in Sir Charles the kind of man who would establish and maintain a community which permitted her to assume her rightful place.[41]

The literary 'daughters' had influenced Richardson so far as to cause him to seek to define the merits of his hero according to how he treated women – his sister, and the two heroines, Harriet Byron and Clementina, in particular, but also a great many lesser characters, of whom Mrs Shirley and Miss Mansfield are especially important, since they are used to show that Sir Charles treats a sagacious grandmother and an old maid without fortune, with respect, as well as women who are young, attractive and portioned. Perhaps that was what George Eliot noticed when she said the morality was perfect, but she also responded to Charlotte Grandison.

Jane Austen was brought up on *Grandison* and first came to it as a novel which her mother enjoyed. Growing up as she did in an age of revolution, when feminism became a subject of political controversy, she understood quite clearly that *Grandison* was a crucial novel in the evolution of changing ideas about the right basis of relationships between the sexes. Her brother tells us that she admired it particularly, though for reasons discussed below we should probably take this with a grain of salt. The evidence of Austen's own writings suggests a highly critical attitude to *Grandison*, and some antipathy to Richardson in general. The two references to *Grandison* in Austen's letters do not suggest admiration of either the work or its heroine. In the first she says she is to have some new caps made, one of which will be 'white satin and lace, and a little white flower perking out of the left ear, like Harriet Byron's feather'. This is a reference to the improper costume worn by Miss Byron at the masquerade from which she was abducted, only narrowly escaping ruin, by Sir Hargrave Pollexfen. The second makes fun of Harriet Byron's excessive gratitude to Sir Charles and his sister for having rescued her from the villain.[42] In *Northanger Abbey*, Mrs Morland is said to read *Sir Charles Grandison* often; Catherine says it is 'very entertaining', though not at all like *Udolpho*. The 'sweet' Miss Andrews, who is suspect, being a friend of Isabella Thorpe's, is said to have been unable to get through the first volume. This looks more like evidence of admiration of *Grandison*, but we should be careful. Mrs Morland is 'a very good sort of woman', but there is nothing to suggest she has a discriminating taste in literature. Catherine has the sense to see that *Grandison* is not to be dismissed by an Isabella Thorpe but, since she is designed as a heroine incapable at this stage of judging books, we should not assume that her finding it 'entertaining' implies strong admiration of the work by her author. *Grandison* is not mentioned in the list of works praised in chapter 5 of *Northanger Abbey*, nor is it ever used in any novel to show the discriminatory powers of a man or woman of sense and developed taste. As Southam says in the Introduction to Austen's '*Grandison*', the Juvenilia include a number of parodies on *Grandison*, *Love and Friendship* being among them. Lastly, there is the recently published dramatisation of 'Sir Charles Grandison' which mocks its parent-novel mercilessly, and makes of Harriet Byron almost as absurd a figure as the inane Mrs Palmer in *Sense and Sensibility*. As in the original, Charlotte Grandison gets the best lines, such as they are, and she becomes a caricature of the sharp-tongued, slightly coarse Jane Austen of some of the early letters. Like George Eliot, Austen shows that she has laughed at Charlotte Grandison's calling her baby a 'marmouset', a 'pug' and a 'brat'.[43]

There can be no doubt that Austen and Eliot agreed in their dislike of Harriet Byron and in their enjoyment of the irreverence of the Good Man's sister but, whereas George Eliot thought 'the morality . . . perfect', Jane Austen thought it very defective. Austen had thought hard and long about *Grandison*, whereas Eliot had not, but I think their differences on the morality of the novel reflect fundamental differences of attitude towards benevolent patriarchy. Eliot shared the Romantic partiality for Great Men, and could find no better life for her heroines than to adopt the role of helpmeet to truly good and great ones. Austen, whose feminism immunised her pretty thoroughly against Romanticism, has little time for those who are too good or great to make equal marriages. Her heroines do not adore or worship their husbands, though they respect and love them. They are not, especially in the later novels, allowed to get married at all until the heroes have provided convincing evidence of appreciating their qualities of mind, and of accepting their powers of rational judgement, as well as their good hearts. As Austen's most lovable and sympathetically defective patriarch, Mr Bennet, says, his daughter's husband must be her 'partner in life' for she will never be happy in an 'unequal marriage'. He means one where her husband lacks her superiority of head and heart, not that the unequal fortunes of Mr Darcy and Miss Bennet will cause trouble. Austen's anti-Romanticism, which is an aspect of her feminism, makes her a critic of the 'Good Man' and of the Great Critic who admired his author. It is also what makes her see *Grandison* as distorting the rational Christianity in which she believed, whereas Eliot lightheartedly remarked that it would take a 'heathen' to dislike it.

In her own novels Austen criticises the belief that women's problems are to be solved by benevolent patriarchs. She does this by showing patriarchal figures as at best defective, like Mr Bennet, and at worst vicious, like General Tilney. Her heroines, especially the later ones, solve their own problems before making marriages with men who see themselves in a fraternal, rather than a patriarchal, relationship as husbands. No doubt she was influenced in this by her understanding of feminist argument, as it was to be found in polemical writing like *A Vindication of the Rights of Woman*, but she also learnt to define her own feminist position through a careful consideration of fiction. *Sir Charles Grandison* was a landmark in the mid-eighteenth century treatment of the 'Man and Woman Question', but after 1788 there was a flowering of female talent in fiction, and there was much that Austen could and did learn from the great variety of women's writing after that date.

5 Women as Authors: 1788–98

In 1788 Fanny Burney published *Evelina* and Mary Wollstonecraft published *Mary*; in 1818 *Northanger Abbey* and *Persuasion* were published posthumously, and Wollstonecraft's daughter, Mary Shelley, published *Frankenstein*. For a period of around thirty years women produced a great variety of interesting and memorable fiction, and, but for the intervention of Scott, they would also be seen as having dominated the development of the novel in English through the whole of this period. Charlotte Lennox, Clara Reeve and Charlotte Smith, who had begun earlier, continued to publish new works which were widely read and admired; Ann Radcliffe became the foremost of the Gothic novelists; Elizabeth Inchbald acquired a considerable reputation; Hannah More turned to fiction, and, above all, there was 'the great Maria'. As is clear at once from this catalogue, the women novelists did not form a school or movement. Their writings included burlesque and Gothic fantasy, moral tale and tale of terror, domestic realism and Rousseauist romantic idyll. Among them were Deists, Dissenters, Roman Catholics, Evangelicals and Latitudinarians. Some were Jacobins or Jacobin sympathisers, some kept out of political engagement of any kind and some were diehard conservatives. Some are known only as novelists, others, like Reeve, were also critics and historians of literature or, like Wollstonecraft, Edgeworth and More, known also through political, religious and educational writings.

However one looks at it, this burgeoning of female talent is extraordinary, and was bound to have a profound effect upon any young woman beginning to write once it had occurred. The lady novelist might publish anonymously, might declare her aversion to the glare of public notice, might assure the world of her lack of learned qualification and her dislike of 'masculine' women, but if she went ahead all the same and published, her actions belied her words. For this reason alone, it will not do to approach the female authors of this period and divide them into genuine feminists versus the rest, for at this period to become an author was, in itself, a feminist act.

In *Jane Austen and her Predecessors* (1966) Frank W. Bradbrook spoke of Austen as belonging to a 'feminist tradition' of fiction. He defined this tradition narrowly, excluding controversial novelists like Wollstonecraft and Mary Hays, and he found little of importance in it:

The feminist tradition in the English novel was well established when Jane Austen began writing, and though not particularly distinguished, the best work embodied a view of life which she could accept as partly valid and relevant.[44]

Lloyd W. Brown attacks Bradbrook's definition of the 'feminist' tradition, claiming that it is no more than

the customary analogical thesis which is based, not on some concept of the novelist as a searching analyst of women's roles, but on what Inga-Stina Ewbank contemptuously dismisses as 'a collective classification as "a female novelist"'.[45]

He seeks to show that Austen was a feminist in the sense of being 'a searching analyst of women's roles', and that she adopts the same point of view on many questions as Mary Wollstonecraft. Austen should be seen, not as belonging to the rather petty female tradition which Bradbrook calls 'feminist', but as sharing with Wollstonecraft a belief in 'a liberationist principle' which is 'the essence of the eighteenth-century feminist tradition within which Jane Austen writes'.[46]

I think Brown is right in connecting Austen with Wollstonecraft, and in criticising the 'feminist tradition' as too narrowly conceived and ill-defined, but it is misleading to bring about a neat separation of lady novelist sheep and liberationist goats. As a feminist moralist, Jane Austen is in agreement with Wollstonecraft on so many points that it seems unlikely she had not read *Vindication* and approved of much of it, but there is no doubt either that she admired Fanny Burney and Maria Edgeworth, and regarded them as her teachers. Burney and Edgeworth had, in her view, demonstrated that women had those 'powers of mind' which Wollstonecraft claimed as belonging to the second, as well as the first, sex. In *Northanger Abbey*, she chooses to cite *Camilla*, *Cecilia* and *Belinda* as works in which 'the greatest powers of the mind are displayed . . . the most thorough knowledge of human nature' (p. 38). Clearly she valued the point of view which these authors brought to fiction and, if we see them as taking on where *Sir Charles Grandison* left off, it is not difficult to see why. *Grandison* was a 'familiar history' and a ponderous representation of the manners and morals of the patriarchal family, seen from a

male point of view. Fanny Burney turns the 'familiar history' into
the 'domestic comedy' and begins to show us how it looks from a
female point of view. Her heroes are rather wooden, like Sir Charles,
and her heroines spend far too long exhausting themselves and the
reader with displays of overwrought sensibility, but they are not
altogether without spirit or intelligence and the novels in which they
appear sometimes raise serious questions about contemporary attitudes to men, women and marriage, even though the solutions
adopted are hardly rebellious. *Cecilia, or Memoirs of an Heiress*, is
about a heroine who inherits a fortune on condition that her husband
take her name on marriage. The trials she goes through derive partly
from this condition, and partly from the defects of her three guardians and one unworthy admirer. *Camilla* includes comic portraits of
some pastors and masters, as well as of the foppish Sir Sedley
Clarendel. Burney's success with her range of comic character
portraits is obviously what Austen most admired about her, as her
references to Madame Duval, Captain Mirvan and Miss Larolles
show. And it was through comedy that she herself was to show not
only that patriarchal manners and morals were unjust to women, but
that they were absurd.

Fanny Burney was a generation older than Austen; brought up in a
musical and literary environment, she was encouraged by Mrs
Delaney, who had been one of Richardson's 'daughters'. Ellen
Moers calls her a 'literary grand-daughter' and she was, like Clarissa
Harlowe, heir to her grandfather's estate. R. Brinley Johnson,
writing of *Evelina* in 1918, says:

Modelled on the work of Richardson, and the fathers of fiction, who had so
recently passed away, it nevertheless inaugurated a new departure – the
expression of a feminine outlook on life. It was, frankly and obviously,
written by a woman for women, though it captivated men of the highest
intellect.[47]

Perhaps we should add 'and women of the highest gifts too'. Fanny
Burney is not a feminist novelist, since she does not make or imply a
critical analysis of patriarchy, but to deny her an important place in
the history of women's literary emancipation is to put too strong an
emphasis on ideas, and not enough on what may be shown by other
means than argument or analysis.

Maria Edgeworth was born only eight years earlier than Jane
Austen, and was still young when the Feminist Controversy was at
its height. Her pedagogic writing is discussed above in connection
with it. Edgeworth made her name as a novelist with *Castle Rackrent*
(1800) and her Irish novels were generally regarded in her own time

as her best and most original works. It was these that Scott particularly admired, and which he said had inspired him to write the
Waverley Novels. It is noticeable, however, that Jane Austen refers
only to *Belinda* (1801) and *Patronage* (1814), novels which belong to
the line of domestic comedy, as written by women, which Fanny
Burney had begun. Austen's admiration of Edgeworth was not
uncritical. She praises *Belinda* in *Northanger Abbey*, chapter 5, but in
the same passage satirises Edgeworth's derogatory remarks about
the novel, and calls for more literary sisterhood among heroines and
their authors.

Jane Austen undoubtedly learnt from the success of Burney and
Edgeworth in their handling of the novel as domestic comedy, but I
think she also learnt from Wollstonecraft's failures – *Mary: A Fiction*
(1788) and the posthumously published fragment, *The Wrongs of
Woman, or Maria* (1798; hereafter referred to as *Maria*). Wollstonecraft, like Burney, sees her novel as following on from
Richardson, though her Advertisement is critical of his work and
makes a clear association of the English Sentimental school of fiction
with the Rousseau of *Emile* (1762):

In delineating the Heroine of this Fiction, the Author attempts to develop a
character different from those generally portrayed. This woman is neither a
Clarissa, a Lady G——, nor a Sophie . . . In an artless tale, without episodes,
the mind of a woman who had thinking powers is displayed.

Wollstonecraft knows that she invites ridicule by talking about the
'thinking powers' of a heroine, but she declares that

in a fiction, such a being may be allowed to exist; whose grandeur is derived
from the operations of its own faculties, not subjugated to opinion; but
drawn by the individual from the original source.

Thus she sets out her intention of portraying a heroine who will
illustrate the central tenet of Enlightenment feminism, that individual women have those powers of mind which enable them to
acquire moral principle through rational reflection upon experience.
However, she attempts this daunting task in a tale which is a great
deal too 'artless' for her to achieve her object.

Mary's mind is shown in contrast to her mother's, which is about
as active as Lady Bertram's. Mary is a rational Christian, having read
'Butler's Analogy, and some other authors' which have made her 'a
Christian from conviction'. But Mary's life does not exemplify
Butlerian ethics, her proper exercise of self-love does not lead to true
happiness as Butler taught that it would. In this world, things are too
heavily weighted against women with 'thinking powers' and Mary,

at the end of the novel, can only look to to the next, 'where there is neither marrying nor giving in marriage', for that 'juster appointment' to which Austen, with some irony, refers in the final chapter of *Mansfield Park*.

Wollstonecraft objected to the creation of 'unmixed' heroines and understood why feminists must object to them. In the Author's Preface to *Maria*, she said:

In many works of this species the hero is allowed to be mortal, and to become wise and virtuous as well as happy, by a train of events and circumstances. The heroines, on the contrary, are to be born immaculate.

Again she shows that she wishes to portray a heroine whose progress through life will exemplify how she learns morals as Butler thought rational beings were meant to learn them. But Maria achieves no happiness, and the notes which Godwin printed as to how the novel was to end show that, after an attempt at suicide, Maria, abandoning self-love altogether, was to decide to live for the sake of her child. *Maria* succeeds in showing 'the partial laws and customs of society' which give rise to the 'misery and oppression peculiar to women',[48] but fails to show how women might live rationally and respectably in a better-ordered society.

Jane Austen may well have profited from consideration of both novels, which would not have been unattainable in Bath. At all events, these similarities are worth noting. *Maria* touches on whether or not a woman, who has no legal or constitutional rights, may be said to have a country. In *Northanger Abbey*, the laws and customs of England are overtly held to protect a wife, even one married to General Tilney, but the ironies of the novel undermine this and raise doubts as to how far all is well in the Midland counties of England. In *Maria* the heroine is literally imprisoned by her husband; she says, 'Marriage had bastilled me for life' (p. 155), and a little later refers to 'the master-key of property' (p. 157). In *Mansfield Park*, Maria sees Sotherton as 'a dismal old prison' (p. 53). She is about to sell herself to Rushworth for the sake of his money and estate and, as she sends him off to fetch the key to the iron gate through which she wishes to pass with Crawford, she quotes Sterne's starling which, imprisoned in the Bastille, sang, 'I can't get out, I can't get out'. There may also be a connection between Fanny Price's surname and the letter in *Maria* in which the heroine's husband says 'that every woman had her price' (p. 161). This may have directed Austen back to Crabbe whose village heroine, like Wollstonecraft's Maria, refuses to see herself as marketable. Whether these similarities amount to allusion or not, the criticisms made of marriage in *Mansfield Park*, as commonly regarded, support Woll-stonecraft's objection to it as a property deal. What Wollstonecraft's fictions illustrate with particular clarity is the problem of represent-ing the injustice suffered by women without assimilating the heroine to the sentimental prototype which she wishes to avoid. I think it likely that Austen's confidence that comedy – by no means artless – was the only means by which this problem could be solved may have been strengthened by her reading of *Mary* and *Maria*.

Elizabeth Inchbald illustrates even more clearly the difficulties experienced by feminists when they became novelists, and our difficulties in attempting to divide liberation feminists from lady novelists. Inchbald's first novel, *A Simple Story*, can quite properly be seen as a feminist work, since it deals at length with female education, showing one heroine, Miss Milner, as corrupted by a false education, and her daughter, Matilda, as benefiting from a serious education through which she learns moral self-discipline. However, it does not differ remarkably in feeling or in moral tone from the novels of some of the 'conservative' women, and was widely praised by many of them, including Maria Edgeworth.[49] But Inchbald, who was described by her biographer as 'all heart',[50] came under the spell of Rousseau. *Nature and Art*, written in 1796, ought not to be spoken of as a feminist novel since it follows Rousseau in representing women as too strong of heart and too weak of head to survive without male protection. Agnes, in this novel, is rather like the Agatha of *Lovers' Vows*. Seduced and abandoned, she becomes a prostitute following the death of her illegitimate child. She says that she can no longer respect herself since no one else does. Years later she is condemned to death for forgery by the man who originally ruined her. Inchbald was soon to become the translater and interpre-ter of Kotzebue's sentimental and Rousseauist comedies. This drew down upon her the wrath of Cobbett's *The Porcupine*, which objected to Kotzebue as a leveller. Austen's objection to *Lovers' Vows*, Inchbald's translation of *Das Kind der Liebe*, has sometimes been taken as indicative of her sympathy with anti-Jacobinism but, as is discussed below, it is on feminist grounds that, like Wollstonecraft, she objects to Rousseau's literary disciples.

6 A Vindication of the Rights of Woman

Mary Wollstonecraft published *Vindication* in 1792 and dedicated it to Talleyrand, but it is a mistake to think of it as drawing inspiration solely from the French Revolution. Condorcet, the *philosophe* most firmly in favour of constitutional rights for women, is not mentioned, and it is uncertain if Wollstonecraft was acquainted with his writings.[51] Women had, in fact, been excluded from the new Constitution in France, and the Dedication of the *Vindication* amounts to a plea to Talleyrand to get this changed. The work has strong roots in pre-revolutionary English radicalism, and Wollstonecraft acknowledges Catherine Macaulay as her teacher, saying that when she began *Vindication* she looked forward to its being read with approval by her, and was much grieved to learn of her death before its completion. She says too that she agrees with Macaulay on educational matters, and refers to her 'valuable work' (*Letters on Education: with Observations on Religious and Metaphysical Subjects*, 1790). Wollstonecraft calls her 'the woman of the greatest abilities, undoubtedly, that this country has ever produced'. She regrets the lack of recognition she received and declares:

Posterity, however, will be more just, and remember that Catherine Macaulay was an example of intellectual acquirements supposed to be incompatible with the weakness of her sex. Her works gave proof that a woman can acquire judgement in the full extent of the word. Possessing more penetration than sagacity, more understanding than fancy, she writes with sober energy and argumentative closeness; yet sympathy and benevolence give an interest to her sentiments, and that vital heat to arguments, which forces the reader to weigh them. (pp. 206–7)

Catherine Macaulay was born in 1731 and died in 1791, and she is an important link in the obscured, if not wholly hidden, history of English women in the Age of Enlightenment. Doris Stenton, who shares Wollstonecraft's high opinion of her, says that she 'challenged most directly the prevalent conceptions of her time', though she died 'before the mass of Englishmen had felt the full impact of revolutionary ideas which stemmed from France', and developed her feminism out of the 'principles of eighteenth-century radicalism for which she had stood'. Those principles led her to criticise the exclusion of women from political and civil rights:

Though the situation of women in Modern Europe, when compared with that condition of abject slavery in which women have always been held in the east may be considered brilliant . . . yet we have no great reason to boast of our privileges, or of the candour and indulgence of the men towards us. For with a total and absolute exclusion from every political right to the sex in general, married women, whose situation demands a particular indulgence, have hardly a civil right to save them from the grossest injuries; and though the gallantry of some of the European societies have necessarily produced indulgence, yet in others the faults of women are treated with a severity and a rancour which militates against every principle of religion and common sense. [52]

Wollstonecraft shows that she is not only in sympathy with Macaulay's ideas but admires her as demonstrating the ability of women to make a serious contribution to learning. The respect with which she speaks of her is in line with Catherine Macaulay's own attitude as a young women to Elizabeth Carter; with Carter's praise of the work of other women, and of Elizabeth Elstob's acknowledgement of the encouragement she had received from Mary Astell. [53] Just as the women novelists praised each other's work, so between the learned ladies of a feminist tendency there was a strong wish to give recognition to female predecessors. Catherine Macaulay first achieved distinction as a learned lady in the mid-century style, but lived to write the first feminist work of the 1790s. When she was young, Mary Astell's name was still spoken of with respect by those who remembered her; the year before she died she wrote the work which exerted a greater influence on *Vindication* than any other. This is important in itself, and also in considering the connections between Wollstonecraft and Austen, for not only was there a direct influence of the older woman upon the younger, but they were both heirs to a common tradition of feminist development. Owing to the way in which our history of the eighteenth century has been written, with the distinguished women usually mentioned, if at all, in connection with their association with better-known men and male-dominated movements, schools or other groupings, the continuity of feminist development, in all its manifestations, is easily overlooked. Our habit of thinking of Mary Wollstonecraft as a Jacobin, and Jane Austen as a Lady Novelist praised by Scott, makes it difficult for us to see connections between them; attention to the 'feminist tradition' of the eighteenth century, in its widest sense, shows that it is by no means bizarre to look for such connection.

Wollstonecraft's first work on the woman question – *Thoughts on the Education of Daughters: with Reflections on Female Conduct, in the more Important Duties of Life* – came out three years before Macaulay's *Letters on Education*, and was less directly political in its implications. By 1792 she was prepared to go further, though the main emphasis was still on education, morals and religion. Janet Todd says of *Vindication*:

Pedagogical like her early works, it goes beyond them in expression and implication. Her previous aim had been to teach women to think. This was still her aim but it is expressed now in more striking terms, with full awareness of its revolutionary implication.[54]

The *Vindication* sums up the feminist ideas which had been developing over nearly a century. It places them in the new context of European change, following the events of 1789, but the manner and the arguments owe more to English sources of the pre-revolutionary period than they do to the *philosophes* or the Jacobins. The first thing that strikes one about it is its emphasis upon the authority of Reason and rational principle as the only true guide to right conduct. Wollstonecraft speaks freely and respectfully of religion, but considers true religion as in accordance with rational principles derived by rational beings from reflection upon experience. In this she follows Bishop Butler and Richard Price. God, or 'the Supreme Being', is also 'that unclouded principle of reason' to which men and women alike owe obedience and 'in whose service is perfect freedom' – an expression taken from the *Book of Common Prayer* of the Church of England, which I think she quotes rather more often than Austen does, just as she quotes Dr Johnson in more clearly favourable contexts than can be found in Austen.

Wollstonecraft is preoccupied in *Vindication* with women of the middle class, and she tells us why: 'I pay particular attention to those in the middle class, because they appear to be in the most natural state' (p. 266). What she means is that they are in that state where moral independence is most likely to be found. Rich women were corrupted by their artificial upbringing. The poor, lacking education and oppressed by physical labour, were in no position to think or act independently. In her mistrust of the rich and her faith in useful employment, Wollstonecraft is not unlike the chastened Sir Thomas Bertram of the final chapter of *Mansfield Park*, where he acknowledges 'the advantages of early hardship and discipline, and the consciousness of being born to struggle and endure'. In the *Vindication* we read:

> In the superior ranks of life how seldom do we meet with a man of superior abilities or even common acquirements? The reason appears to me to be clear, the state they were born to is an unnatural one. The human character has ever been formed by the employments the individual or the class pursues; and if the faculties are not sharpened by necessity, they must remain obtuse. (pp. 139–40)

Not only does the *Vindication* concern itself mainly with women of the middle class, but with women who are, or who will be, married. Mary Wollstonecraft quotes Lord Bacon's remark that 'the best works and of the greatest merit for the public, have proceeded from the unmarried or childless men'. She adds, 'I say the same of women.' But she gives nearly all her attention to women as daughters, wives and mothers, since it is in these roles that the great majority of women play their parts in the secular world, and she shows that the education they receive does not equip them to acquit themselves creditably even here. Girls brought up to be idle and unself-critical make poor mothers:

> The management of the temper, the first, and most important branch of education, requires the steady hand of reason; a plan of conduct equally distant from tyranny and indulgence. (p. 161)

Nor can women be acceptable companions to their husbands once initial passion has subsided, unless they bring other qualities besides beauty and sensibility. The two main objects of a married woman's life – to be of service to her husband and their children – cannot be fulfilled by the Rousseauist woman of sensibility. Those who advocate a trivialising education of women do most to unfit them for the only roles in life which they allow them. Girls subjected to it are like 'flowers planted in too rich a soil; strength and usefulness are sacrificed to beauty':

> One cause of this barren blooming I attribute to a false system of education, gathered from the books on this subject written þy men who, considering females rather as women than as human creatures, have been more anxious to make them alluring mistresses than affectionate wives and rational mothers . . . the civilised women of the present century, with a few exceptions, are only anxious to inspire love, when they ought to cherish a nobler ambition, and by their abilities and virtues exact respect. (p. 179)

Wollstonecraft supposes that girls, like boys, benefit from roughing it a little, and she opposes the belief that girls should be taught to cultivate an artificial weakness of body in order to make themselves attractive to men, and to excite in them noble feelings of protectiveness:

the first care of mothers and fathers who really attend to the education of females should be, if not to strengthen the body, at least not to destroy the constitution by mistaken notions of female excellence; nor should girls ever be allowed to imbibe the pernicious notion that a defect can, by any chemical process of reasoning, become an excellence. (pp. 111–12)

Girls and boys should 'play harmlessly together', and Mary Wollstonecraft affirms, 'as an indisputable fact', that

most of the women, in the circle of my observation, who have acted like rational creatures, or shown any vigour of intellect, have accidentally been allowed to run wild, as some of the elegant formers of the fair sex would insinuate. (pp. 129–30)

That physical weakness or lassitude could enhance a girl's sexual attractiveness may seem strange now: nor is religiosity thought alluring, but it was not always so. The prurience which found sexual excitement in 'angelic' girls did not begin in Victoria's reign. Mary Wollstonecraft has some harsh things to say about it, especially when men of religion give it a spurious respectability. She berates James Hervey, whose *Meditations and Contemplations* were 'still read', although they were written between 1745 and 1746. Hervey thought that:

Never, perhaps, does a fine woman strike more deeply, than when, composed into pious recollection, and possessed with the noblest considerations, she assumes, without knowing it, superior dignity and new graces; so that the beauties of holiness seem to radiate about her, and the bystanders are almost induced to fancy her already worshipping among the kindred angels. (pp. 193–4)

Wollstonecraft cannot stand that sort of thing. 'Should', she asks, 'a grave preacher interlard his discourses with such fooleries? . . . Why are girls to be told that they resemble angels: but to sink them below women?' Like Austen, she has no patience either with Dr Fordyce, whose *Sermons to Young Women* (1766) contain a remarkable passage in which the awfulness of abusing young angels is discussed with salacious relish:

Behold these smiling innocents, whom I have graced with my fairest gifts, and committed to your protection; behold them with love and respect; treat them with tenderness and honour. They are timid and want to be defended. They are frail; oh do not take advantage of their weakness! Let their fears and blushes endear them. Let their confidence in you never be abused. But is it possible, that any of you can be such barbarians, so supremely wicked, as to abuse it? Can you find in your hearts to despoil the gentle, trusting creatures of their treasure, or do anything to strip them of their native robe of virtue? Curst be the impious hand that would dare to violate the unblemished form of chastity! Thou wretch! thou ruffian! forbear; nor venture to provoke Heaven's fiercest vengeance. (pp. 192–3)

Wollstonecraft says, not unreasonably,

I know not any comment that can be made seriously on this curious passage, and I could produce many similar ones; and some, so very sentimental, that I have heard rational men use the word indecent when they mentioned them with disgust. (p. 193)

Austen knew how to deal with Dr Fordyce. These same sermons are chosen by Mr Collins, after rejecting a novel, to read aloud to the Bennet ladies in the drawing-room at Longbourn. It must have been during just such a passage that Lydia, 'a stout well-grown girl of fifteen', interrupted him to inform her mother of some interesting gossip about the regiment quartered nearby. In both Wollstonecraft and Austen there is the same objection to the sentimental treatment of girls as 'angels'; it makes them less than rational human beings and it invites hypocrisy, since everyone who has much to do with them knows that girls are not really much like angels anyway. Some may be taught to affect an angelic demeanour, and some men may like it, but observers and analysts of human nature ought not to be deceived.

Wollstonecraft associates lack of a proper education with women's exploitation of the marriage market:

[If they were better educated] women would not then marry for support, as men accept places under Government, and neglect the implied duties. (p. 261)

But as things are, the employments open to them 'far from being liberal are menial'. Even a girl of good education could look forward to nothing better than being a governess:

But as women educated like gentlewomen are never designed for the humiliating situation which necessity sometimes forces them to fill: these situations are considered in the light of degradation; and they know little of the human heart, who need to be told, that nothing so painfully sharpens sensibility as such a fall in life. (p. 261)

Taught to think of themselves as 'angels' or 'queens', middle-class girls without exceptional beauty and/or fortune are, as Wollstonecraft sees it, quite unfitted for the only opportunities actually open to them, and this cannot be changed until women are seen not as 'relative creatures' or 'objects' in a male-devised scenario, but as equal human beings, subject to the same moral principles:

For man and woman, truth, if I understand the meaning of the word, must be the same; yet in the fanciful female character, so prettily drawn by poets and novelists, demanding the sacrifice of truth and sincerity, virtue becomes a relative idea, having no other foundation than utility, and that utility men pretend arbitrarily to judge, shaping it to their own convenience.

Women, I allow, may have different duties to fulfil; but they are *human* duties, and the principles that should regulate the discharge of them, I sturdily maintain, must be the same.

To become respectable, the exercise of their understanding is necessary, there is no other foundation for independence of character; I mean explicitly to say that they must bow to the authority of *reason*, instead of being the *modest* slaves of opinion. (p. 139)

In these opinions, Wollstonecraft draws on the feminist tradition going back to Astell, but a new edge is given to them by her reading of Rousseau. As Susan Moller Okin shows, Rousseau, in one sense the apostle of liberty enlightened by reason,

argues all the most commonly held assertions that have, as part of our patriarchal culture, rationalised the separation and oppression of women.

Rousseau was a major inspiration of the Romantic movement in European literature, and may be seen as revolutionary in so far as he taught men and women to want change and to believe that it was possible. But, like the great English poet of liberty, John Milton, Rousseau excluded women from liberation through enlightenment. Okin says:

In keeping with a long tradition that, as we have seen, reaches back to Aristotle and beyond, Rousseau defines woman's nature, unlike man's, in terms of her function – that is her sexual and procreative purpose in life. While man has been categorised in terms of a generally limitless potential, for rational thought, creativity, and so on, woman has been viewed as functionally determined by her reproductive role, and her actual and potential abilities perceived as stunted, in accordance with what have been regarded as the requirements of this role. Woman's function is seen as physical and sensual, whereas man's potential is seen as creative and intellectual. For centuries, the extreme disparities between the method and extent of the education of the two sexes have been conveniently glossed over, as they are in Rousseau, as the case is made that women, while intuitive and equipped with a talent for detail, are deficient in rationality and quite incapable of abstract thought[55]

The refusal of Rousseau to admit the second sex into the new Garden of Eden, except on terms which perpetuated Eve's fall, though not

Adam's, was a bitter blow to those women who understood it, and saw the effects it had.

Mary Wollstonecraft shows as much embarrassment about the necessity of attacking Rousseau as the necessity of attacking Milton, for in both she goes against major inspirational figures with whom, apart from their exclusion of women from the benefits of liberty, under the law of Reason, she would have been in sympathy. All the same, she does not shirk the task of revealing the flaws in Rousseau's argument, starting with a false inference drawn from the physical differences between men and women. Rousseau

> then proceeds to prove that woman ought to be weak and passive, because she has less bodily strength than man; and hence infers that she was formed to please and to be subject to him, and that it is her duty to render herself *agreeable* to her master – this being the grand end of her existence. (p. 173)

Rousseau had thought that men and women should not be educated in the same manner, for 'the education of women should be always relative to men'. Wollstonecraft has difficulty in keeping her temper; she even indulges in a little irony:

> But granted that woman ought to be beautiful, innocent and silly, to render her a more alluring and indulgent companion; – what is her understanding sacrificed for? . . . only, according to Rousseau's own account, to make her the mistress of her husband for a very short time? For no man ever insisted more on the transient nature of love. (p. 187)

Wollstonecraft associates, among othes, Dr Fordyce, James Hervey and Dr Gregory with Rousseau. She complains that some women, including Madame de Genlis and Madame de Staël, have gone a good deal too far in their Rousseauist discipleship, contrasting them with Hester Chapone and Catherine Macaulay, of whom she approves.

Mary Wollstonecraft does not mention August von Kotzebue, for in 1792 he had not yet begun to write. Had she been revising the *Vindication* in 1800, or thereabouts, she would undoubtedly have included him in her list of 'writers who have rendered women objects of pity, bordering on contempt', for Kotzebue is entirely a Rousseauist in his treatment of women. English feminism in the Age of Reason was not 'liberated' in the sense that liberty was thought of in the Romantic way as 'making one's own world' or 'doing one's own thing'. Perfect liberty, as Wollstonecraft says – and Austen implies – was, for man or woman (but especially for woman), to be found in the service of that Rational Principle which good Butlerian Anglicans still called God. The underlying argument of the Austen novels – and they are novels in which argument matters – is entirely in accord with this. It looks old-fashioned now, but it should be noted that Austen is often most radical, *as a feminist*, where she sounds most out-dated (and most like Mary Wollstonecraft).

7 The Great Wollstonecraft Scandal of 1798

The resemblance between Wollstonecraft and Austen as feminist moralists is so striking that it seems extraordinary that it has not always been recognised, but that is to leave out of account the Great Wollstonecraft Scandal of 1798. The effects of this upon the development of feminism in England were profound. Before 1798, there were marked differences between those who advocated political rights for women and those who merely advocated that they receive an education fit for rational beings, but the bolder and the more timid might still be seen as moving in the same direction. The Scandal, which directed attention away from the perfectly respectable arguments of Enlightenment feminism to the 'Irregularities' of Mary Wollstonecraft's sexual conduct, had the effect of polarising women with any kind of public reputation into 'Unsex'd Females' or paragons of sexual virtue, without a rebellious thought in their heads.

As Claire Tomalin shows,[56] Wollstonecraft's death was noticed without an outbreak of hostility against her, but five months later, against the advice of many of her friends, Godwin published *Memoirs of the Author of a Vindication of the Rights of Woman*. With a genuine respect for truth, but a total lack of interest in how the truth would be received and what effects it would have, he disclosed full details of his wife's relationship with Imlay, her suicide attempts, and her having conceived his child before marriage. He also praised, without full regard for the truth, her rejection of Christianity. Some of Wollstonecraft's friends found it hard to acquit Godwin of culpable stupidity. The anonymous author of *A Defence of the Character and Conduct of the Late Mary Wollstonecraft Godwin, founded on the Principles of Nature and Reason, as Applied to the Peculiar Circumstances of her Case* (1803) was one. His *Defence* is addressed to an anonymous lady, and it is made clear that both knew Wollstonecraft well, and were distressed by the unjust attacks made upon her. I believe that Joseph Johnson, the Dissenting publisher, must have been the author of this work, and that Anna Barbauld, who wrote in defence of Wollstonecraft without endorsing all her opinions, was the lady to whom it was addressed. Johnson, if it were he, says of Godwin:

> Yet, with an unaccountable inconsistency, no sooner was she deposited in the cold lap of our common mother, than her husband, as if *sworn to declare the truth and the whole truth*, promulgated to the world the very circumstance, which he must know would injure her credit with the respectable part of the community, and thus undermine the influence which she had been labouring to acquire. He knew the shafts of calumny had already been launched against her, and yet, most unaccountably he added to the cause, by giving a publicity to circumstances, over which common discretion would have endeavoured to draw an eternal veil. After such an unfortunate oversight, I feel astonished at his neglecting to vindicate her character and account for his own conduct: had he done this with the ability he confessedly possesses, and the glowing ardour that, as a party so nearly interested he ought to feel; I am persuaded that any remarks of mine would have been unnecessary, as the extenuation of her conduct would have issued from a much more able hand. (pp. 52–3)

Everything written on the subject of female emancipation for the next two decades, if not for much longer, has to be understood in the light of public reaction to the *Memoirs*, and the violent personal abuse which they provoked. Wollstonecraft was now branded as a whore and an atheist, and other women who dared to show sympathy with her ideas could not expect to escape calumny. Mary Hays, who defended her friend and supported her claims on behalf of women, was subjected to personal attack, although there were no sexual scandals to mull over in her case. She was, with Wollstonecraft, the subject of the Rev. Richard Polwhele's anti-feminist satirical poem, *The Unsex'd Females*, published in 1798. Anna Barbauld, who had been a friend of Wollstonecraft's since the Newington Green days, avoided joining in the general condemnation, and was probably the anonymous author of two articles in which her sincerity and genius were praised, although her feminist views were not endorsed. Mrs Opie, who had also been a close friend, now made public her condemnation. Half a century later, Mary Russell Mitford shows she found it impossible to forgive Mrs Opie's treatment of Wollstonecraft.

Among the women who wrote on the sensitive subject of female education after 1798, many were at pains to deny that their wish to see girls taught to think carried any radical political implications. Some, like Mrs Jane West, were especially slavish about it;[57] others, like Maria Edgeworth and Hannah More, were simply cautious to the point of half-denying the case they argued. There is no reason to suppose that, had the Wollstonecraft scandal not occurred, women like Edgeworth and More would have written on feminist subjects in the same spirit as Wollstonecraft, but I doubt if they would have needed to display their acceptance of social restrictions upon women quite so ostentatiously. Given the circumstances in which they actually wrote, the similarities between Wollstonecraft, Hays, Edgeworth and More on the subject of female education seem quite as remarkable as their differences.

II The Publication and Reception of Jane Austen's Novels, 1797–1818

8 The Feminist Controversy and the Received Biography

Jane Austen was born in December 1775 and was thus sixteen when the *Vindication* was published. She grew up and became a novelist in the following decade when the Feminist Controversy, in which fiction played an important part, was at its height. Many critics have noticed that feminist feeling and feminist ideas are easily apparent in her novels, yet the full importance of the Controversy, as exercising an influence upon the development of her work and its publication, has not been made apparent, nor has it been taken sufficiently into account in considering the way Jane Austen was presented to the public after her early death. Yet one has only to take note of one or two dates to see that, given her subject-matter, the events of 1797–8 must have been significant.

In 1797 Jane Austen felt ready to publish 'First Impressions' and her father wrote to Messrs Cadell about it on her behalf, taking care to say that he was 'well aware of what importance it is that a work of this sort [the unstated implication was that it was by a lady, though Mr Austen's daughter was not actually mentioned] should make its first appearance under a respectable name'.[1] He meant the name of the publisher, and the wary note indicates his, and perhaps his daughter's, apprehension of the kind of attack which *First Impressions* might attract. Why nothing came of this we do not know (the story about the instant, dismissive reply of the publisher is late and not reliable).[2] In January 1798 Godwin published *Memoirs of the Author of a Vindication of the Rights of Woman* and the full fury of the anti-feminist backlash was let loose.

At this time Jane Austen was twenty-two and unmarried. Had her name or one of her novels become associated in any way with the Controversy, she would have been a vulnerable subject of attack, despite her being 'of good family' – indeed, her family might well have suffered a great deal of embarrassment. Her novels made no attempt to disguise 'the sparkle of confident intelligence' and went so far as to criticise those who thought this necessary in young women. If 'First Impressions' was substantially *Pride and Prejudice* unrevised, it must have included an implied criticism of the practice of entailing property in the male line, a strongly satirical portrait of a clergyman, and a condemnation of such meal-ticket marriages as that made by Charlotte Lucas, in terms reminiscent of the *Vindication*. Had *First Impressions* appeared early in 1798 we dare not guess what such moralists as the Rev. Richard Polwhele might have said about it. But it was not published and we neither know why, nor what the author thought about it – though I have sometimes wondered whether her unaccountable aversion to the name 'Richard', and her making the Rev. Mr Morland in the novel written between 1798 and 1799, 'a very respectable man, though his name was Richard', amounted to an obscure dig at Polwhele and what he stood for.

Leaving such flippant speculation aside, we surely ought to ask if there is evidence that Jane Austen's development as a novelist was affected by the reaction against feminism after 1798. We know, of course, that there was a long gap between the writing of the early novels and the later ones, and that the later novels were different in style and tone as well as in complexity. Could this have anything to do with the clamp-down on feminism between the completion of *Northanger Abbey* and the delayed publication of *Sense and Sensibility*? Biographers have not thought so. Noticing an apparent abandonment of authorship at this period, and a lack of information about Jane Austen's life, it has been suggested that she was unhappy, possibly preoccupied with what R. W. Chapman calls 'Romance' and therefore gave up writing. There is little, if any, reliable evidence about it. 'Family sources', round about 1870, suggested that in 1801, or thereabouts, Jane Austen became attached to a rather nebulous gentleman whose name is uncertain. He may, if he existed, have gone to Sidmouth (or some other West Country seaside place) while Jane Austen was there, and soon after died or disappeared without trace. Even if the story were more convincing, would it amount to a sufficient explanation of the hiatus in the novelist's development, let alone of the curious history of her early failure and later success in achieving publication? It seems to me that it would not. Biographers, even the careful and scholarly Dr Chapman and Jane Aiken Hodge (whose *The Double Life of Jane Austen* is intelligent, as well as readable) have been led away from the one public matter of consequence with which Jane Austen was seriously involved, and which has an important bearing on the whole development of her art. Aiken Hodge says, at the start of her Introduction,

In Jane Austen's lifetime, it occurred to no one that she would one day be famous, that future generations would be eager for details of the intensely private life of 't' other Miss Austen'. Burying her, in 1817, in Winchester Cathedral, her grieving family paid due tribute to 'the benevolence of her heart, the sweetness of her temper, and the extraordinary endowments of her mind', but did not think to mention the six novels that would bring people from all over the world to look at the plain, stone slab that marks her grave.[3]

The full text of what Jane Austen's 'grieving family' put as a permanent memorial to her is as follows:

In Memory of
JANE AUSTEN
youngest daughter of the late
Revd. GEORGE AUSTEN
Formerly Rector of Steventon in this County.
She departed this Life on the 18th. of July 1817
aged 41, after a long illness supported with
the patience and the hopes of a Christian.

The benevolence of her heart
the sweetness of her temperament
the extraordinary endowment of her mind
obtained the regard of all who knew her and
the warmest love of her intimate connections.

Their grief is in porportion to their affection
they know their loss to be irreparable
but in their deepest affliction they are consoled
by a firm though humble hope that her charity
devotion, faith and purity have rendered
her soul acceptable in the sight of her
REDEEMER

It is certainly remarkable in its insistence upon Christian virtue and total silence about the literary distinction which had, presumably, earned her the honour of a cathedral burial. Were the words on the stone engraved in naïve unawareness that the author of '*Pride and Prejudice &*' might attract further notice, or was this the first attempt at dealing with what Caroline Austen, nearly fifty years later, called 'the vexed question of the Austens and the public'?[4]

As it happens, we can be sure that some of the Austens were aware of the possibility that posterity might be interested in her, for Henry Austen, in the *Biographical Notice*, written only five months after her death, says that her works, which he compares with those of Fanny Burney and Maria Edgeworth, 'may live as long as those which have burst on the world with more éclat'. And he says that she had already received applause from that part of the public 'competent to discriminate'. This was not written by one who had no premonition of the fame that was later to come to Jane Austen and it is important to see how he wrote, bearing in mind not only 'future generations' but those who, at the time, were likely to take an interest in her. Jane Austen had made her sister Cassandra her literary executrix, but it was Henry who saw to getting *Northanger Abbey* and *Persuasion* published, and he who wrote the *Biographical Notice* which was prefaced to them. Jane Austen had declared her sex on the title-page of *Sense and Sensibility*, but she was responsible for nothing else that was made public about her. Henry, undertaking publication of *Northanger Abbey* – the novel Crosby had suppressed in 1803 – together with *Persuasion*, whose moral tendency was objected to by an 1818 reviewer because it encouraged young people to trust their own judgement, sounds a guarded and defensive note in presenting the author to the public. He hopes his 'brief account of Jane Austen will be read with a kindlier feeling than simple curiosity'. Not only does he stress her domesticity and contentment but, at the end, he places the utmost emphasis upon her piety:

One trait only remains to be touched on. It makes all others unimportant. She was thoroughly religious and devout; fearful of giving offence to God, and incapable of feeling it towards any fellow creature.[5]

Would it have been necessary to have put it quite like that had Henry Austen been writing about a brother? It is followed by some excerpts from the letters, designed to emphasise domesticity, and discount serious authorship. The first is the notorious 'little bit of ivory' letter.[6]

Every reader of Jane Austen since 1818 has been provided with a portrait of the author which stresses the lack of incident in her life, and her preference for a retired, domestic existence. Perhaps nobody takes Henry Austen's portrait quite literally – it so clearly fails to match the character we know through the novels and the surviving letters – yet, because it is the only biographical work written by a contemporary who knew Jane Austen intimately, we feel that it must have some authority. And, if Jane Austen were at all like the woman described by Henry, she could hardly have written works which, through their irony, make serious criticisms of gross error in contemporary life and literature. To suggest that the sainted spinster-aunt of Chawton was a feminist who agreed, on a number of issues, with Mary Wollstonecraft, might seem little short of blasphemy. And that, I think, is exactly what Henry Austen intended. He knew that, given the prejudice of the time, his sister's personal reputation might not escape embarrassing comment were the full force of her irony to be understood. No matter how blameless her life, a woman known to have avoided marriage and to have held independent views of a feminist kind might not be kindly or respectfully treated.

The *Biographical Notice*, – which might be better entitled the *Hagiographical Notice* – seeks to establish the author's respectability, and to inhibit speculation about her personal life. As such, it is a remarkably effective piece of writing and no wonder, for we have it on good authority that Henry Austen was a clever, witty, sophisticated man. Had Jane Austen really been the pious mouse that he turns her into, she would not have been his favourite sister and life-long friend, yet he assures us that she 'never uttered either a hasty, a silly or a severe expression', that she 'recoiled from everything gross', that she was censorious about Fielding, that she regarded the £150 she received for *Sense and Sensibility* as 'a prodigious reward for what had cost her nothing', that she was nervous about being known as an author, although willing, within the family circle, to discuss her works, being 'thankful for praise, open to remark and submissive of criticism' and, to crown it all, he represents her Christian faith, not as the faith of conviction, but of timidity and subservience: she was 'well-instructed' on 'serious subjects' and held opinions according 'strictly with those of our Established Church'.

This nonsense has sometimes been read as the naïve sentimentality of an affectionate brother who after all (everything else having failed) did, in the end, become a clergyman. I give Henry Austen more credit than this. The *Biographical Notice* is an absurdity but, in an age when a young, unmarried woman could not be accounted respectable unless she was represented in this ridiculous way, its absurdity is understandable. The *Notice*, in so far as it asserts that the author of *Northanger Abbey* was a good woman, deserving of respect despite her cleverness, may be seen as true in spirit, but modern readers, free of the prejudices of the early nineteenth century, should no longer allow their idea of the narrator of '*Pride and Prejudice* &' to be uncritically guided by it.

The Austen novels require the reader to form an idea of the narrator, at least to the extent of ascertaining her point of view about morals, marriage and authority within the family, and her attitudes to particular authors and literary movements. Henry Austen's account of his sister's life and character was, I believe, designed to disarm ill-natured and illiberal criticism. Unfortunately, it has also had the effect, long after the feminist views of Jane Austen have become entirely respectable and a little old-fashioned, of giving a

false, unduly limited impression of the novelist and of her engagement with feminist issues, as they were seen in her time.

In order to read the *Biographical Notice* aright, one should recall
that, in 1803, the year that Crosby's did *not* publish *Susan*, Joseph
Johnson (if it were he who wrote *A Defence of the Author of A
Vindication of the Rights of Woman*) had quoted Laertes – 'A Ministering Angel will my Sister be/When thou liest howling' – in rebuking
those churlish moralists and divines who had insulted the memory of
Mary Wollstonecraft:

the world was not worthy of her; for its absurdities, its prejudice, its vices
and its vanities, she was much too intelligent, too independent, too good
and too great.[7]

The point was not lost on Henry Austen, who would certainly have
been familiar with the controversy sparked off by Godwin's
Memoirs. It fell to him, as the brother of another 'intelligent',
'inependent', 'good' and 'great' woman, to present her unpublished
works to the world at large, and he was more astute than Godwin in
taking account of the 'absurdities, prejudices, vices and vanities' of
the age. The *Biographical Notice* should be read with that in mind. It
served the purpose for which it was intended well, as the critical
literature up to 1870 shows. The author who was made 'sick and
wicked' by 'pictures of perfection' was herself established as an
exemplary daughter, sister and aunt, who happened to write some
very good novels without in any way offending against the strictest
standards of female delicacy and self-effacement.

Henry Austen's portrait gave a firm outline of an exemplary
feminine character, but spared us the minutiae of games of Spillikins
and the making of patchwork quilts. All that was filled in by James
Edward Austen-Leigh in the *Memoir* of 1870. In 1942, Q. D. Leavis
protested against the 'conventional account of Miss Austen as prim,
demure, sedate, prudish and so on, the typical Victorian maiden
lady'.[8] It did not, she rightly noted, match the evidence of the
published letters, highly selected and censored though these are. But
the Jane Austen created by family biographers in the Victorian age,
and finalised in 1913 by W. and R. A. Austen-Leigh's *Life and Letters*,
is still frequently and uncritically referred to in modern critical
writing. This is not the place to consider in detail the reliability of the
biography which took shape substantially in 1870, more than fifty
years after Jane Austen's death. It is, however, worth noting that
J. E. Austen-Leigh, although the novelist's nephew, had not known
her intimately, as he admits, and that, by the time he undertook the
task of writing a substantial account of her life, a great deal of the

first-hand material on which it ought to have been based had disappeared. What survived was very selective, and the biographer's own attitudes ensured that what was known, as well as what was believed (sometimes without clear foundation), was presented in a way which emphasised the domestic contentment of the devoted aunt, rather than the professionalism of the determined novelist.

James Edward Austen-Leigh had been little more than a school-boy when his aunt died. He was a clergyman of over seventy at the time he put the *Memoir* together. His assimilation of Jane Austen to a Victorian ideal is neatly illustrated by the portrait which he published in the first edition of the *Memoir* which, despite its spuriousness, remains the most frequently reproduced 'likeness'. It is, as Chapman called it, 'tediously familiar', and continues to exert a harmful influence upon the reading of the novels.

Two portraits of Jane Austen are reproduced as frontispiece to this book. The top one, drawn by Cassandra when both were still young, is the only authentic portrait known. It shows a young woman with penetrating dark eyes, sitting with arms rather aggres-sively crossed and staring boldly ahead. The mouth is caustic, and there is no more than the suspicion of a smile; the curls are slightly absurd. The subject is plainly attired and sits on what appears to be a simple, country-made, ladder-back chair. The lower portrait is the one commissioned for the *Memoir*, and executed by Mr Andrews of Maidenhead, on the basis of Cassandra's unacceptable sketch and the advice of the now elderly relations, who told him what their recollection of the appearance of the author was, as they saw her more than half a century earlier. Mr Andrews' Jane Austen is altogether more decorous than Cassandra's. The face is no longer slightly alarming, the cap and curls are prettier, the pose is more ladylike and the chair would belong comfortably in a Victorian dining room. The dress is right for the turn of the century, but this is a Victorian lady, dressed up in the fashion of another age, who could not have read Mary Wollstonecraft or sympathised with some of her ideas, although the young woman of Cassandra's sketch looks as though she might.

The received biography informs us about Jane Austen's family and domestic life, but leaves out a great deal that matters to the develop-ment of the novelist. The published letters are but a small selection of all those written, and have been subjected to a good deal of cen-sorship. Our accepted portrait of the novelist is too often treated as though it were a fuller and more accurate likeness than it really is. In particular, the idea that Jane Austen was reluctant to publish and that the years she spent in Bath were unimportant need questioning, for there is reason to think that her failure to become a publishing author was connected with the Feminist Controversy; that she was well aware of this; and that the change in style and manner between the early and late novels came about partly as a response to the difficulties she encountered. There is also reason to think that the period spent in Bath was of great importance in widening her intellectual and literary horizons, and in giving her greater independence in her choice of reading, as well as bringing her into contact with people she would not have met at Steventon.

Virginia Woolf, relying on the *Memoir* which she quotes, formed the impression that Jane Austen not only lived in obscurity, but was quite unacquainted with the ways of fashionable and literary people. In *The Common Reader* she considers what would have happened had her life been longer: 'She would have stayed in London, dined out, lunched out, met famous people, made new friends, read, travelled, and carried back to the quiet country cottage a hoard of observations to feast upon at leisure.' As a result of such experiences,

She would have devised a method, clear and composed as ever, but deeper and more suggestive, for conveying not only what people say, but what they leave unsaid; not only what they are, but what life is. She would have stood farther away from her characters, and seen them more as a group, less as individuals. Her satire, while it played less incessantly, would have been more stringent and severe.[9]

I think that, through her frequent visits to London, where she stayed with Henry Austen and his wife, the former Countess de Feuillide, who was their cousin, Jane Austen had, throughout her adult life, more acquaintance with the fashionable world than is generally supposed. But between 1801 and 1806, from the age of twenty-five to thirty, her life in Bath must also have given her whatever advantages could be gained from such experience and this did in fact have something of the effect which Virginia Woolf speaks of, for in the later novels Jane Austen does stand further away from her characters, does see them more as a group, less as individuals, and her satire does become more stringent and severe. It seems worth taking a new look at this period of the novelist's life.

9 Residence in Bath

Since what is believed, on the strength of family tradition, continues to exert so strong an influence upon our beliefs about Jane Austen, we had better start by examining what is known about this period. First the letters: there is a marked lack of letters written at this time, and it has been assumed by R. W. Chapman and others that they were destroyed because they were concerned with 'intimate' feelings, especially about the two sisters' love relationships. This assumption should not be accepted uncritically, for Cassandra's censorship of the letters, finally made about 1843 when she was seventy, may well have been designed to expugn from the record evidence of her sister's interest in matters of a more public nature, including her opinions of plays seen, reviews read, books borrowed from the circulating libraries, and of people met or observed.

Secondly, the family biographies: the *Biographical Notice* tells us only that Jane Austen lived in Bath with her parents after her father retired, and that he died there. Curiously, since he must surely have known, or been easily able to check, how long she lived there, he says it was 'a period of about four years'. It was actually five. The *Memoir* repeats this error and, observing that the author can find only three letters (all written to Cassandra) from this time, says: 'They shew that she went a good deal into society, in a quiet way, chiefly with ladies' (p. 68). It is a masterly dismissal of five vital years in the author's life in such a way as to inhibit further interest in them. Later, it came to be accepted that Jane Austen disliked Bath and was unhappy there, the evidence for this being the story of her having fainted away when told of her father's decision to leave Steventon, and two references in later letters to feelings of relief at having escaped from Bath to Clifton in the hot weather of July 1806. To take the second and less important point first: complaints about the weather in Bath in midsummer were common. Bryan Little, in his *Bath Portrait*, comments on this, saying: 'The better air of Upper Clifton, as I know from living in both places, was preferable to Bath's long drowsy days of summer heat.' He quotes Lady Nelson who, in 1797, wrote to her husband that Bath was 'so hot in summer, and so stinking that very few remain in it'. Jane Austen's comments on pleasure in leaving Bath both occur in letters written in midsummer and in which the unpleasantness of heat are under discussion; there is therefore no reason to suppose that she is voicing anything more than the general opinion about the summer climate of the place.

The 'fainting' story is more important because it illustrates the way in which the life of the legendary Jane Austen has been created. In the 1913 *Life* (p. 154), we are told that:

> Tradition says that when Jane Austen returned home accompanied by Martha Lloyd the news was abruptly announced by her mother, who thus greeted them: 'Well, girls, it is all settled: we have decided to leave Steventon in such a week and go to Bath'; and the shock of the intelligence was so great to Jane that she fainted away.

That was what 'tradition' said in 1913. The story was derived from a letter written by Jane Austen's niece Caroline, to her brother James Edward, in 1869. It is quoted by Chapman in *Facts and Problems:*

> My aunt was very sorry to leave her native home, as I have heard my mother relate. My Aunts had been away a little while and were met in the Hall on their return by their Mother who told them it was all settled, and they were going to live in Bath. My Mother who was present said my Aunt was greatly distressed. All things were done in a hurry by Mr. Austen. (p. 46)

This is a tame version compared with the later one, and it is inaccurate in one respect, as Chapman points out and as the author of the *Life* must have surmised. Jane Austen returned from Ibthorpe with Martha Lloyd; Cassandra was away from home in that year for more than six months.

Although Chapman, with his concern for accurate detail, spotted this error, he did not allow it to modify in any way the traditional family view of how Jane Austen reacted to this change. His handling of this phase of her life and Jane Austen's own remarks are in amusing contrast. He says:

> We cannot doubt that the loss of her native county and of the multitude of associations which made up her girlish experience was exquisitely painful. Her feelings cannot have been less acute than Marianne's on leaving Norland, or Anne's on leaving Kellynch. Her return to her own country, eight years later, was the long delayed return of an exile.

Jane Austen's own account of her feelings are quite different:

> I get more and more reconciled to the idea of our removal. We have lived long enough in this Neighbourhood, the Basingstoke Balls are certainly in

decline, there is something interesting in the bustle of going away, and the prospect of spending summers by the Sea or in Wales is very delightful. For a time we shall possess many of the advantages which I have often thought of with Envy in the wives of Sailors and Soldiers. – It must not be generally known however that I am not sacrificing a great deal in quitting the Country – or I can expect to inspire little tenderness in those we leave behind. (*Letters*, p. 103)

There is no support here for the idea that Jane Austen had a settled dislike of Bath; nor in the letters that survive from this period (some written a year or two earlier) when she was staying there, but before the move, is there support for J. E. Austen-Leigh's assertion that she went into society 'in a quiet way, chiefly with ladies'. The Leigh-Perrots entertained in style in the Paragon, sometimes giving parties for ninety guests, and they invited a wide assortment of people, by no means all ladies. Jane Austen seems to have participated in the general social life of the place, including the public breakfasts in Sydney Gardens and other gaudy entertainments. There is no reason to suppose she did not get a good deal of amusement out of them, and she shows that she welcomed the chance to mix with a new set of people. In 1801, for example, she reports having met Mr Pickford, who was as 'raffish in his appearance as I would wish every disciple of Godwin to be', and his elegant wife. A day or two later, when she is looking forward to another party, she says she hopes they will be there, and does not distance this with a joke or any sign of disapprobation.

The two letters of April 1805 show that even in the period after her father's death she was much engaged with the social round and the public concerts and other entertainments of Bath, and expressed no particular dissatisfaction with it. She shows her awareness of the importance of this period in her own development when she says, after a reference to December 1797, 'What a different set we are now moving in! But seven years are enough to change every pore of one's skin and every feeling of one's mind.'

At the time the Austens moved to Bath, the city was just about to experience a short revival of the social brilliance it had known in its earlier hey day. Because the Napoleonic Wars made it impossible to make the Grand Tour, people of fashion once again came to Bath. In February 1802, the Duke and Duchess of York, who had made previous visits to Bath, came for the latter half of the season and they were followed, in 1803, by the Prince and Princess Grassalkotine and Prince and Princess Esterhazy. The presence of these aristocratic parties brought Bath into favour not only with the English but, to some extent, with foreign visitors who were deprived of their usual haunts. The Bath newspapers of the time were full of reports of masquerades, firework displays and fancy dress balls on an extravagant scale and attended by the rich and famous. And Bath continued to attract well-known literary people. William Beckford's return to Fonthill in 1803 was well covered by the gossip column of the *Bath Journal*. Hannah More was often to be seen there, as was Wilberforce. Sophia Lee, the author of *The Recess*, lived in Bath, and Mrs Piozzi settled there in 1804. Among those who came as visitors were Sir John Hawkins, Thomas Holcroft, Shelley (aged seventeen), Southey and Landor. Jane Austen must, at this period, have seen, read and heard about a good many 'famous people', even if she did not get to know any of them personally. We know from her letters that she read the Bath papers, especially the 'Arrived Here' column, with interest.

At this period there were, apart from good bookshops, some ten circulating libraries in Bath. For 15 shillings a year, or 2s 6d a month, a subscriber might borrow two books, to be changed as often as desired, and the libraries made a point of stocking new books in French and Italian, as well as in English. As V. J. Kite shows, it was not true that novels formed the greater part of their stock, nor that women comprised the majority of their subscribers.[10] In Bath, Jane Austen must have had access to virtually any author she wished to read and a quiet reading-room too if she wanted it, since these were provided by the bigger libraries.

Lastly, there was the theatre which, as *Mansfield Park* shows, provided a new stimulus for later work. In letters written after 1811 from London, Jane Austen shows that she had been familiar at an earlier period with the acting of Robert Elliston, Charles Matthews, Mrs Edwin and Mrs Siddons, all of whom performed in Bath while she lived there. It must have been at this period that she had the best opportunity of acquiring a love of 'good hardened acting', which she was later to contrast with the 'raw efforts of those who have not been bred to the trade'. The Theatre Royal at Bath had probably the best company outside London. Most of the actors migrated to London, and those who had already done so frequently came back to play there during the season. The repertory was substantially the same as in the London theatres, with performances on two or three nights a week and a change of programme for each occasion. The arrival and departure of actors was given some prominence in the Bath press, and the merits of their performances noticed at length. Thus, during the years 1801–6, Jane Austen had the chance of seeing not only those plays of Shakespeare which held a regular place in the repertory, but the many new ones, like those by Kotzebue, which were both very successful and highly controversial.

10   The Curious History of
Mrs Ashton Dennis (M.A.D.)

Jane Austen would have liked to see *First Impressions* in print in 1798, but she did not actually succeed in publishing anything until 1811, when *Sense and Sensibility* appeared at her own expense. By 1799 the first drafts of three novels had been completed and there may have been other attempts at publication of which no record survives. If Cassandra Austen's memorandum is to be trusted, no new work, apart from *The Watsons*, was begun until 1811, when *Mansfield Park* was started, but there is no need to assume that Jane Austen was not actively concerned with the writing *and publishing* of novels during this time. We know that she went on thinking about the possibilities of short early pieces like *Lady Susan*, which Q. D. Leavis thought important to the germination of *Mansfield Park*. There may have been other short or incompleted pieces of writing which also had their place in the germination of the later novels, for there is evidence that ideas used in *Mansfield Park* and *Emma* were slowly worked on from as early as 1799.[11] We also know that she played about with some apparently aimless spoofs, like the theatrical burlesque of *Sir Charles Grandison*.

What is certain is that before she embarked on the seven-year period of intensive literary work from 1809 to 1816, during which time she revised two early novels pretty thoroughly, and wrote three new ones, Jane Austen had made two more attempts to get her work published. We know too that she was angry and disappointed at her failure in both of them, but the possibility that this, rather than dislike of Bath or disappointment in love, had a profound effect upon her development as a novelist has not been sufficiently thought about. The novel which failed to get into print in its author's life-time was *Susan* – later *Northanger Abbey* – and its history is of crucial importance to an understanding of how Jane Austen's development as an author was affected by the Feminist Controversy and its aftermath, and what lay behind the long gap between the writing of 'the lost originals' of the three early novels and the three later novels.

It begins with an inconsistency: Cassandra Austen's memorandum records that 'North-hanger Abbey was written about the years 98 & 99',[12] but the 'Advertisement', prefaced to it in Henry Austen's edition as 'by the authoress', says that it 'was finished in the year 1803, and intended for immediate publication'. What this probably means is that *Northanger Abbey*, the last of the early novels, underwent pretty thorough revision while Jane Austen was in Bath where she was living when she succeeded in selling it to Messrs Crosby and, for a brief period, thought she had, at the age of twenty-seven, become a publishable novelist. This turned out not to be the case because, although Crosby's advertised the novel, they never actually published it. Whether Jane Austen protested earlier we do not know, but when she wrote to them tartly on their negligence in 1809 they were, to say the least, unhelpful. Yet we know that, in 1809, two years before she decided to publish *Sense and Sensibility* off her own bat, Jane Austen would have liked to see *Northanger Abbey* in print as her first publication. We do not know what the title-page would have looked like, but we do know that *Northanger Abbey* shows an awareness of sexist bias in 'the Tradition' and in the way that works written by women were received by reviewers. It includes in chapter V a remarkable passage in which the novel is defended against its detractors and in which the undervaluing of women's writing is attacked. The 'Northanger Defence of the Novel' is uncharacteristic of the author in that it amounts to an interpolation in her work of matter not strictly to the point of the 'story'. It is the *only* statement about the novel which she ever intended for publication. It is quite different in tone from her scattered remarks on the same subject in family letters, and indicates a very different idea of the scope and value of fiction (including her own) from that suggested in 'the blessed bit of ivory' letter.

The 'Northanger Defence' is of such importance to the present study of feminism, as a moral interest which informs the development of Jane Austen's art, that it must be quoted in full. The 'Defence' comes in the last section of the unusually long chapter V, which begins with a satirical account of the rapid progress to intimacy of Catherine Morland's friendship with the hypocritical Isabella Thorpe. The transition from this to the subject of fiction occurs as their resolution to meet 'in defiance of wet and dirt, and shut themselves up, to read novels together' is recorded. The author then distances herself from her heroine and anti-heroine in an aside which leads into the 'Defence' itself:

Yes, novels; – for I will not adopt that ungenerous and impolitic custom so common with novel writers, of degrading by their contemptuous censure the very performances, to the number of which they are themselves adding – joining with their enemies in bestowing the harshest epithets on such works, and scarcely ever permitting them to be read by their own heroine, who, if she accidentally takes up a novel, is sure to turn over its insipid pages with disgust. Alas! if the heroine of one novel be not patronised by the heroine of another, from whom can she expect protection and regard? I cannot approve of it. Let us leave it to the Reviewers to abuse such effusions of fancy at their leisure, and over every new novel to talk in threadbare strains of the trash with which the press now groans. Let us not desert one another; we are an injured body. Although our productions have afforded more extensive and unaffected pleasure than those of any other literary corporation in the world, no species of composition has been so much decried. From pride, ignorance, or fashion, our foes are almost as many as our readers. And while the abilities of the nine-hundredth abridger of the History of England, or the man who collects and publishes in a volume some dozen lines of Milton, Pope and Prior, with a paper from the *Spectator*, and a chapter from Sterne, are eulogised by a thousand pens, – there seems almost a general wish of decrying the capacity and undervaluing the labour of the novelist, and of slighting the performances which have only genius, wit, and taste to recommend them. 'I am no novel reader – I seldom look into novels – Do not imagine that *I* often read novels – It is really very well for a novel.' Such is the common cant. – 'And what are you reading, Miss——?' 'Oh! it is only a novel!' replies the young lady; while she lays down her book with affected indifference, or momentary shame. – 'It is only Cecilia, or Camilla, or Belinda'; or, in short, only some work in which the greatest powers of the mind are displayed, in which the most thorough knowledge of human nature, the happiest delineation of its varieties, the liveliest effusions of wit and humour are conveyed to the world in the best chosen language. Now, had the same young lady been engaged with a volume of the *Spectator*, instead of such a work, how proudly would she have produced the book and told its name; though the chances must be against her being occupied by any part of that voluminous publication, of which either the matter or manner would not disgust a young person of taste; the substance of its papers so often consisting in the statement of improbable circumstances, unnatural characters, and topics of conversation, which no longer concern any one living; and their language too, frequently so coarse as to give no very favourable idea of the age that could endure it. (pp. 37–8)

The most striking thing about this passage is the strength with which the novel, as a literary form, is defended and the idea given of its scope and importance. A novel is a 'work in which the greatest powers of the mind are displayed . . . the most thorough knowledge of human nature'. Such works are not written without the exercise of mental powers of a high order, nor without the expenditure of time and energy, and yet 'there seems almost a general wish of decrying the capacity and undervaluing the labour of the novelist'. The passage is impassioned and the author's language, as she develops her point, becomes less discreet. She is disrespectful, yet impersonal, about 'the abilities of the nine-hundredth abridger of the History of England', but, as she warms to her polemic, she pours scorn not on the 'miscellanist' but the 'man' who acquires a literary reputation at second hand. It can hardly be accidental that the three novels cited in justification of her claims for the genre are all by women. The plea 'Let us not desert one another; we are an injured body', wryly made to heroines and authors alike, does not specify women authors, but the cry is a cry for literary sisterhood, associated with the literary form in which women had, at long last, acquired a voice. The novelists addressed here are, by implication, women novelists, the 'Reviewers' who abuse their work, men. The 'Northanger Defence' shows that Jane Austen did not regard herself as practising an art at all like that of the miniaturist or worker in ivory. And it shows that she held a self-conscious, feminist view of the tradition in which she, and other women, were establishing themselves as reputable novelists.

At sixteen she had written a burlesque *History of England*, in which scepticism as to the value and validity of a great deal of historical writing is implied. In *Northanger Abbey*, 'the nine-hundredth abridger of the History of England' takes his place with other literary men who do not deserve the respect accorded them. Later, in chapter XIV, Catherine, who often functions as the child who sees that the emperor has no clothes, explains why she is not fond of History:

'I read it a little as a duty, but it tells me nothing that does not either vex or weary me. The quarrels of popes and kings, with wars or pestilences, in every page; the men all so good for nothing, and hardly any women at all – it is very tiresome: and yet I often think it odd that it should be so dull, for a great deal of it must be invention.'

Jane Austen's scepticism about 'History' is a feminist scepticism in which she anticipates a later age, as well as agreeing with Mary Astell.

The 'man' of whom she speaks contemptuously is a miscellanist and incurs scorn because he lacks the original creative gifts of the novelist, but his choice of authors also has a feminist point. Milton, Prior and Pope had all written works to which a feminist might take exception. Milton, being the greatest, and one whom no enlightened man or woman could dismiss, comes first, because his sexist treatment of Adam, Eve and the Fall was, to the women of Jane Austen's age, particularly painful. *Paradise Lost* (Book IV, 11. 291–301) stuck in the throat of the author of *Northanger Abbey* as awkwardly as it did in that of the author of *A Vindication of the Rights of Woman*. Nor was the description of Adam as 'Patriarch of Mankind' thought well chosen. Prior had done *The Nut Brown Maid* into eighteenth-century English in *Henry and Emma*, where he brought out all her 'Patient Griselda' characteristics, leaving out her weather-beaten toughness. (He had also written a rather awful Pastoral, called *Love and Friendship*, and attributed it to a Mrs Elizabeth Sinclair.) Pope's *Of the Character of Women*, despite its praise of Martha Blount, was remembered largely for its much quoted first lines:

> Nothing so true as what you once let fall,
> 'Most Women have no Characters at all'.

The Spectator, like other periodicals of the time, was well-known for its frequent papers in which women as authors or readers were mocked. Sterne gets into the pack of this literary Autolycus because Yorick's treatment of Mad Maria and La Fille de Chambre, in *A Sentimental Journey*, illustrated precisely the conjunction of sentimentality and licence which feminists thought unbecoming – if not much worse – especially in a parson.

Had *Northanger Abbey* (or *Susan*) been published in 1803, or even in 1809, this passage might well have caused a small stir. It was pretty outspoken coming, as it did, in the first work of a *young* woman author. But, of course, it was not published. For reasons which have never been made clear it was, to all intents and purposes, suppressed. Messrs Crosby advertised it in their 'Flowers of Literature' catalogue, but they never published it and, when challenged by the author about the suppression of her work in 1809, they informed her that they had no intention of publishing it, would prosecute her if she sought to get it published elsewhere (as she had threatened to do) and would not return the MS. or release it from their toils unless she stumped up the sum of £10, which was the amount they had paid her six years earlier. The correspondence about this shows quite clearly Jane Austen's urgent interest in achieving publication and, in the curious manner in which she signs her letter, a rising sense of persecution, only partially controlled by making a silly joke of it:

Gentleman, – In the spring of the year 1803 a MS. novel in two vols. entitled *Susan*, was sold to you by a gentleman of the name of Seymour, and the purchase money £10 recd. at the same time. Six years have passed, and the work, of which I am myself the Authoress, has never to the best of my knowledge appeared in print, tho' an early publication was stipulated for at the time of the sale. I can only account for such an extraordinary circumstance by supposing that the MS. by some carelessness to have been lost, and if that was the case am willing to supply you with another copy, if you are disposed to avail yourselves of it, and will engage for no farther delay when it comes into your hands. It will not be in my power from particular circumstances to command this copy before the month of August, but then if you accept my proposal you may depend on receiving it. Be so good as to send me a line in answer as soon as possible as my stay in this place will not exceed a few days. Should no notice be taken of this address, I shall feel myself at liberty to secure the publication of my work by applying elsewhere.

I am, Gentlemen, etc., etc.,
M.A.D.

Direct to Mrs. Ashton Dennis,
Post Office,
Southampton.
April 5, 1809.

She was soon slapped down. She received the following reply:

Madam, – We have to acknowledge the receipt of your letter of the 5th. inst. It is true that at the time mentioned we purchased of Mr. Seymour a MS. novel entitled *Susan*, and paid him for it the sum of £10, for which we have his stamped receipt, as a full consideration, but there was not any time stipulated for its publication, neither are we bound to publish it. Should you or anyone else we shall take proceedings to stop the sale. The MS. shall be yours for the same as we paid for it.

For Crosby & Co.
I am yours, etc.
Richard Crosby.

How Jane Austen felt about this we do not know, but we know what she did. She decided to forget *Susan* and Messrs Crosby for the time being, and went ahead instead with a revision of the earlier 'Elinor and Marianne', which by 1811 she was ready to publish under a new title, at her own expense, and with a new firm.

Some time around 1816, when four other novels had appeared, she sent £10 to Messrs Crosby, and *Susan* was returned. By then, the literary climate had changed, but she still hoped to publish it and wrote an 'Advertisement' for it. It was this which Henry Austen had printed by way of Preface to the posthumous double edition (1818) of *Northanger Abbey* and *Persuasion*. It does not suggest that Jane Austen had forgiven Messrs Crosby, and it leaves wide open the possibility that, despite her arch disclaimer, she had a pretty clear idea of why this publishing house had acted as it did. The 'Advertisement' reads as follows:

This little work was finished in the year 1803, and intended for immediate publication. It was disposed of to a bookseller, it was even advertised, and why the business proceeded no farther, the author has never been able to learn. That any bookseller should think it worth while to purchase what he did not think it worth while to publish seems extraordinary. But with this, neither the author nor the public have any other concern than as some observation is necessary upon those parts of the work which thirteen years have made comparatively obsolete. The public are entreated to bear in mind that thirteen years have passed since it was finished, many more since it was begun, and that during that period, places, manners, books and opinions have undergone considerable changes.

Despite the assertion that Crosby's suppression of this novel concerns neither the author nor the public, she makes rather a point of including it, and of saying that no rational explanation has ever come her way. A novel begun in the late 1790s and ready for publication in 1803 would, of course, be somewhat out of date by 1816. This must be especially true of a novel in which contemporary literary allusion plays a large part, but was that all? As late as 1813, Eaton Stannard Barrett had published *The Heroine*, which Jane Austen described as 'a delightful burlesque, particularly on the Radcliffe style' (*Letters*, p. 377). Peacock did not publish *Nightmare Abbey* until 1818 and, thirty years later, Charlotte Brontë, in *Shirley*, still assumes that readers are familiar with Mrs Radcliffe's works.[13]. *Northanger Abbey* was not outmoded in so far as it was a burlesque of Gothic romance, but in so far as it attempts a more penetrating criticism of literature and life than is common in the burlesque genre, and does so from a feminist point of view, it had less chance of being read with understanding in 1816 than in the late 1790s when it was begun, or in 1803, when it was ready for publication. It is but one of the many ironies in the history of her eventual success that when *Northanger Abbey* at last appeared it was prefaced by an account of her life and character which effectively inhibited readers from seeing how strongly and overtly it displayed that 'sparkle of confident intelligence' which had once made it a work worth suppressing.

After her failure to get *Northanger Abbey* published in 1809, Jane Austen seems to have settled down to the thorough revision of the two other early novels and to ensuring that these were published. In this she was successful and, particularly after *Pride and Prejudice* came out, began to acquire a high reputation among the more discriminating. But there were further ironies of literary history in store. The first of the new novels, *Mansfield Park*, appeared in the late spring of 1814; *Waverley* was published in late July or early August. It thus happened that, just at the point when Jane Austen was ready to start publishing her new works, in which the Enlightenment feminist tradition of fiction culminates, English fiction found its Great Romantic (male) novelist, and the twenty-five years in which fiction in England had been dominated by women came to an end. Scott's success could not stop Jane Austen from further publication since she was by now an established author, but it could and did have a profound influence upon the way in which her works were received into the critical tradition.

As a wry comment in a letter to her niece Anna, written some two months after the publication of *Waverley* makes clear, Jane Austen was aware that Scott's entry into fiction marked the end of 'the feminist tradition' as the central development of the English novel – or at least of its recognition as such. *Mansfield Park*, the first entirely new work of her maturity, and the most ambitiously feminist of all her novels, received little notice. In late September, she wrote to her niece commenting on *her* novel, but making an ironic comment on the emergence of the great Romantic novelist:

Walter Scott has no business to write novels, especially good ones. – It is not fair. – He has Fame and Profit enough as a Poet, and should not be taking the bread out of other people's mouths. – I do not like him, & do not mean to like *Waverley* if I can help it – but I fear I must. (*Letters*, p. 404).

Writing a year or so earlier to Cassandra, with some facetious suggestions for damping down the 'too light, and bright, and sparkling' *Pride and Prejudice*, she mentioned the possibility of inserting some 'solemn specious nonsense, about something unconnected with the story; an essay on writing, a critique on Walter Scott, or the history of Buonaparté' (*Letters*, p. 300). Worse was yet to come. It was Scott's review of *Emma* that was to set the accolade of literary distinction upon Jane Austen.

11 Scott's Review of 'Emma'

By 1815, when the publication of *Emma* was foremost in Jane Austen's mind, she became the subject of embarrassing attentions from the Rev. James Stanier Clarke, librarian to the Prince Regent. He wrote her some remarkably stupid suggestions about how she might write in future, and put her in the awkward situation of having either to dedicate *Emma* to the Prince Regent or making a point of refusing to do so. She agreed to the dedication, but she was not happy about it. In 1813, is one of the few surviving letters to anyone outside her immediate family, she wrote thus to Marthy Lloyd about Caroline of Brunswick and her husband:

I suppose all the World is sitting in Judgement upon the Princess of Wales's Letter. Poor woman, I shall support her as long as I can, because she *is* a Woman, & because I hate her Husband – but I can hardly forgive her for calling herself 'attached & affectionate' to a Man whom she must detest – & the intimacy said to subsist between her & Lady Oxford is bad – I do not know what to do about it; but if I must give up the Princess, I am resolved at least always to think that she would have been respectable, if the Prince had behaved only tolerably by her at first. (*Letters*, p. 504)

Soon after his marriage, the Prince had insisted upon introducing his mistress into the royal household and Caroline, desperate by 1813 about his treatment of her and their daughter, but failing to get any reply from her husband when she wrote to him about it, sent a copy of one of her letters to the press. Jane Austen's feminist sympathy in this unhappy and unedifying matter could hardly be more plain. When she did, under a mixture of pressures, agree to dedicating *Emma* to the Prince, she wrote to Cassandra: 'I hope you have told Martha of my first resolution of letting nobody know that I might dedicate, & for fear of being obliged to do it – and that she is thoroughly convinced of my being influenced now by nothing but the most mercenary motives' (*Letters*, p. 436).

If she were at fault she certainly received her deserts, for it is very likely that the dedication of *Emma* had something to do with Scott's agreeing to review it. This review, which appeared in the *Quarterly*

Review of March 1816, is the first important piece of critical writing about Jane Austen – and it misses the point. Scott makes it clear that he has recognised an author of distinction and that her novels are outstandingly good examples of a comparatively new kind of work, which has 'arisen within the last fifteen or twenty years'. That this kind of novel is realistic rather than romantic he makes clear, but that this has anything to do with the feminist viewpoint of its author he avoids saying. In his last paragraph he shows some embarrassment, as he makes his most serious criticism of this kind of fiction in general:

One word, however, we must say in behalf of that powerful divinity, Cupid, king of gods and men, who in these times of revolution, has been assailed, even in his own kingdom of romance, by the authors who were formerly his devoted priests. We are quite aware that there are few instances of first attachment being brought to a happy conclusion, and that it seldom can be so in a state of society so highly advanced as to render early marriages among the better class, acts generally speaking, of imprudence. But the youth of this realm need not at present be taught the doctrine of selfishness. It is by no means their error to give the world or the good things of the world all for love; and before the authors of moral fiction couple Cupid indivisibly with calculating prudence, we would have them reflect, that they may sometimes lend their aid to substitute more mean, more sordid, and more selfish motives of conduct, for the romantic feelings which their predecessors perhaps fanned into too powerful a flame. Who is it, that in his youth has felt a virtuous attachment, however romantic or however unfortunate, but can trace back to its influence much that is his character may possess of what is honourable, dignified, and disinterested? If he recollects hours wasted in unavailing hope, or saddened by doubt and disappointment; he may also dwell on many which have been snatched from folly or libertinism, and dedicated to studies which might render him worthy of the object of his affection, or pave the way perhaps, to that distinction necessary to raise him to an equality with her. Even the habitual indulgence of feelings totally unconnected with ourself and our own immediate interest, softens, graces, and amends the human mind; and after the pain of disappointment is past, those who survive (and by good fortune those are the greater number) are neither less wise nor less worthy members of society for having felt, for a time, the influence of a passion which has been well qualified as the 'tenderest, noblest and best'.[14]

The playful nonsense about 'Cupid' is used to obscure the fact that the Austen novels are about cupidity disguised by sentiment. Earlier in the review, Scott had spoken of the author of *Emma* as a woman and, in associating the attack upon sensibility with 'these times of revolution', he perhaps reveals a partly conscious awareness that the point of view of this author implies a radical criticism of the society in which she lives and its literary conventions. However, he chooses not to discuss this openly, but launches instead into a generalised defence of 'romantic feelings' which, he claims, ennoble those who, in youth, experience them. His choice of language suppresses the very different effect that such romanticism actually had upon women, as against men, and thus fails to take account of the subject of the novels which ostensibly provokes this polemic. Jane Austen, it is implied, teaches a 'doctrine of selfishness' and 'calculating prudence' which 'the youth of this realm' does not need to be taught. A general argument about the value of sensibility is advanced in terms which exclude consideration of the differing effects of the cult of sensibility upon the two sexes. There can be few examples of writing in which the assumption that 'masculine' words can be used to include both sexes so clearly distorts understanding. What with 'Cupid', 'king', 'gods', 'men', 'priests', 'youth', we are already invited to forget that the subject under discussion is fiction, written by men and women novelists, speaking to the men and women who read them. We are quite prepared for the non-neutral use of the 'common' pronoun 'he'. 'Who is it that in his youth . . . ?' The rest of the paragraph, ignoring the fact that 'the youth of this realm' consists of young women as well as young men, extols the value of 'a virtuous passion' from a wholly male point of view. As Mrs Bennet could have told Scott a first attachment, resulting in early marriage to a rich young man, far from being imprudent was, *for a young woman*, the best means by which she could secure a 'respectable' future for herself, in the 'highly advanced society' where girls 'of the better class' were everywhere expected to use their youth, beauty, and the well cultivated charms of 'softness', and 'sweetness of manner', to catch an eligible husband while such attractions lasted.

There is little doubt that Jane Austen knew that it was Scott who had reviewed *Emma*, and none at all that she felt the irony which life, and the vagaries of publishing, had imposed upon her by bringing her work before the public, as it was praised and misunderstood by the Great Romantic Novelist. Returning to John Murray, her current publisher, the copy which he had sent her, she wrote as follows:

Chawton, April 1, 1816.

Dear Sir,
    I return you the 'Quarterly Review' with many thanks. The Authoress of 'Emma' has no reason, I think, to complain of her treatment in it, except in the total omission of 'Mansfield Park'. I cannot but be sorry that so clever a man as the Reviewer of 'Emma' should consider it as unworthy of being noticed. You will be pleased to hear that I have received the Prince's thanks for the *handsome* copy I sent him of 'Emma'. Whatever he may think of *my* share of the work, yours seems to have been quite right.

In consequence of the late event in Henrietta Street, I must request that if you should at any time have anything to communicate by letter, you will be so good as to write by the post, directing to me (Miss J. Austen), Chawton, near Alton; and that for anything of a larget bulk, you will add to the same direction, by *Collier's Southampton coach.*

I remain, dear Sir,

Yours very faithfully,

J. Austen.

This is more discreet than the earlier letter to Crosby, but it shows the same disillusionment with the way in which her work has been treated. Instead of the rather crude 'M.A.D.' by way of signature, the letter is sent and dated on All Fool's Day. Although, at a surface level, it is polite, 'the Authoress of *Emma*' manages to say that the clever man who has reviewed her has chosen to ignore a major work which ought not to have been ignored; that the Prince Regent's appreciation of her work is, as might be expected, confined to the handsomeness of its binding and printing and, although she pays Murray himself a compliment about *his* share of the work, it is a compliment which shows that he is not in her confidence so far as any real understanding of her writing goes.

The Scott review must have shown Jane Austen that her ingenuity in combining a feminist criticism of life and literature with a warm humanity and an abiding love of the ridiculous was not likely to be understood. In 1813, writing to Cassandra about *Pride and Prejudice*, she had parodied some lines from Scott's *Marmion*:

> I do not rhyme to that dull elf
> Who cannot image to himself

This became:

> I do not write for such dull elves
> As have not a great deal of ingenuity themselves
> (*Letters*, p. 298)

and was said in connection with the observation that, in the proofs of *Pride and Prejudice*, there were still 'a few typical errors; and a "said he, or a said she" would sometimes make the dialogue more immediately clear'.

Yes indeed. Perhaps Jane Austen should have stressed the 'said he' and the 'said she' of it a little more than she did, for not all her readers have been bright elves, and some of the brightest have, through habituation to linguistic convention perhaps, rather than pride or prejudice, found it difficult to take what 'he' says and what 'she' says as at the heart of the comedy and the moral involvement of the Austen novels.

III Allusion, Irony and Feminism in the Austen Novels

'for she partook largely in all the best gifts of
the comic muse' (Henry Austen, 1817)

12 Comedy and the Austen Heroines: The Early Novels

F. R. Leavis placed Jane Austen as the inaugurator of the 'great tradition' of English nineteenth-century fiction. But she is unlike the later novelists of this tradition in that she writes *comedies*, that is, her novels preserve, and call attention to, certain formal features proper to comedy in its theatrical sense, and this is used to distance what is represented from life itself, even though character and events are made, for the most part, to look natural and probable. In George Eliot, Henry James and Joseph Conrad, the distinction between comedy and tragedy is no longer of importance, for their form of realism attempts to embrace the whole of life under a single vision. Auerbach speaks of the *comédie larmoyante* and *Sturm und Drang* as opening the way to the realism of Balzac and the naturalism of Zola, in which 'random individuals from daily life in their dependence upon historical circumstances' are made the subject of 'serious, problematic and even tragic representation'.[1] But the Austen heroine is not realistic in quite this way, for what is 'serious, problematic and dependent upon historical circumstances' about her is subsumed under the formal, comic role which she is required to play. In the Austen novels the narrator, at crucial moments, when everything has been made to look natural and probable, draws the reader's attention to the way in which character and action also fulfil the formal requirements of comedy and, in this way, directs us *not* to mistake what is represented for a straightforward imitation of life itself. Sometimes the conventions adhered to are mocked and this, as Lloyd W. Brown has shown, is especially true of the 'happy endings'.[2]

Some critics with a social conscience, including feminist ones, have found the Austen novels complacent in their optimism, but Jane Austen's vision does not seem complacent or superficial if we take the formal comic features of her novels seriously, as part of their total meaning. The comic vision is partial, but it need not be untruthful provided it is not mistaken for more than it is. Jane Austen puts pressure on the limits of comedy, but she does not seek to break down the distinction between tragedy and comedy, only to enlarge the scope of comedy in prose fiction, by making it capable of embodying a serious criticism of contemporary manners and morals *and of contemporary literature*. As a feminist moralist, Jane Austen criticises sexist pride and prejudice as embedded in the laws and customs of her age, but she was also a critic of the same faults in literature itself. Her interest in the conventions of art is not a means of escaping from her central moral interest, but a way of showing, through drawing attention to them, that they must be questioned critically if true understanding is to be achieved. As her work developed she became more, not less, aware of literary form as in need of the conscious critical attention of the discerning reader. In her later novels she relies upon a greater awareness of contemporary conventions and their accustomed meanings than the modern reader always possesses, and this has led to the belief that she became more conservative in her outlook, whereas she became more radical and more subtle, demanding more in the way of intelligent, critical co-operation in the reader.

The full strength of Austen's feminist criticism of life and literature, and the consistency with which she went on developing new ways of making it, does not appear unless one takes account of literary and theatrical irony as controlling the total meaning of the major late novels, *Mansfield Park* and *Emma*, as well as of the earlier ones. Part Three of this study is mainly about allusion, irony and feminism in these two novels but, before discussing that, a little more needs to be said about the character of the Austen comedy, and the way in which it accommodates both an ideal vision – the *idyllic* element which Lionel Trilling[3] saw in it – together with forceful and sometimes *subversive* (to use D. W. Harding's[4] word) criticism of life and letters as they actually were.

Jane Austen is the major comic artist in English of the age we call 'Romantic', her scepticism about Romanticism being largely a product of her feminism, but, in her confidence that the comic vision remained capable of bringing enlightenment, and of reaching towards the ideal, she is the representative of that true comic spirit which the Romantics admired in Shakespeare, and which Shelley thought lost in a corrupt age, like that in which he and Jane Austen lived. Where 'the calculating principle' predominates, he tells us, in *A Defence of Poetry*,

Comedy loses its ideal universality: wit succeeds to humour; we laugh from self-complacency and triumph, instead of pleasure; malignity, sarcasm and contempt succeed to sympathetic merriment; we hardly laugh, but we smile.

There is, in the Austen comedy, a great deal of wit, some sarcasm and a trace of malignity here and there (for example, in the portrayal of Aunt Norris and Sir Walter Elliot) but there is more sympathetic merriment than sarcasm, and the wit is tempered by humour. Jane Austen's comic vision includes a glimpse of something ideal and universal, together with a sharp, ironic awareness of how far short we mostly are of it, especially when 'dressed in a little brief authority'. The feminism is in the laughter, sometimes rather harsh laughter, but it is also in the visionary ideal, for Austen manages to create a few brief oases where men and women experience equal relationships with one another, and where it would appear that the idea of their being otherwise, at least for those of such superior mind as her heroes and heroines, has never been heard of.

This is not to say that the Austen heroines lead extraordinary lives, or are endowed with extraordinary genius. The difficulties they experience are not, in many instances, the same as those experienced by men, but the way they learn to solve them is what matters. Mary Wollstonecraft, arguing that 'for man and woman . . . truth must be the same', says:

Women, I allow, may have different duties to fulfil; but they are *human* duties, and the principles that should regulate the discharge of them, I sturdily maintain, must be the same.[5]

That is the central moral principle developed in the Austen novels and, though it goes against Rousseau and Richardson, it does not go against the author's Butlerian, secularised Christianity. Gilbert Ryle, observing that Jane Austen's

heroines face their moral difficulties and solve their moral problems without recourse to religious faith or theological doctrines. Nor does it ever occur to them to seek the counsels of a clergyman,

suggests that Austen 'draws a curtain between her Sunday thoughts, whatever they were, and her creative imagination'.[6] Perhaps she did think more about revealed religion on Sundays than other days, but even so there would have been no reason for her Sunday thoughts to come into conflict with her weekday ones. The Austen heroines act as independent moral agents because that is the way in which the Creator intended those with powers of reason to act. Since the novelist wishes to show us heroines capable of learning morals through experience and the exercise of their own judgement, she does not send them off to get the advice of the few rational clergymen available in her fiction, for to do so would prevent her showing that, while the Church of England ordains such moral teachers as Mr Collins, Mr Elton and Dr Grant, the natural moral order of things allows Miss Bennet, Miss Woodhouse and Miss Price (under Providence) to do very well without them, having within themselves, as Miss Price puts it, 'a better guide . . . than any other person can be' (*Mansfield Park*, p. 412).

Jane Austen's heroines are not self-conscious feminists, yet they are all exemplary of the first claim of Enlightenment feminism: that women share the same moral nature as men, ought to share the same moral status, and exercise the same responsibility for their own conduct. As Austen's understanding of the problem of presenting heroines fit to take the place of central moral intelligence in her novels increased, so did their moral stature. It is all done, apparently without effort, as though it were perfectly natural for young women to think, to learn through what passes under their own observation, and to draw conclusions the author thinks valid from it. It looks natural, but it is done by playing with the mirror of art and producing an illusion. The illusion is both visionary and salutary, for it suggests how we might live, and criticises the way we actually live, in a world where women, however marked their abilities, are not thought of (except by a few, mostly *heroes*) as equals and 'partners in life'.

E. H. Gombrich, in his study of *Art and Illusion*, takes John Constable's *Wivenhoe Park*, painted in 1816, as an illuminating example of how what appears an unpremeditated representation of natural landscape is the outcome of lengthy testing of the painter's fresh vision against models of landscape painting in his immediate tradition. Gombrich speaks of Rousseau's assertion that Emile must copy nature and never other men's work as 'one of those programmes charged with explosive ignorance', since a greater appearance of fidelity to Nature is achieved through adaptation and adjustment of earlier models or, as he summarises it, through '*schema* and correction'. *Wivenhoe Park*

looks so effortless and natural that we accept it as an unquestioning and unproblematic response to the beauty of the English countryside. But, for the historian there is an added attraction to this painting, he knows that this freshness of vision was won in a hard struggle.[7]

These remarks are apposite to Jane Austen as well as to Constable, for her fresh vision of how things might be in a more natural social order was arrived at in a comparable way, and her art is no more an 'unquestioning and unproblematic response' to English society than

Constable's was to the English landscape. There is, however, an important difference between the painter and the novelist: Constable wished it to be thought that he drew directly from Nature and played down his debt to Cozens.[8] Austen, being less disturbed than Constable by awareness of how 'the tradition' of any art impinges upon 'the individual talent', and sometimes has to be consciously resisted, draws attention to the models or schemas employed in the formation of her distinctive, feminist vision, expecting the reader better than a 'dull elf' to see their point.

In her earlier work, Jane Austen came up against a major difficulty: the literary models which she needed to use could not, even when adjusted and corrected, be easily freed of anti-feminist bias. It came naturally to her, as her earliest writings show, to write burlesque, and two of her early novels – *Northanger Abbey* and *Pride and Prejudice* – develop out of well established burlesque plots. But such burlesque plots, which turn on the early folly of the heroine, make it difficult to establish her as the central moral intelligence of the novel in which she appears. An alternative model, taken from the moralistic tradition of female writing in which contrasting sister-heroines are portrayed, and utilised in *Sense and Sensibility*, also proved to have intractable difficulties. Austen's earlier attempts at the adjustment and correction of such schemas must be considered before going on to *Mansfield Park* and *Emma*.

13 *Sense and Sensibility*

The schema used in *Sense and Sensibility* – that of contrasted heroines, one representing female good sense and prudence, the other led into error and difficulty by impulsiveness and excesses of feeling and conduct – was to be found in many women novelists, especially those of an 'improving' tendency. In Maria Edgeworth's *Letters of Julia and Caroline* (1795) and Jane West's *A Gossip's Story* (1796) this schema is used in a straightforward, didactic way. The sensible sister judges aright all the time and eventually, partly as a result of the homilies she delivers, the imprudent sister is brought to acknowledge her faults and amend her ways. The purpose is simply to recommend prudence and self-control without emphasis upon the abilities of the heroines, which make them the proper judges of what is prudent and how self control should be exercised.

Sense and Sensibility is an early work, probably less drastically revised than *Northanger Abbey* or *Pride and Prejudice*, and Jane Austen shows some uncertainty about her own purposes in employing the schema, but she modifies it in two important ways, both of which increase the stature of her pair of heroines. She shows that both sisters have superior abilities, neither being totally lacking in either sense or sensibility, and she introduces a range of other characters against whose defects Elinor and Marianne shine.

In the first chapter, we are told that Elinor 'possessed a strength of understanding and coolness of judgement', and that 'she had an excellent heart; her disposition was affectionate, and her feelings were strong, but she knew how to govern them'. Marianne, although over-eager and immoderate, is not represented as lacking more solid powers of mind: 'She was sensible and clever.'

As the novel develops, Marianne and Elinor each begin to take on the rounded character of a single, central heroine. Elinor's response to the contrite Willoughby goes beyond what is quite appropriate in a representative of Sense. Marianne's critical self-analysis after her illness, which is induced by her own reflections and not the moralising of her sister, is too intelligent to fit a representative of Sensibility.

Austen may have started off with the intention of using this type of schematic plot and characterisation much as it had been used before, merely pruning it of its tendency to encourage moralising and solemnity. But, because she creates heroines fully representative of human nature in a larger sense than the schema allows, she discovers its inadequacies. They become particularly clear in the final chapters, where Marianne's marriage to Colonel Brandon fulfils the requirements of the schematic design, but is felt as a betrayal of the developed character she has become. The schema entailed the showing up of one sister against the other, rather than the endorsements of their superior judgement in the face of prejudice and error in less sensitive and sensible people. It did not therefore permit the adequate representation of a single heroine with a good head and a sound heart.

14 Northanger Abbey

Northanger Abbey is developed from a schema used by Charlotte Lennox in *The Female Quixote* (1752), by Beckford in *The Elegant Enthusiast* (1796), and by Eaton Stannard Barrett in *The Heroine* (1813), which Austen was later to enjoy, and by a number of other eighteenth- and early nineteenth-century writers of burlesque. It presented particular difficulties for a feminist since, although it turned on the condemnation of romantic illusions inspired by literature, it characteristically made a heroine the victim of such delusions, and called on a hero of sense, perhaps aided by a sensible clergyman, to dispel them. *Northanger Abbey* follows the schema in making its heroine the subject of absurd delusions following on the reading of romantic novels, but it corrects the schema in several important ways. First, the heroine, although young and naïve, is always shown as possessing sound, healthy affections and a good deal of native common sense. Her errors, it is pretty plain, are not likely to be long-lasting, for her own abilities, with a little experience, are bound to correct them. Second, the hero, although he is also a clergyman, is not shown as always superior in his judgements. He has the sense to value novels, saying – in reply to Catherine's suggestion that 'gentlemen read better books' – ' "The person, be it gentleman or lady, who had not pleasure in a good novel, must be intolerably stupid." ' He knows how to admire and how to read Ann Radcliffe:

'I have read all Mrs. Radcliffe's works, and most of them with great pleasure. *The Mysteries of Udolpho*, when I had once begun it, I could not lay down again; – I remember finishing it in two days – my hair standing on end the whole time.' (p. 106)

And he learns to see in Catherine's unaffected character qualities which inspire true affection. But he is not without some of the affectations of a clever young man as is shown in his strictures on Catherine's use of 'nice', and in his expounding of the fashionable doctrines of the 'picturesque' in chapter XIV. In both instances he is clever, rather than sensible. Third, although the heroine's delusions about General Tilney and the 'forbidden gallery' at Northanger are exposed as absurd, they lead the reader to something more substantial. Austen's handling of this episode amounts to a major criticism of assumptions associated with the schema of the burlesque novel in which a heroine learns that her romantic notions are all mistaken, and that the world of the everyday is better ordered than that of imagination. Catherine accepts the truth of things as Henry Tilney puts them to her, and is bitterly ashamed of herself for having indulged in wild fantasies about the General's conduct to his late wife but, as events show, she was not so far out as might at first appear.

Henry Tilney's account of his mother's life and death makes it clear that she did suffer greatly during her years as the General's wife and his abstract arguments, in support of the idea that English wives in the Midland counties of England are protected by better laws and more humane customs than those to be found in Mrs Radcliffe's Alps and Pyrenees, ought to raise doubts in the intelligent reader's mind, though they satisfy Catherine. Dismissing her dreadful suspicions, he says:

'What have you been judging from? Remember the country and the age in which we live. Remember that we are English, that we are Christians. Consult your own understanding, your own observation of what is passing around you – Does our education prepare us for such atrocities? Do our laws connive at them? Could they be perpetrated without being known, in a country where social and literary intercourse is on such a footing; where every man is surrounded by a neighbourhood of voluntary spies, and where roads and newspapers lay everything open?' (pp. 197–8)

This is a powerful rejection of the gothic fantasy of the wicked husband who secretly murders his wife, or locks her up for years on end in a turret, and Catherine, on reflection, accepts it. However things might be in Italy, Switzerland and France,

in the central part of England there was surely some security for the existence of a wife not beloved, in the laws of the land, and the manners of the age. Murder was not tolerated, servants were not slaves, and neither poison nor sleeping potions to be procured, like rhubarb, from every druggist. (p. 200)

This can be read as a complete dismissal of Catherine's nonsense, yet there is something really evil about the General, and his wife had, in a sense, been imprisoned by her marriage to him, perhaps even brought to an early grave through unhappiness; for General Tilney is allowed by the laws of England and the manners of the age to exert near absolute power over his wife and daughter, and he does so as an irrational tyrant. What must a more experienced Catherine see in observing what passes around her? What do our marriage laws connive at? What does our education prepare us for? A wife not beloved cannot easily be murdered, but perhaps the 'laws of the land and the manners of the age' do little to protect her as an equal citizen. Servants are not slaves, but how does a wife's status differ from that of a slave? Is she not her husband's property?

In view of the General's subsequent conduct, it is clear that the correct answers to these questions are not quite so straightforward as Henry Tilney thinks. As to the matter of sleeping potions, as Austen was to show through Lady Bertram, these are scarcely needed in a country where a woman, if 'well married', may pass away thirty years half asleep on a sofa, with a lap-dog, and a tangled, useless bit of needlework, and still be reckoned a respectable wife of a respected public man.

Northanger Abbey includes some of Austen's strongest criticism of the society in which she lived, but the schema does not permit her to make the heroine herself sufficiently aware of its real defects. Ann Radcliffe's novels, which ought, according to the schema, to be exposed as foolish, are here made into something more complex: a test of the literary intelligence of the hero and heroine. Henry Tilney shows his superiority by responding to Radcliffe's powers of invention and imagination without supposing that *The Mysteries of Udolpho* is an imitation of life. Catherine also shows her responsiveness, but is required to make a childish confusion of life and art. Austen then, through her own more realistic invention, shows that there is a further truth which neither of them has quite seen. This modifies and corrects the schema, but at risk of confusing readers.

15 Pride and Prejudice

Under its earlier title of *First Impressions* what was to become *Pride and Prejudice* was thought ready for publication as early as 1797. As its first title suggests, it must have been at that stage fairly close to a burlesque schema similar to that of *Northanger Abbey* – a novel in which the heroine's romantic confidence in first impressions (a common article of faith in such heroines) was corrected by experience. *Pride and Prejudice*, as it eventually appeared in 1813, had been extensively and recently revised by the author who had already published *Sense and Sensibility*, and had begun to think about *Mansfield Park*. In its final form, therefore, it comes closer to the later work than either of the other early novels and the schema is very drastically modified. Elizabeth Bennet's role, as the heroine who puts too high a value on first impressions, can still be seen in her infatuation with Mr Wickham, and in her initial dislike of Mr Darcy, but it becomes unimportant as the novel develops. Half way through the second volume Elizabeth receives the letter from Mr Darcy in which a true account of past events is made plain to her. Once she has read it and reflected upon its contents, which she does with speed and a remarkable display of judicious critical acumen, taking due note of the interest of the writer and the quality of his language, as well as of events and conduct which she had previously misunderstood, she becomes the best informed, as well as the most intelligent character in the entire novel. Quicker and cleverer than the hero, she soon sees that he has solid virtues of head and heart which largely outweigh his tendency to solemnity and self-importance – qualities which his education and upbringing, as well as his wealth, have imposed upon a naturally affectionate heart and a critical mind. From this point onwards Elizabeth Bennet takes on the character of the later Austen heroine; she becomes the central intelligence through whose eyes and understanding events and character are mediated to the reader. Through the use of the 'indirect free style' of narration, Elizabeth's powers of rational reflection, as well as her personal point of view, are made plain.

None of the Austen heroines is more attractive than Elizabeth Bennet, none more clearly possessed of intelligence and warm affections, but as she develops she effectively destroys the role she is supposed to play. The result is that she begins to look too much like a heroine without a part, a real–life character, not a creature in print, and this will not do, for her extreme, and improbable, good luck in marriage is acceptable only if it is properly distanced from life by the formal requirements of plot and part. That is why Jane Austen spoke of *Pride and Prejudice* as 'too light and bright and sparkling', and why she developed new ways of dealing with the heroine's role, so that the plot should no longer turn on a major reversal of her beliefs or judgement. The later heroines may make mistakes, sometimes serious ones like Emma's, and their author continues to mock their absurdities, but they are conceived, from the start, as the central and most enlightened minds of the novels in which they appear. They no longer (except incidentally) miscast themselves, their difficulties arise from a miscasting imposed upon them by the society in which they live, where intelligent young women of the middle class have no role appropriate to their abilities.

In the three late novels, the main thrust of irony is against the errors of law, manners and customs, in failing to recognise women as the accountable beings they are, or ought to be; and against those forms of contemporary literature which render them 'objects of pity, bordering on contempt', by sentimentalising their weaknesses and making attractive what ought to be exposed as in need of correction. Austen's adherence to the central convictions of Enlightenment feminism becomes more marked and more forceful, and the scope of her comedy is enlarged, not by taking in a wider social spectrum, but by widening and deepening the range of allusive irony. The catalyst was the popular German dramatist, August von Kotzebue.

16 *Kotzebue and Theatrical Allusion in Mansfield Park and Emma*

I am sure that though none of my plays will be staged in fifty years yet the poets of posterity will use my plots and more often my situations . . . Turn the play into a story and if it still grips it will live. (August von Kotzebue)[9]

Had Jane Austen not made Kotzebue's *Das Kind Der Liebe* (*Lovers' Vows*) the play-within-the-novel in *Mansfield Park* it is unlikely that his name would be familiar to many English readers. His importance to her later work is, however, not confined to this one novel, but plays a part in the plot of *Emma* and is still, though more weakly, felt in *Persuasion*. In the first two, Austen used his plots and situations and turned the plays into stories which still grip and still live, but perhaps not quite in the way Kotzebue hoped. Kotzebue becomes the grit which irritates Austen into the production of pearls, but her obvious scorn for his plays has not been fully understood as in line with her views as a feminist moralist to whom Kotzebue was the latest and most influential of those disciples of Rousseau, castigated by Wollstonecraft.

Kotzebue's plays enjoyed an enormous success in England from 1798 to about 1810. L. F. Thompson says that, at this time, his 'name was a household word from John O'Groats to Land's End', and his plays, 'especially *The Stranger*, *Pizarro*, *The Birthday* and *The Natural Son [Lovers' Vows]*, were represented not only in London season after season but on the boards of every market town that could boast such an ornament'.[10]

Kotzebue's great popularity, however, did not make him admired among the intelligentsia. He became a figure of controversy and was condemned by a good many writers, including Wordsworth, de Quincey, Coleridge and Scott. The chief complaint against him was that he pandered to the public love of sensational plots, created characters who did not resemble human beings as we know them to be, and, through excesses of sentimentality, aroused disgust rather than compassion. Since Kotzebue was also attacked in some right-wing periodicals on account of his revolutionary political sympathies, the view that all hostility to him was on this account has gained ground, especially in studies of Jane Austen which discover in her novels the point of view of an anti-Jacobin. But this is simplistic and hides differences which ought to be considered.

A review of *Lovers' Vows*, which appeared in Cobbett's *Porcupine and Anti-Gallican Monitor* in 1801, has been much quoted in support of the belief that Austen's contempt for this play is a mark of her political conservatism. In it, the reviewer says:

It is the universal aim of German authors of the present day to exhibit the brightest examples of virtue among the lower classes of society; while the higher orders, by their folly and profligacy, are held up to contempt and detestation. This is fully exemplified in *Lovers' Vows*. The Cottager and his Wife are benevolent and charitable; Frederick, the hero of the piece, a common soldier, the offspring of cupidity, presents an amiable pattern of filial love; while Count Cassel, a travelled nobleman, is a caricature of every odious and contemptible vice.[11]

This view of *Lovers' Vows* is further discussed below in connection with *Mansfield Park*, but it ought also to be considered together with what Wordsworth had to say in the following year. In the Preface to *Lyrical Ballads*, in which he sets out his purposes in representing such examples of virtue as appear in men like Michael, Simon Lee the Huntsman, and the Leech-Gatherer, he says that such portraits as these are especially needed at a time when

a multitude of causes, unknown to former times, are now acting with a combined force to blunt the discriminating powers of the mind, and unfitting it for all voluntary exertion to reduce it to a state of savage torpor.

Among the causes named is the 'craving for extraordinary incident' which is encouraged not only by the press, but the corruption of contemporary literature:

The invaluable works of our elder writers, I had almost said the works of Shakespeare and Milton, are driven into neglect by frantic novels, sickly and stupid German tragedies, and deluges of idle and extravagant stories in verse.

There can be little doubt that Kotzebue was high on Wordsworth's list of those German dramatists who thus corrupted the ability of the public to think or feel adequately.

It might, of course, be said that Wordsworth, even in 1802, had strong conservative impulses and that therefore to quote him, in arguing that an objection to Kotzebue was not necessarily the mark of a reactionary, carries little weight. But even if there are signs in the Preface of the conflict between Wordsworth's 'levelling muse' and his conservatism, it must surely be difficult to deny that part of his purpose in *Lyrical Ballads* comes close to what the *Porcupine* reviewer complains of in Kotzebue. If it must be allowed that the great poet of 'humble and rustic life', in the 1802 edition of *Lyrical Ballads*, objected to Kotzebue as corrupt, we ought not to convict Jane Austen of a reactionary political motive in making him the target of her scorn, unless we can be sure that she had no other interest more obviously germane to her subject-matter and consistent with the whole development of her work.

Jane Austen must have thought little of Kotzebue and less perhaps of the public taste which clamoured for his works, on account of the extreme silliness of his plays, but she had also a feminist motive in satirising him. Here it is important to insist that, whatever later readers and critics may think of Kotzebue's sentimentalising of innocent adulteresses, or pathetic victims of 'noble' seducers, as revolutionary and liberationist, this view is not in accord with that of Enlightenment feminism. We can see why if we consider L. F. Thompson's remarks, bearing in mind what Wollstonecraft had to say about Rousseauist attitudes to women:

> Kotzebue's plays were excellently suited for a female audience. He is never guilty of an expression to which one can take exception. . . . One of Shakespeare's plays held the stage only a night or two because the cast was too exclusively male. Kotzebue gave almost undue prominence to the other sex and catered especially for their taste with his humanitarianism, his happy endings, his introduction of children and his appeal rather to the heart than to the head.[12]

This explanation of why 'Kotzebue found favour with the ladies' is surely a sufficient explanation of why he did not find favour with the Lady who first appeared in print with *Sense and Sensibility*, and who may have wondered, as she watched Bath audiences lapping him up (they can't have included many revolutionaries), whether men or women were really much guided by Reason or Nature, at least in their buying of theatre tickets.

Jane Austen's ability to use the most depressing evidence of folly to advantage came to the rescue. We know that she saw the first performance in Bath of Thomas Dibdin's *The Birthday* (a version of Kotzebue's *Die Versöhnung*) in 1799. It may have been the first time she had seen a Kotzebue play in the theatre at all. It must have stirred her a good deal, for fifteen years later it provided the schema against which *Emma* was constructed. We may assume that she did not share the view of the *Bath Herald and Register* (surely not a journal controlled from Paris by Jacobins) reviewer, who said:

The pleasing spectacle of *Bluebeard* . . . was again brought forward Saturday evening last . . . preceded by Kotzebue's admirable drama of *The Birthday*. If the German author has justly drawn down censure for the immorality of his productions for the stage – this may be accepted as his *amende honorable* – it is certainly throughout unexceptionably calculated to promote the best interests of virtue and the purest principles of benevolence and, though written much in the style of Sterne, it possesses humour without a single broad Shandyism.[13]

The Birthday is about two brothers who have quarrelled over 'a garden', and been at daggers drawn about it for fifteen years. They are eventually reconciled by the heroine, Emma, the daughter of one of them, who believes (falsely as it turns out) that she can never marry because of her duty to devote herself to her irascible and stupid father. How Jane Austen used this schema in *Emma* is discussed below; all that I wish to establish here is that she became acquainted with Kotzebue's work almost as soon as his success in England came about, and that her opinion of it was not in accord with that of the reviewer of a respectable Bath newspaper whose circulation was maintained by its bourgeois (or better) readership, in a city never much associated with revolutionary sympathies. Her use of ironic allusion to Kotzebue in two of the new novels begun after 1812 shows how strongly she reacted to him, and also suggests, as is confirmed by other evidence, that, although the writing of *Mansfield Park* did not begin until 1813, the working on ideas that eventually came to fruition in the later work began much earlier under the stimulus of influences away from Steventon.

In developing her later comedy as a criticism of contemporary literature and theatre as well as life, Jane Austen made use of Shakespeare, the touchstone of truth and nature in art not only for Dr Johnson, but for the major poets of her own generation. Johnson says, in the 1765 Preface to his edition of Shakespeare:

Other dramatists can only gain attention by hyperbolical or aggravated characters, by fabulous and unexampled excellence or depravity, as the writers of barbarous romances invigorated the reader by a giant and a dwarf; and he that should form his expectations of human affairs from the play, or from the tale, would be equally deceived. *Shakespeare* has no heroes; his scenes are occupied only by men, who act and speak as the reader thinks that he should himself have spoken or acted on the same occasion. Even where the agency is supernatural the dialogue is level with life.

Jane Austen's references to Shakespeare in *Mansfield Park* (chapter III of the third volume) show that she is here invoking him in such a light to contrast with Kotzebue. Coleridge also contrasts the two. In

Shakespeare there is a 'signal adherence to the great law of nature, that all opposites tend to attract and temper each other'. This adherence prevents him from exaggeration of vice and virtue and from the sentimentalising of morals, in the interest of particular classes or groups:

Keeping at all times in the high road of life, Shakespeare has no innocent adulteries, no interesting incests, no virtuous vice: he never renders that amiable which religion and reason alike teach us to detest, or clothes impurity in the garb of virtue, like Beaumont and Fletcher, the Kotzebues of the day . . . Let the morality of Shakespeare be contrasted with that of the writers of his own, or the succeeding, age, or of the present day, who boast their superiority in this respect. No one can dispute that the result of such a comparison is altogether in favour of Shakespeare . . . he inverts not the order of nature and propriety, – does not make every magistrate a drunkard or glutton, nor every poor man meek, humane, and temperate; he has no benevolent butchers, nor any sentimental rat-catchers. (*Lectures*, 1818)

Jane Austen's view, as shown in her later novels, is partly in accord with this, for she too sees Shakespeare as upholding what 'religion and reason alike' teach us about Nature and morals, and Kotzebue as distorting it by the sentimental treatment of a particular class of characters. But the class which concerns her is not that of the poor contrasted with the rich, but of women contrasted with men. What she thought about benevolent butchers and sentimental rat-catchers, the figures who, in Coleridge's rhetoric, become the representatives of 'the poor', we can only guess for she avoids dealing with them, but we can see, from her treatment of schemas derived from Kotzebue, that she thought his treatment of women, whether village girls or aristocrats, objectionable, because he does not depict them as full human beings accountable for their own actions, but as relative creatures whose highest moral function is to excite compassion in men.

Austen's criticism of Kotzebue is, above all, that he does not draw women as 'mixed characters', whereas Shakespeare, 'who has no heroes' and no heroines either, if by these we mean 'pictures of perfection', does. Kotzebue's innocent female victims may not be guilty of broad Shandyisms, but their language ought to excite disgust, for it was not fit for Englishwomen of sense. Beside it, the languages of a Portia or a Rosalind (allowing for a little coarseness, common in a less polished age) was from a pure and undefiled well, fit for Englishwomen who valued their liberty under the law of reason and nature.

Some of the most perceptive nineteenth-century critics of Austen – Whately, G. H. Lewes, Richard Simpson – found themselves comparing her with Shakespeare as a humourist and as a faithful portrayer of human nature. And it was her greatest achievement that she brought the central argument and subject matter of English feminists from Astell to Wollstonecraft under the humane influence of Shakespearian comedy, seeing in the poet of Nature an enlarged understanding of men and women which might guide her own age towards something better than Kotzebue. Of course, she also rejoiced, like Shakespeare, in human folly, and relished her own role of female-philosopher-turned-Puck – never more so, perhaps, than when she associated Mansfield Park with the truths of the woods near Athens. For *Mansfield Park*, in which the domestic government of an English estate is exposed as based on false principles, makes the education of Sir Thomas Bertram, Bart, MP, rather than of Miss Fanny Price, one of its central ironic themes. The benevolent, but mistaken, Patriarch lives to profit by such 'a contrast . . . as time is for ever producing between the plans and decisions of *mortals*, for their own instruction, and their neighbours' entertainment' (p. 472; my italics). The sparkle of confident, feminist intelligence was never more boldly displayed than in Austen's invocation of Puck's 'Lord what fools these mortals be', in her presentation of the august and formidable Sir Thomas, whose Northamptonshire seat cannot have been many miles distant from that of Sir Charles Grandison.

*IV Feminist Criticism of Society
and Literature in the Later Novels*

17 Mansfield Park

Mansfield Park has been thought to lack irony. Lionel Trilling, who spoke of Jane Austen's irony as a way of comprehending the world through 'awareness of its contradictions, paradoxes and anomalies', believed that it had been abandoned in this novel, 'which undertakes to discredit irony and affirm literalness'.[1] Such a view arises from failure to recognise the author's feminist point of view and the play of ironic allusion upon the whole construction, plot and characterisation. Allusion in this novel is particularly wide ranging and various, but, since the character of the heroine has proved so troublesome to critics, we had better start with her and leave the wider allusive references until later.

Fanny Price and Sophie in *Emile*

Fanny Price is made to look a natural character, her behaviour and attitudes being well accounted for in the upbringing she has experienced both at Portsmouth and Mansfield, but she is not presented in a wholly naturalistic way, for we are meant to notice that she is her author's fictional creature. 'My Fanny' is not the same as Crabbe's guileless village girl from whom she takes her name, though she plays something of the same role.[2] She is drawn in such a way as to make comparisons and contrasts between her character and that of a number of more sentimental models, of which the most important are Rousseau's Sophie, the perfect wife for Emile; and the exemplary young women of the more sentimental kind of conduct book.

Writing to her niece Fanny Knight (the one with a weakness for Evangelical gentlemen), in 1817, she discussed faultless heroines. Her remarks occur in connection with the opinions of a Mr Wildman, who had been reading some of her novels, without finding them much to his taste:

Do not oblige him to read any more. – Have mercy on him . . . He and I should not in the least agree of course in our ideas about Heroines; pictures of perfection as you know make me sick and wicked – but there is some very good sense in what he says, and I particularly respect him for wishing to think well of all young Ladies; it shows an amiable and delicate Mind – And he deserves better than to be obliged to read any more of my Works. (*Letters*, pp. 141–2)

This could hardly be clearer, its impish irony adding to its force. If Jane Austen created a conduct-book heroine, it cannot have been without an ironic intention of some kind.

A clue to what it was occurs in an unsigned article on the 'Female Novelists', published in *New Monthly Review* in 1852:³ 'Then again, in *Mansfield Park*, what a bewitching "little body" is Fanny Price.' The writer of this review had seen what Trilling missed, in designating her 'a Christian heroine', Fanny's apparent innocence and religiosity is an aspect of her sexiness, a veneer of the 'angelic' which makes her sexually exciting to men like Crawford, who wish to find in their wives such vulnerable 'virtue' as will excite both sexual passion and manly protectiveness. The conduct-book genre included works like Fordyce's *Sermons*, in which religiosity in pretty young women was thought of in a salacious way. Fanny Price, with her timidity, her apparent submissiveness, and her gentle manner looks like Emile's Sophie translated into the Midland counties of England, where she awaits a man of sense and sensibility, like Crawford, to perceive her merits, and to be aroused by her vulnerability. And, as he falls in love with her and comes to wish to marry her, it is made clear that her apparent saintliness is closely connected with her ability to excite sexual passion. In chapter XII of the second volume, where he tells his sister of his intention to marry Fanny, his appreciation of her 'graces of manner and goodness of heart', of her 'being well-principled and religious', is mingled with his dwelling on her 'charms', 'her beauty of face and figure', and her 'beautifully heightened colour', as she attends to the service of 'that stupid woman', her Aunt Bertram, with the neat arrangement of her hair softened by 'one little curl falling forward . . . which she now and then shook back' (pp. 296–7).

Rousseau had recommended that girls should be obedient to their mothers, despite his supposing that their mothers would lack understanding, because the habit of obedience was so important in a wife. A girl should learn her religion from her mother, who ought to teach her that, upon marriage, she should follow the instruction of her husband. Fanny's devoted service to her stupid aunt and her respect for religion are wrongly interpreted by Crawford as signs of unthinking docility. His view of her is deeply sentimental, and by the third volume he discovers 'some touches of the angel' in her. What he never sees, as the hero does, is that Fanny's powers of mind fit her to be an equal and friend of her marriage partner, but unfit her for any other role. Edmund, in reply to a question about whether Fanny has 'come out', says: 'My cousin is grown up. She has the age and sense of a woman, but the outs and not outs are beyond me' (p. 49). Mary Wollstonecraft says in *Vindication* 'what can be more indelicate than a girl's *coming out* in the fashionable world? Which . . . is to bring to market a marriageable miss' (p. 289). Edmund's refusal to understand the question is a mark of his ability to respect his cousin, and his reply, in which her status as an adult with the mental attributes of an adult are acknowledged, stands against the wrong understanding of Crawford, whose idea of 'a woman' does not include recognition of adult human qualities.

Fanny's physical fragility and her somewhat undeveloped, childish appearance contribute to making her seem close to the sentimental ideal of woman. Wollstonecraft objects to Rousseau's belief that genuine weakness, and the affected exaggeration of weakness, are natural to women and a means by which they gain an ambiguous power over men. She quotes, with disgust, a passage from *Emile*, in which it is asserted that women

So far from being ashamed of their weakness, they glory in it; their tender muscles make no resistance; they affect to be incapable of lifting the smallest burdens, and would blush to be thought robust and strong. (p. 174)

And declares that

the first care of mothers and fathers who really attend to the education of females should be, if not to strengthen the body, at least not to destroy the constitution by mistaken notions of female excellence; nor should girls ever be allowed to imbibe the pernicious notion that a defect can, by any chemical process of reasoning, become an excellence. (p. 126)

She then attacks such conduct-book authors as have taken their cue from Rousseau and encouraged girls to cultivate either real or affected weakness and low spirits. Among these she reluctantly places Dr John Gregory, whose *A Father's Letters to his Daughters* (1774)

actually recommends dissimulation and advises an innocent girl to give the lie to her feelings, and not dance with spirit, when gaiety of heart would make her feel eloquent without making her gestures immodest. 'In the name of truth and common sense,' says Wollstonecraft, 'why should not one woman acknowledge that she has a better constitution than another? (pp. 111–2).

Austen did not admire physical weakness, ill-health, or ignorance in young women, but a lot of people did, including those who ought to have known better. The relevance of this to Miss Price is obvious. Austen created, in her, a heroine whom the unwary might take for something like the Rousseauist ideal of the perfect woman, but she expects her more discerning readers to see through it, and gives them a good many indications that this is not a proper reading. The most important of these is, of course, the category mistake of the anti-hero, but there is a good deal else. The true hero is never shown as encouraging Fanny in her partly self-imposed fragility and timidity, although he is kind to her when he observes her genuine tendency to tire easily. He gets her a horse, encourages her to ride regularly, and tells her to speak up for herself, even to her uncle. But the major comic emphasis, through which Austen shows that she does not admire hypochondria in women, even beautiful ones, comes through the splendid portrait of pampered indolence in Lady Bertram.

Fanny is quite different from her aunt in that she has, as a child and as a very vulnerable adolescent, experienced both neglect and hardship. Given Mrs Price's predilection for sons, and her slatternly housekeeping, there is little reason to think that the health (whether of body or mind) of her eldest daughter had ever received much attention. At Mansfield, the somnolence of Aunt Bertram, the sadism of Aunt Norris and the false regard for wealth and status of Sir Thomas Bertram, his elder son and his daughters, have all combined to ensure that Fanny's mental and physical health are put in jeopardy. She does not have a strong constitution, but she was not, as a child, devoid of normal impulses to active life. She did not enjoy such freedom as Catherine Morland did, rolling down green slopes with her brothers, and it is never positively established that she preferred cricket to dolls or nursing dormice; but Fanny, in her early years at Portsmouth, was important as '*play-fellow*' as well as 'instructress and nurse' to her brothers and sisters. The single instance of remembered childhood activity which Austen mentions concerns dancing. William recalls how he and Fanny used to dance together as children. It is what prompts him to ask Sir Thomas if his sister is not a good dancer, Sir Thomas being forced to reply that he does not know. William says, 'I should like to be your partner once more. We used to jump about together many a time, did not we? when the hand organ was in the street?' (p. 250). Fanny's excessive fragility of body and lack of self-confidence is the result of inconsiderate, and sometimes humiliating, treatment by her illiberal, selfish aunts, but it has not quite stamped out of her an impulse to life which is to be seen in her continued love of dancing. At her first ball, 'she was quite grieved to be losing even a quarter of an hour . . . sitting most unwillingly among the chaperons . . . while all the other young people were dancing' (pp. 116–17). Later, when a ball is given in her honour, the narrator tells us: 'She had hardly ever been in a state so nearly approaching high spirits in her life. Her cousins' former gaiety on the day of a ball was no longer surprising to her; she felt it to be indeed very charming' (p. 273). And she actually practises her steps in the drawing-room, when she is sure Aunt Norris won't see her. She gets tired later at this ball, partly because she is jealous of Miss Crawford, but it is three o'clock in the morning, and she is up earlier than anyone else, apart from William, next day in order to see him off.

Fanny's feebleness is not a mark of Clarissa Harlowe-like saintliness, but it alludes to it and mocks it. Unlike Clarissa, who starts well and ends up as a rape victim resigned to death, Fanny improves in strength of mind and body as the novel progresses, and ends up married to the cousin she loves both passionately and rationally. But her lack of robust health contributes to her attraction of Henry Crawford. The affectation of fragility, which it took an expensive and artificial education to produce, Fanny lacks; but a genuine fragility of body and spirit, largely the result of oppression and neglect, she has, and Crawford is 'fairly caught' by it. Moreover, it does arouse in him strong, protective feelings, for he looks forward to being able to demonstrate to Maria and Julia Bertram how Fanny ought to be treated and to raising her status generally:

'Yes, Mary, my Fanny will feel a difference indeed, a daily, hourly difference, in the behaviour of everyone who approaches her; and it will be the completion of my happiness to know that I am the doer of it, that I am the person to give the consequence so justly her due. Now she is dependent, helpless, friendless, neglected, forgotten.' (p. 297)

But Fanny is not Henry Crawford's, she is Jane Austen's, which means that she has to earn respect on her own merits and not because an attractive man with a good estate has fallen in love with her. For, housed within the 'bewitching little body', lurking behind the 'soft light eyes', is a clear, critical, rationally-judging adult mind, quite unlike the tractable, child-like mind of the true conduct-book heroine or sentimental novel. Mary Wollstonecraft says 'the conduct of an accountable being must be regulated by the operation of its own reason; or on what foundation rests the throne of God?'

(*Vindication*, p. 121). The moral climax of *Mansfield Park* occurs when Fanny insists on acting in accordance with this principle. Sir Thomas, once he is able to comprehend that she intends to refuse Henry Crawford, thunders away at her about ingratitude, selfishness, perversity and sheer obtuseness as to her own best interest. He is forced to wonder if she does not show:

'that independence of spirit, which prevails so much in modern times, even in young women, and which in young women is offensive and disgusting beyond all common offence.' (p. 318)

Thus Fanny, in whom the 'sparkle of confident intelligence' never shines, is forced, despite herself, to stand up for those rights which her given moral nature, not her own wish, impose upon her. To add to the irony, and to ensure that readers interested in moral argument cannot miss the point, Austen makes Sir Thomas, before he knows that Fanny will not have Crawford, attribute to her precisely those powers of mind which cause her to act as one accountable to herself and her God even before him. Speaking of Mrs Norris's severities, he says:

'You have an understanding, which will prevent you taking things only in part, and judging partially by the event, – You will take in the whole of the past, you will consider times, persons, and probabilities. (p. 313)

And so she does, especially in remembering Crawford's conduct towards Julia and Maria. Never perhaps was female silence so clearly made to speak as it is in the East Room, when the well-meaning but blind Sir Thomas moralises, in a lengthy speech, about 'wilfulness of temper' and 'ingratitude', while the heroine applies her handkerchief to her streaming eyes, unable to whisper anything but that she is 'very sorry indeed' for being unable to act otherwise than in accordance with the incongruously stout, rational conscience, shown to the reader through her interior monologues. Jane Austen mocks her heroine even as she shows her to be in the right, for the scene is highly theatrical, and essentially comic. Through theatrical allusion, the moral argument of *Mansfield Park* is made entertaining as well as instructive and its scope is enlarged, for we are expected to see Austen's characters and action in relation to other literary and dramatic works, from which they derive ironic meaning.

Theatrical Allusion

In *Mansfield Park* allusion to plays and the theatre takes the place of allusion to fiction, and the novel itself is constructed in a quasi-theatrical way. Possibly the idea of adopting this mode, and of developing fictional characters partly in relation to their perform-ance as actors, first occurred to Jane Austen when she read Maria Edgeworth's *Belinda*, in which Kotzebue is damned as the idol of the Rousseauist Mr Vincent. Edgeworth employs allusion to the theatre in a fairly straightforward way, associating addiction to masks, routs and play-going with insincerity, and affectation, and describing Lady Delacour (a Woman of Fashion) as like a spoilt actress in public, all boredom and melancholy at home. The final chapter, 'Dénoue-ment', was described by Anne Thackeray Ritchie, in her 1896 edition, as 'a sort of epilogue [spoken by Lady Delacour] with all the characters assembled round about as the curtain drops upon the scene in which Clarence Harvey and Belinda Portman come to a happy understanding'. In fact, *Belinda* ends with a sort of tableau in which the characters smilingly take up emblematic positions. It is compara-ble with the ending of *Lovers' Vows*, though there everyone is close to tears – apart from Agatha, who is drowned in them.

In *Mansfield Park* the three volumes correspond to the three acts of a play, and the final chapter, which is quite different in style from the rest, forms an author's epilogue. Volume I ends with the highly dramatic appearance of Julia, her face all aghast, exclaiming: ' "My father is come! He is in the hall at this moment." ' Volume II opens with the chapter in which Sir Thomas makes 'his first appearance on any stage', and ends with Fanny's letter to Miss Crawford and her false confidence that she has now done with Henry Crawford. Volume III opens with Sir Thomas's coming to the East Room to bring the glad tidings of Crawford's proposal, and ends on an ironic, almost Chekhovian note, as Fanny and Edmund sit together on a wet Sunday evening in an English country house, consoling one another for their disappointments, real and supposed. In the epilogue chapter the author comments on her characters and their conduct. The opening sentence – 'Let other pens dwell on guilt and misery' – reminds us that Austen's novel is a comedy, and that the rewards and punishments dispensed will be appropriate to it.

In fact the narrator's stance in this chapter is difficult, for it combines Puck with Female Philosopher. The heroine, upon whom the author has played a good many tricks, is now allowed her happiness, the hero's falling in love being treated more cursorily and ironically than in any other novel. Sir Thomas is shown to have learnt better wisdom through the misfortunes of his children, his mistakes serving, like those of other 'mortals', for his own 'instruction and his neighbours' entertainment'. Maria, now an Adulteress and Ruined Woman, is not punished by Agony of Mind leading to Decline, but, like a curst dairymaid, left to torment and be tormented by Aunt Norris. Mary Crawford is abandoned to the enjoyment of her £20,000 and her smart, silly London friends. Dr Crawford, having first been promoted to a stall at Westminster Abbey, kills himself by over-eating and drinking. With all these Puck predominates, but the Female Philosopher comes out strongly in the comments on Henry Crawford, with whose future is associated a condemnation of the double standard of sexual morality and an allusion to Bishop Butler's ideas about rewards and punishments in the hereafter:

That punishment, the public punishment of disgrace, should in a just measure attend *his* share of the offence, is, we know, not one of the barriers, which society gives to virtue. In this world, the penalty is less equal than could be wished; but without presuming to look forward to a juster appointment hereafter . . . (p. 468)

In *Belinda*, Edgeworth makes a simple association of the actor's art with insincerity and some have thought that Austen does the same, but what she attempts is more complex. Through word-play on 'act', 'acting' and 'action', she explores the kinds of responsibility appropriate to art on the one hand, and to the conduct of 'moral agents' in daily life on the other. An actor has a responsibility to his art, and will not, if he is a professional, betray it in order to achieve trivial personal satisfaction, as Henry Crawford does. A clergyman, whose role, as Austen shows it, is to be guide, philosopher and friend to his parishioners, need not despise acting, but will respect it only when it is serious, with its own kind of integrity. Edmund admits that he loves a play better than most people, and would go further than most to see one well acted:

'True, to see real acting, good hardened real acting; but I would hardly walk from this room to the next to look at the raw efforts of those who have not been bred to the trade – a set of gentlemen and ladies, who have all the disadvantages of education and decorum to struggle through.' (p. 124)

And it is noticeable that, in objecting to playing Anhalt, he does not say that he thinks he would disgrace his profession through 'insincerity', but through lack of professional skill, 'for I should be sorry to make the character ridiculous by bad acting. It must be very difficult to keep Anhalt from appearing a formal, solemn lecturer; and the man who chooses the profession itself is, perhaps, one of the last who would wish to represent it on the stage.' (p. 145)

The distinction made here is comparable to that made in *Northanger Abbey* about how to read Mrs Radcliffe. A man of real sense and sensibility will value a good novel and admire good acting, but he won't confuse the two, having too much respect for art, as well as a proper sense of the difference between life and art, to mix them up and make both trivial.

The ability to respond to acting and to value it is used to define the true sensibility of the heroine as well as the hero. Fanny declares she cannot act, but she quickly warms to Crawford's acting:

Fanny believed herself to derive as much innocent enjoyment from the play as any of them; Henry Crawford acted well and it was a pleasure to *her* to creep into the theatre and attend the rehearsal of the first act. (p. 165)

Everyone also is busy with their own concerns and 'after the first rehearsal or two Fanny began to be their only audience' (p. 165). In Volume III her pleasure in the play and in acting is again referred to:

His acting had first taught Fanny what pleasure a play might give, and his reading brought all his acting back before her again, nay, perhaps with greater enjoyment for it came unexpectedly and with no such drawback as she had been used to suffer in seeing him on the stage with Miss Bertram. (p. 337)

Fanny herself reads plays aloud to her aunt and, although we are not told how well she did it, we have no reason to suppose that she was mangling Shakespeare when Henry took over from her. Her admiration for Crawford the actor, is always contrasted with her dislike of Crawford the man; whereas her cousins wish to act with him because they are already half in love with him, they, in contrast to her, are *not* shown admiring him for his performance.

Insensitivity to the art of acting is not shown as a sign of moral worth, but of stupidity. Mr Rushworth impresses Sir Thomas with his good sense when he says, 'I am not so fond of acting as I was at first. I think we are a great deal better sitting comfortably here and doing nothing' (p. 186). But the truth is that Rushworth is fit for nothing at all, being too stupid to play a creditable part in real life, or to think of acting as anything more than the excuse for dressing up and showing off. But the best irony about acting is reserved for Lady Bertram, who cannot stay awake long enough to hear a play any more than she can attend to what ought to be her real-life responsibilities. On the evening that Sir Thomas returns from Antigua, she lets the cat out of the bag with this splendid piece of ineptitude:

in the elation of her spirits Lady Bertram became talkative and what were the sensations of her children upon hearing her say, 'How do you think the young people have been amusing themselves lately, Sir Thomas? They have been acting. *We have all been alive with acting.*' (p. 181, my italics)

'Lovers' Vows'

E. M. Butler, in an article published in 1933, argued that '*Mansfield Park* is nothing more nor less than *Lovers' Vows* translated into the terms of real life with the moral standard subverted by Kotzebue neatly re-inverted.'[4] In the same year William Reitzel quoted a hostile review of *Lovers' Vows* which had appeared in Cobbett's *Porcupine and Anti-Gallican Monitor*, and suggested that the purpose of *Mansfield Park* was to mock Kotzebue's revolutionary morals and assert the political beliefs and moral code of the readership of the *Porcupine*, 'persons of property, rank and respectability; in the public offices as well as in the best private families'. Reitzel adds that Sir Thomas Bertram was a born member of this class, 'in which it cannot be too often repeated, Jane Austen herself contentedly and proudly lived'.[5] From these two articles a number of beliefs, now firmly entrenched in the critical literature, are derived: that *Mansfield Park* is peculiarly literal in the treatment of Sir Thomas Bertram and everything under his patronage; that it discredits the revolutionary ideals of liberty, equality and fraternity, opposing to them the 'traditional', hierarchic ordering of society; and that it dismisses Kotzebue's sexual morality in favour of that adhered to by the upper-class English establishment (represented by Sir Thomas and Lady Bertram, Mr Rushworth, the Honourable Mr Yates and the Rev. Dr Grant, presumably). The first point is the most important for, if it is true that Austen presents us with an unironic portrait of Sir Thomas Bertram and of the domestic government of Mansfield Park, then the rest follows but, as a good many critics have perceived, Sir Thomas *is* treated ironically. Not only does Austen mock his solemnity and portentousness, she makes him wrong in almost all his assumptions. How, then, is *Lovers' Vows* to be seen in relation to *Mansfield Park*?

Kotzebue's play is about the patriarchal family, about bastardy and about class distinctions as they affect sexual relationships. His intention is to attack what Wollstonecraft called 'unnatural distinctions in society' but his handling of his subject is inconsistent, as well as lacking credibility. His village girl ends up a Baroness and his 'natural son' as a man of property. Moreover, his treatment of Agatha, although intended to be sympathetic, could hardly be admired by a rational feminist since it 'renders her an object of pity, bordering on contempt'. Frederick's illegitimacy is treated in such a way as to disconnect it from the material deprivations he and his mother have endured, and the curtain comes down on the following tableau:

(Anhalt leads on Agatha – the Baron runs and clasps her in his arms – supported by him, she sinks on a chair which Amelia places in the middle of the stage – the Baron kneels by her side, holding her hand.)

Baron: Agatha, Agatha, do you know this voice?
Agatha: Wildenhaim.
Baron: Can you forgive me?
Agatha: I forgive you (embracing him).
Frederick (as he enters):   I hear the voice of my mother! – Ha! mother! father!

(Frederick throws himself on his knees by the other side of his mother – She clasps him in her arms. – Amelia is placed on the side of her father attentively viewing Agatha – Anhalt stands on the side of Frederick with his hands gratefully raised to Heaven. The curtain slowly drops.)

Anyone who does not take it for granted that Jane Austen laughed at this had better re-read *Love and Friendship*.

Jane Austen satirises Kotzebue's (and Rousseau's) attitude to women through her portrayal of Fanny Price and Lady Bertram. Keeping her representatives of the rich and the poor within the same broad social class – Sir Thomas Bertram being the richest, Fanny the poorest – she deals with some of the unnatural distinctions in society in a more realistic way than Kotzebue, avoiding a fairy-tale happy ending. Fanny does not, as some critics have said, inherit Mansfield Park, for she marries the younger son, the heir being pointedly restored to health. Edmund will have a comfortable home and income, but compared with his older brother's wealth it is quite modest. Fanny will be much less well-off than she would have been had she married Crawford, and bids fair, with her husband, to fulfil a role she admires: 'To be the friend of the poor and oppressed! Nothing could be more grateful to her' (p. 404) – albeit in an unmelodramatic way. In Kotzebue, Anhalt, the poor clergyman, marries the girl he loves, for she has plenty of money and does not require further riches. In *Mansfield Park*, Edmund loses the woman with whom he is in love because he is not rich enough for her. In Kotzebue, Baron Wildenhaim makes amends for his youthful misconduct towards Agatha by marrying her twenty-odd years late. In *Mansfield Park*, Sir Thomas, who was thirty years earlier 'captivated' by Miss Ward, lives to see his children punished through the ill effects of an unequal marriage, in which his wife has lacked the ability to educate her daughters. Attempting to 'bind by the strongest securities all that remained to him of domestic felicity', he comes to give 'joyful consent' to the marriage of 'the two young friends', whom he once believed could never marry, since the distinction between even a second son of a baronet and the unportioned Miss Price must be too great.

In these respects, Jane Austen may be said to reverse characters and situations found in Kotzebue, but she goes a good deal further, calling in Shakespeare to assist her preference for an English sense of what is natural and reasonable, against the German disciple of Rousseau. Like Johnson and Coleridge, Austen takes it for granted that Shakespeare's English is the language of truth and nature, yet she is far from uncritical of his acceptance in *King Lear* of some 'unnatural distinctions in society' associated with patriarchy and of his male-biased treatment of English history. In *Mansfield Park* she uses allusion to Shakespeare's language to establish the rights of her heroine and the superior sense of her hero, but she 'corrects' the schema of *King Lear* as well as the schema of *Das Kind der Liebe* (translated into English as *The Natural Son* as well as *Lovers' Vows*) and associates her heroine's rights to true English justice with those of Henry VIII's first Queen, to whom Shakespeare had given some memorable lines, well rendered in the theatre of her own time by Mrs Siddons.

Before examining what Austen's allusions to *King Lear* and *King Henry VIII* in *Mansfield Park* mean in the context of Enlightenment feminism, it had better be noted that, at around the time when she had every reason to expect to become, at an early date, a published author and was prepared to accept whatever music publication might excite, Jane Austen had the opportunity in Bath of seeing the three plays to which important allusion is made in *Mansfield Park*. In January 1803 *King Lear*, improved by Nahum Tate, was performed in the Orchard Street Theatre Royal; so was *Lovers' Vows*. In March 1803 *King Henry VIII* was put on in the same theatre. There is no need to assume that these were the first or only performances seen by Jane Austen, but it is worth nothing that, so far as we know, she was in Bath at these times and likely to have seen them. What matters, so far as this study is concerned, is her treatment of primogeniture (associated with bastardy) and of the claims of female speakers of the

English tongue (whether they be Spanish Queens or poor relations of well-intentioned Baronets) to English justice and English liberty.

Between 1681 and 1823 Shakespeare's great tragedy of patriarchal error and mis-government was not performed on the English stage except in the form in which Tate had adapted it to the tastes of a politer age, leaving out the blinding of Gloucester, and leaving Cordelia alive to marry Edgar, his eldest son and legitimate heir. Austen takes Tate's plot and rewrites it so as to preserve the essence of the patriarch's errors about his elder daughters, and of his discovering in the natural 'bond', understood only by the youngest, all that Nature authorises. In Sir Thomas the figures of the king and Gloucester are combined, for he has, as well as three daughters, two sons, both legitimate, but one, the scape-grace Tom, being destined to riches and authority, the other, Edmund, being 'some twelve or fourteen moonshines/Lag of a brother', destined only for retirement and obscurity in the role of a country clergyman, his brother's first servant and dependant.

In *King Lear*, as Shakespeare wrote it, Edmund's younger son-ship and his bastardy were closely associated, a point brought out by Coleridge who, praising the truth to life with which he is represented, condemns Gloucester for the way in which he humiliates Edmund, in his manner of referring to his mother, and associates with this 'the law of primogeniture' as occasioning 'the mournful alienation of brotherly love . . . in children of the same stock'.[6] Shakespeare's plot, constructed to uphold 'Degree' as the great string which binds mankind to heaven in a mystical order, requires that Edmund, the younger son and bastard, should prove himself 'unnatural' although he carries the ironic title of 'natural son'. Austen's younger son, although quite clearly better qualified by natural gifts of prudence, sensitivity to other people, and habits of self-critical reflection to make a good ruler, better than his elder brother, is humiliated on account of his birth-order. In chapter 8 of Volume I, Tom pointedly reminds him that his interest in their father's property is inferior to that of the heir. Later, when Mary Crawford, with whom Edmund is by this time in love, says that he ought to go into Parliament instead of into the Church, he replies: ' "I believe I must wait till there is an especial assembly for the representation of younger sons who have little to live on" ' (p. 214). Sir Thomas is a member of Parliament as, presumably, his elder son will also be. It is suggested (p. 161) that Mr Rushworth will also enter the House when Sir Thomas is able to find him a borough. (A rotten borough is not specified but would, undoubtedly, be appropriate.)

King Lear, having no sons, divides his kingdom between his daughters, disinheriting the youngest because, when asked to obtain her share through flattery, she has nothing to say – except that she loves him according to the natural bonds which give rise to affection and filial duty. Cordelia's truth is grounded in her obedience to the moral law inherent in Nature, which makes her appear to her father, in his pride, disobedient and ungrateful. The schematic similarity between Sir Thomas's three daughters (the youngest being an adopted niece, whom he exiles to Portsmouth, following her disobedience) is fairly obvious. In Tate's *Lear*, Cordelia marries Gloucester's older son, Edgar. In *Mansfield Park*, Fanny marries the younger, who bears the name of Shakespeare's bastard younger son, though not his character. Mary Crawford and Fanny (in chapter 4 of Volume II) are made to discuss Edmund's name. Miss Crawford begins:

'I am so glad your eldest cousin is gone that he *may* be Mr. Bertram again. There is something in the sound of Mr. *Edmund* Bertram so formal, so pitiful, so younger–brother–like, that I detest it.'
'How differently we feel!' cried Fanny, 'To me, the sound of *Mr.* Bertram is so cold and nothing-meaning – so entirely without warmth and character! – It just stands for a gentleman, and that's all. But there is a nobleness in the name of Edmund. It is a name of heroism and renown – of kings, princes and knights; and seems to breathe the spirit of chivalry and warm affections.'
'I grant you the name is good in itself, and *Lord* Edmund or *Sir* Edmund sound delightfully; but sink it under the chill, the annihilation of a Mr. – and Mr. Edmund is no more than Mr. John or Mr. Thomas.' (p. 211)

The different attitudes of the heroine and anti-heroine towards 'unnatural distinctions in society' are made plain, and Austen, by making her younger son the moral superior of the heir to Mansfield Park, implicitly questions the validity of primogeniture which not only divides brothers and is associated with the disqualification of sisters, but also dissociates government, whether in the family, Church or State, from Reason and Nature, as they appeared to a mind formed in the Age of Enlightenment.

In chapter 3 of Volume III, Henry Crawford and Edmund Bertram discuss Shakespeare's language and the familiarity of English speakers with it. Henry speaks of Shakespeare as 'part of an Englishman's constitution'. Edmund, avoiding a terminology which excludes women, replies:

'No doubt, one is familiar with Shakespeare in a degree, from one's earliest years. His celebrated passages are quoted by everybody; they are in half the books we open, and we all talk Shakespeare, use his similes, and describe with his descriptions.' (p. 338)

The hero's rather awkward choice of pronouns here is important, for Fanny, who was herself reading Shakespeare before the two young men came into the drawing-room, is listening intently to this conversation. Henry shows through his language an attitude of mind which excludes her from the liberty which belongs to those who 'speak the tongue that Shakespeare spoke'; Edmund does not. It is no accident either that the play Fanny had chosen to read aloud while her aunt dozed was *King Henry VIII*. This play was frequently per-formed in the theatre of the time, where it had become a vehicle for one of Mrs Siddons' most admired performances. Like *King Lear*, it was not played with a pedantic regard for the text as Shakespeare wrote it, cuts being made and speeches from other history plays inserted. The three scenes which made it popular were the trial of Queen Katherine, her confrontation with Wolsey (Act III, (i)), and the spectacular procession scene at the end, in which the infant Elizabeth is borne round the stage before her christening, while Cranmer prophesies as to the blessings England is one day to enjoy under her government.[7]

Criticism has paid a good deal of attention to Henry Crawford's reading from this play, but not enough to Fanny's choice of it, nor its relevance to a novel about the moral status of women and domestic government as the paradigm of the government of England. When this chapter opens Fanny has already had her 'trial scene' in the East Room, and is sitting quietly at her needlework with her aunt, the play hastily put down as the footsteps of Henry and Edmund are heard approaching. This parallels the opening of *Henry VIII* (III (i)) where Queen Katherine is also at her needlework with her ladies when Cardinals Wolsey and Campeius come to bring her counsels which she believes to be unjust, but which she must accept. Shakespeare makes her strongly sympathetic and adds to her appeal to English audiences by allowing her to stress that, though she is not a native of England, she has lived here many years and speaks the native tongue. She will not allow Wolsey to address her in Latin, for plain English will serve her cause better:

> I am not such a truant since my coming,
> As not to know the language I have lived in:
> A strange tongue makes my case more strange, suspicious;
> Pray speak in English. (III (ii), 42–5)

We are not told which speech Fanny was reading, but we may be sure it was *not* the speech of Cardinal Wolsey which was 'quite near enough to satisfy Lady Bertram'. Perhaps readers who knew their Shakespeare well were expected to wonder what would have been a more likely choice on her part. Throughout the rest of the chapter Fanny maintains a speaking silence, apart from the one point at which Crawford pesters her into breaking it. She is, throughout, conscious of the pressure upon her to accept Sir Thomas's advice and marry Crawford, intensified here by her aunt's assumption that this is her duty and by Edmund's encouragement of the match. Although she is silent, Crawford is aware of her intelligent, critical listening, and he is pleased to think that, if Lady Bertram has been moved by his reading, her niece, 'alive and enlightened as she was', must feel a great deal more. Yet it does not strike him that Fanny's feelings about the play itself may bear on her perception of her own situation as one in which, like the Queen, she is being forced to submit to male authority against her wishes and conscience.

'You shook your head at my acknowledging that I should not like to engage in the duties of a clergyman always, for a constancy. Yes, that was the word. Constancy I am not afraid of the word. I would spell it, read it, write it with anybody. I see nothing alarming in the word. Did you think I ought?'
   'Perhaps, Sir,' said Fanny, wearied at last into speaking, – 'Perhaps, Sir, I thought it was a pity you did not always know yourself as well as you seemed to do at that moment.' (p. 342)

Fanny says no more, but what she has said is in sufficiently direct and thoughtful an English as to persaude Crawford, had he a proper respect for her, to leave her alone and to reflect on what she has said. Of course he does not; 'delighted to get her to speak at any rate, he was determined to keep it up' and he goes on tormenting her with assurances of his own fidelity and misplaced confidence in her having the qualities of an angel until 'the solemn procession, headed by Baddeley, of tea-board, urn, and cake-bearers, made its appearance, and delivered her from a grievous imprisonment of body and mind' (p. 344). Perhaps, in a chapter so full of allusion to the Shakespearean history play, we ought to ask how Baddeley relates to the Burleigh of *The History of England*, the tea-urn to Gloriana and the 'cake-bearers' to what-you-will, but I shall not pursue it, except to say that it is all a joke and not at the expense of Miss Price.

Mansfield Park and the Mansfield Judgment

The title of *Mansfield Park* is allusive and ironic, but the allusion in this case is not to philosophical fiction like *Emile* nor to the theatre, but to a legal judgment, generally regarded as having ensured that slavery could not be held to be in accordance with the manners and customs of the English. In this title, in making Sir Thomas Bertram a slave-owner abroad, and in exposing the moral condition of his wife in England, Jane Austen follows an analogy used in the *Vindication* between the slaves in the colonies and women, especially married women, at home.

Wollstonecraft says that a 'truly benevolent legislator always endeavours to make it the interest of each individual to be virtuous; and thus private virtue becoming the cement of public happiness, an orderly whole is consolidated by the tendency of all the parts towards a common centre' (*Vindication*, p. 257). Women, however, are not taught to be virtuous in their domestic life and so are not to be trusted in either private or public life. They learn to be subject to propriety, 'blind propriety', rather than to regulate their actions in accordance with moral law, as 'an heir of immortality' ought. She asks, 'Is one half of the human species, like the poor African slaves, to be subjected to prejudices that brutalise them, when principles would be a surer guard of virtue?' (p. 257).

In England, agitation against the slave-trade had gone on all through the last quarter of the eighteenth century. The arguments against it were rehearsed widely in the early nineteenth century, leading up to the passing of the Act of Abolition, which became effective in 1808. Jane Austen must have been familiar with them and, in a letter of 1813, speaks of having been in love with Thomas Clarkson's writings (*Letters*, p. 292). In 1808, Clarkson published *The Abolition of the African Slave Trade* in which he says:

We have lived in consequence of [abolition] to see the day when it has been recorded as a principle of our legislation that commerce itself shall have its moral boundaries. We have lived to see the day when we are likely to be delivered from the contagion of the most barbarous opinions. Those who supported this wicked traffic virtually denied that man was a moral being. They substituted the law of force for the law of reason. But the great Act, now under our consideration, has banished the impious doctrine and restored the rational creature to his moral rights.[8]

It is easy to see here that a woman, who rejoiced that the slave-trade had been ended, might ask whether it had yet been recorded 'as a principle of our legislation that commerce itself shall have its moral boundaries' – so far as women were concerned. Was it universally accepted that woman was 'a moral being'? Had the rational creature been restored to *her* 'moral rights'?

Clarkson goes over the history of the anti-slavery movement and refers to a particularly famous legal judgment, which established that slavery was illegal in England. This was the Mansfield Judgment, given by the Lord Chief Justice of England in 1772, in a case concerning a black slave, James Somerset, the question being whether, having been brought to England, he could still be held to be 'owned' by his master. Arguing that he could not, counsel for the defence, referring to an earlier judgment given in the reign of Queen Elizabeth, said:

It was resolved that England was too pure an air for slaves to breathe in . . . and I hope my lord the air does not blow worse since – I hope they will never breathe here; for this is my assertion, the moment they put their feet on English ground, that moment they are free.[9]

Lord Mansfield found in favour of Somerset and, by implication, of this view of English air.

In *Mansfield Park*, the English patriarch is also the owner of Antiguan plantations and of the slaves who work them. When he returns to England, his niece puts a question to him about the slave-trade (p. 198). We are not told what the question was, nor what answer was given but, through the title, the making of Sir Thomas a slave-owner abroad, and the unstated question of Miss Fanny, *her* moral status in England is implicitly contrasted yet also compared with that of the Antiguan slaves. Since it is often assumed that Jane Austen could not have thought much about anything which did not impinge upon her domestic life and familial relations, or else been said by Dr Johnson, it may be worth noting that, at the house of her brother Edward Knight, she met Lord Mansfield's niece on a number of occasions, and that Boswell reported Johnson's view on another slavery case – Knight versus Wedderburn – as follows: 'No man is by nature the property of another. The defendant is therefore by nature free.'[10]

In *Mansfield Park* the ideals of 'liberty, equality and fraternity' are given an English, feminist meaning. The equal moral status of women is made clear through exposure of the absurdity of any other belief. As in Wollstonecraft, the language of law and property, and the language of capture and captivation as applied to marriage and sexual relationships, is shown to be indecent. The opening sentence of the novel, in which the *captivation* of an English Baronet by Miss *Ward* of Hun*t*ingdon, although her uncle, the *lawyer*, allowed her £3000 short of an *equitable claim*, amounts to an ironic denunciation of what Wollstonecraft called 'the master key of property'. Images of lock and key, imprisoning East Rooms, Sotherton as 'quite a dismal old prison', the bastilled starling who 'couldn't get out' recur. Yet the soil at Mansfield, especially at the parsonage where the Moor Park apricot thrives, is good, and so is the air. The young people, oppressed by the prison-like atmosphere of Mr Rushworth's house, share 'one impulse, one wish for air and liberty'. Fanny's need for fresh English air is stressed again and again; 'she requires', as Crawford ironically sees, 'constant air and exercise . . . ought never to be long banished from the free air and liberty of the country' (pp. 410–11).

Mansfield Park is also pointedly concerned with fraternity. What ought to be, and sometimes is – as in the relationship between Fanny and her brother William – the paradigm of equal, affectionate relationships between men and women is always held up as an ideal, having implications beyond the literal meaning of 'brother' and 'sister'. Edmund Bertram treats his inferior little cousin as a sister early in Volume I. He does not fall in love with her until the final chapter, where this is treated cursorily and ironically. This is not because Jane Austen had suddenly and unself-consciously become interested in incest; it is because the marriage which provides the necessary happy ending of this comic work carries implications about the right relationships between men and women, both in marriage as a social institution, and in society at large. As John Stuart Mill was to say some fifty or more years later:

The moral regeneration of mankind will only really commence when the most fundamental of the social relations is placed under the rule of equal justice, and when human beings learn to cultivate their strongest sympathy with an equal in rights and cultivation.[11]

Austen, in *Mansfield Park*, shows that such an ideal is more readily to be found in contemporary society between brothers and sisters than husbands and wives, though she seeks a transference to the marriage relationship of the ideal. With William, Fanny experiences a 'felicity' which she has never known before in an 'unchecked, equal, fearless intercourse' (p. 234). Her marriage to Edmund allows the reader to hope that she will know such felicity in her adult married life.

Conclusion

Mansfield Park, far from being the work of conservative quietism that much twentieth-century criticism has turned it into, embodies Jane Austen's most ambitious and radical criticism of contemporary prejudice in society and in literature. Confining herself to 'two or three families in a village', working within the conventions of the domestic comedy which had become the special strength of the women novelists, through allusion, she enlarges its scope so that it carries philosophical and political resonance far beyond its surface meaning.

It is the only novel set in a county she had never visited, except through the pages of *Sir Charles Grandison*, the novel in which, according to C. Griffin-Wolff, Richardson attempted to solve the special problem of Woman by depicting the ideal patriarch as one who would 'establish and maintain a community which permitted her to take her rightful place'.[12] Austen's novel is about a benevolent patriarch who does not know that the rightful place of woman is that of a 'partner in life' who ought to share in domestic government. It carries a further implication about 'government' in a wider sense.

Born in December 1775, Jane Austen was only thirteen when the French Revolution began and too young to experience any of the euphoria felt in England in its early days. Growing up after England was already at war with France, she shared in the mood of hostility to it which became characteristic also of Wordsworth, Coleridge and Southey, her slightly older contemporaries, but, like Wordsworth, she held dear the native tradition of respect for liberty and individual rights. In *Mansfield Park* she shows that Englishwomen, even though they may lack 'genius' or large fortunes, are not, where they demonstrate the characteristics of 'the rational creature', to be denied the 'moral rights' appertaining to such beings. A little absurdity here and there is no bar, since 'rational beings' of both sexes are also 'mortals' and uncommonly prone to absurdity, even in their best moments.

18 Emma

Emma was perhaps the *most* 'gradual performance' of all Jane Austen's novels. Written between January 1814 and August 1815, there is reason to think that ideas embodied in it were first formed some twelve to fifteen years earlier. The novel alludes in particularly interesting ways to two works: Thomas Dibdin's *The Birthday*, an English version of Kotzebue's *Die Versöhnung* (1799); and Eaton Stannard Barrett's burlesque novel, *The Heroine, or Adventures of Cherubina* (1813). An archaeological account of *Emma* would, I think, show how it was built from material belonging to the phase before Austen became interested in Kotzebue and theatrical allusion (*The Watsons*), takes its essential framework from the Kotzebue period (*The Birthday*), and assumed its final shape as the author's early interest in burlesque (*The Heroine*) was revived. These phases, and the external evidence for them, are discussed in the conclusion of this chapter, which is mainly concerned with Jane Austen's use of allusion and the ways in which it was developed so as to allow the expression of a feminist point of view within the comic mode. However, it should perhaps be mentioned here that she first saw *The Birthday* in 1799, and read *The Heroine* early in 1814.

The Birthday

The Birthday was one of the four most successful of Kotzebue's plays in England, performed frequently in London and in provincial theatres for a period of about twenty-five years from 1799, and its plot familiar to contemporary theatre-goers. It is about twin brothers, Captain and Mr Bertram, who have been estranged for fifteen years over the ownership of a garden. They are coming up to their sixty-third birthday when the play opens. Captain Bertram is a gouty, irrascible retired seaman, looked after by his man Junk, who has a heart of gold and a salty vocabulary. He has a son, Harry. Mr Bertram is an invalid, cared for by his devoted and lovely daughter,

Emma. Emma and Harry fall in love, she being ignorant that he is
her cousin. The son and daughter bring about a reconciliation
between the brothers on their birthday, thus defeating the machina-
tions of Mrs Moral, the Captain's dishonest housekeeper, and
Circuit, the rascally lawyer who hoped to see Emma and Harry
disinherited. Emma is able to marry after all, since her lover is her
father's nephew, and therefore acceptable by his fireside. There are
also two aged servants, who had known the brothers as boys – Ann,
their former nurse, and William.

The points of comparison between *The Birthday* and *Emma* are
these: both heroines believe that they cannot marry because of their
duty to their invalid fathers. In both cases they are enabled to do so
because they fall in love with a relation (in one case a cousin, in the
other a brother-in-law) peculiarly acceptable in the invalid father's
house. In *The Birthday* the brothers have quarrelled over property. In
Emma, the Knightley brothers are drawn in contrast as preserving an
amicable, though undemonstrative relationship, in which each is
prepared 'to do everything good for the other'. In *The Birthday*
William's concern for Mr Bertram helps to establish the invalid as a
sympathetic figure in the eyes of the audience. In *Emma*, William
Larkins' relationship with his employer, Mr Knightley, is used to
show both master and man in a favourable light, Mr Knightley
putting up with a certain amount of mock-tyranny, William thinking 'more of his master's profit than any thing' (pp. 238–9).

In *Emma*, the sentimental stereotype of the devoted daughter
whose love of her father is an obstacle to her marriage is subjected to
realistic treatment and the theme of filial devotion is enlarged
through the representation of Miss Bates and her mother. In *The
Birthday*, soon after Emma and Harry have met and Harry has shown
kindness to her father, this dialogue follows:

Emma: Don't you think my father will live to be a very old man now?
Harry: If he is careful not to exert himself too much.
Emma: That shall be my care.
Harry: And will you always remain with him?
Emma: Always, always.
Harry: But if other duties should call upon you?
Emma: Other duties! What duties can be more sacred?
Harry: The duties of a wife or a mother.
Emma: No – I never intend to marry.
Harry: Never marry?
Emma: Not if I should be obliged to leave my father.
Harry: Your husband would supply the place of a son.
Emma: And the son would take the daughter from the father.

Harry: But if a man could be found who would bestow on your father a
          quiet old age, free from every sorrow; who far from robbing the
          father of a good daughter would weave the garland of love round
          three hearts, who would live under his roof and multiply your joys.

In Kotzebue, everything is solved by improbable discoveries of
unsuspected kinship and tears which obliterate old grievances instan-
taneously. In *Emma*, the same basic situation is transformed so as to
allow a serious, ironic and problematic examination of the relationship of father and daughter and its effect upon her character.

Emma Bertram's mother, like Emma Woodhouse's, is dead. At
seventeen, she is a lively, affectionate girl, whose health and beauty
evoke a warm response in other people. She charms Captain Bertram with her winning ways and old William, seeing her approach
with her father, says: 'I do love the very sight of her.' Emma
Woodhouse, at twenty-one, is a much less idealised character, but
she has something of the same effect upon other people. Mrs Weston
speaks in glowing terms of Emma's beauty, as well as her merits as a
friend and daughter, she is 'the complete picture of grown-up health.
She is loveliness itself.' Mr Knightley, although busy criticising her,
confesses: 'I have seldom seen a face or figure more pleasing to me
than hers . . . I love to look at her' (p. 39). Jane Austen, for all that she
subjects her grown-up Emma to realistic pressures which remove
her far from Emma Bertram, gives her a strong power of calling
forth warm affection, as Newman recognised when he said, 'I feel
kind to her whenever I think of her.'

At the end of *Emma*, after Mr Knightley has proposed, but before
Mr Woodhouse knows anything about it, Emma's father enquires
after his health, anxious that he should not have taken cold from his
ride. Jane Austen comments: 'Could he have seen the state of the
heart, he would have cared very little for the lungs' (p. 434). I suspect
that here an exchange between old Ann and William, at the start of
The Birthday, is parodied. William asks how her master is:

Ann: He has slept well, William; he mends every day.
William: I'm main glad for Miss Emma's sake and ecod, for your sake,
          Mrs. Ann. But I be afraid he is not quite tightish yet. I often do
          hear un cough.
Ann: Ay, ay, but the doctor says if the heart be sound, never mind the
          lungs.
William: Ecod! and so do I say. Better lose all the lungs than only have half
          a heart.

Given the popularity of *The Birthday*, the certainty that Jane
Austen knew it, and that she had made use of allusion to another play

of Kotzebue's, it is surely impossible to suppose that the similarities between the plot of *The Birthday* and of *Emma* are not the result of conscious adaptation. How then is it adapted, and for what purpose?

First, although the plot of *Emma* is particularly complex and includes many elements not present in Kotzebue at all, his basic situation, so far as the heroine is concerned, is kept. Instead of being reversed, the daughter's obligation to her father is retained and not only she, but other sensible characters, including Mr Knightley and Mrs Weston, see an insuperable obstacle to her marrying while her father lives, unless she can remain with him. Emma's virtues as a devoted and considerate daughter are emphasised throughout the novel, and with dramatic irony she comforts herself, when she comes to believe that Harriet Smith is to be Mr Knightley's wife, by considering that: 'Marriage in fact would not do for her. It would be incompatible with what she owed to her father. She would not marry, even if asked by Mr. Knightley' (p. 416).

After she *has* been asked, her attitude does not alter: 'a short parley with her own heart produced the most solemn resolution of never quitting her father. She even wept over the idea of it as a sin of thought. While he lived it must be only an engagement; but she flattered herself that, if divested of the danger of drawing her away, it might become an increase of comfort to him' (p. 435). Emma repeats the first part of this to Mr Knightley when he raises the subject with her (p. 448); he has himself come to the conclusion that Mr Woodhouse cannot be moved, and it is he who suggests that he, Knightly, should become a part of the Hartfield household.

The rightness of Emma and Mr Knightley as marriage partners is established both morally and psychologically, but it is also required by the demands of the plot: to that extent Austen retains Kotzebue's schema and does so in a comparable way with a final *ménage à trois*. Mr Knightley, unlike Harry Bertram, is not made acceptable because he turns out to be a long-lost nephew, but because he already occupies a place as a supernumerary son-in-law long before he and Emma ever think of marrying. He is 'not only a very old and intimate friend of the family but particularly connected with it as the older brother of Isabella's husband' (p. 9). He speaks to Emma with the freedom of an older brother, and he is received without ceremony as though he were a near-relation. When the engagement is revealed to Mrs Weston, she feels that it is

in every respect so proper, suitable and unexceptionable a connexion and in one respect one point of the highest importance, so peculiarly eligible, so singularly fortunate, that it now seemed as if Emma could not safely have attached herself to any other creature and that she had been the stupidest of beings in not having thought of it and wished it long ago – How very few of these men in a rank of life to address Emma would have renounced their own house for Hartfield: And who but Mr. Knightley could know and bear with Mr. Woodhouse so as to make the arrangement desirable! (p. 467)

The final precipitation of the marriage, by Mr Woodhouse's anxieties about a local poultry thief, is plainly intended to be taken lightly. While it fits perfectly with his character, the author expects us to enjoy the joke as she finds a piece of comic business with which to facilitate the wedding without which the book cannot be ended. I think that the reader is also supposed to see by this time what the schematic structure has been, and how an unlikely, even an absurd, plot has been worked upon so that it does not violate Nature or probability. At this point, if not before, we are to stand back from the fiction and its characters – to experience the mild alienation which results from being shown the constructional nuts and bolts – and, as we see that there was never any possibility of things working out in any other way, to ask what this particular handling of a stock situation shows us about it.

Jane Austen said that in *Emma* she intended to portray a heroine whom no one but herself would much like, and Emma Woodhouse is, certainly, the furthest of all the Austen heroines from 'a picture of perfection'. And yet she does, in her role of devoted daughter, come quite close to a sentimental stereotype. What Austen does is to show this aspect of her life and character in such a way as to criticise the romanticisation of devoted daughters. Emma's concern for her father, although endearing and amiable, is attended by many ill consequences, for it is a relationship in which a good deal of exploitation goes on, and in which Emma, through excessive devotion to him, fails to take adequate account of her responsibilities outside her family, and particularly towards other women.

In *The Birthday*, Mr Bertram is a genuinely sick man; in *Emma*, Mr Woodhouse is a hypochondriac. Mr Bertram is quite unselfish about his daughter and welcomes his nephew as her husband. Mr Woodhouse does not agree to let a son-in-law in until he becomes frightened of a poacher. By reducing Mr Woodhouse's claims to consideration and respect, Jane Austen satirises the sentimental ideal of the devoted daughter. Emma, self-critical as she learns to be in other ways, never questions her attitude to her father, yet we see him as a bad influence upon her. Although he is a splendid comic figure like Lady Bertram, he is stupid and selfish, a much worse influence on his daughter than is Harriet Smith. Mr Knightley's description of her as 'a flatterer in all her ways' is really more apposite to him. Emma 'dearly loved her father, but he was no companion for her. He could not meet her in conversation, rational or playful . . . for having been a valetudinarian all his life, without activity of mind or body, he was a much older man in his ways than in his years; and though everywhere beloved for the friendliness of his heart and his amiable temper, his talents could not have recommended him at any time' (p. 7). Although Emma knows that his constant '"Emma never thinks of herself, if she can do good to others"'; '"Dear Emma bears everything so well"' are not well judged, she is affected by their constant repetition, for they have done more than anything to make her think too well of herself.

By making Mr Woodhouse a selfish 'old woman', Jane Austen mocks her heroine in the one respect where she believes herself to be above reproach. Unable to see him as he really is, Emma suffers from a peculiarly insidious form of parental tyranny for, with all her apparent independence, she is prevented from growing up.

On the subject of duty to parents Mary Wollstonecraft says:

I never knew a parent who had paid more than common attention to his children disregarded. On the contrary, the early habit of relying almost implicitly on the opinion of a respected parent is not easily shook, even when the matured reason convinces the child that his parent is not the wisest man in the world. This weakness – for a weakness it is, though the epithet amiable may be tacked to it – a reasonable man must steal himself against; for the absurd duty, too often inculcated, of obeying a parent only on account of his being a parent, shackles the mind, and prepares it for a slavish submission to any power but reason. (*Vindication*, pp. 267–8)

These remarks are applicable to Emma, for all that her father is the most absurd of tyrants.

Beside Emma, as the romanticised daughter of a rich, indulgent father, is set Miss Bates, whose situation as a middle-aged spinster with an aged mother and little money, comes much nearer to what is commonly observed in daily life of devoted daughters. Writers of lectures and sermons for young ladies were apt to glamourise the youthful daughter of an invalid father, but the poorly-off old maid with an aged mother was more likely to be an object of scorn. Miss Bates had not married, but it does not appear that this is because she made a romantic sacrifice of her happiness, as Emma Bertram and Emma Woodhouse think they should, but because she has never received an offer. Yet she is cheerful, active and 'her contented and grateful spirit were a recommendation to everybody and a mine of felicity to herself' (p. 21). Jane Austen's portrayal of Miss Bates is part of her correction of Kotzebue, and Emma's moral growth is closely associated with an improvement in the respect she accords to her. Emma's early announcement to Harriet that she 'has very little intention of ever marrying' is followed by a discussion of Miss Bates in which she reveals a patronising and insensitive attitude. She does not call on the Bateses as often as she ought, deeming such calls 'a waste of time – tiresome women' (p. 155). Her rudeness at Box Hill is the culmination of a long period in which the young, rich, spoilt, devoted daughter has not acted well towards the ageing, poor one. Emma's resolution, once she is brought to see her conduct in a truer light, to initiate 'a regular, equal, kindly intercourse' with Miss Bates marks the starting-point of her beginning to grow up, and to accept her social responsibilities as a woman.

Die Versöhnung treats fraternal as well as filial love in a sentimental fashion. The elderly Bertram brothers, who have been estranged for fifteen years over the ownership of 'a garden', end up weeping tears of joy and congratulating one another on having sound hearts. In *Emma*, the fraternal affection and conduct of George and John Knightley is contrasted with such sentimental models as this. When the Knightley brothers are first seen together, ' "How d'ye do, George?" and "John, how are you?" succeeded in the true English style, burying under a calmness that seemed all but indifference the real attachment which would have led either of them to do everything for the good of the other.'

There follows an account of their conversation in which the keen interest that both brothers take in the Donwell estate is shown as a bond between them:

The plan of a drain, the change of a fence, the felling of a tree and the destination of every acre for wheat, turnips or spring corn, was entered into with as much equality of interest by John as his cooler manners rendered possible; and if his willing brother ever left him anything to enquire about, his enquiries even approached a tone of eagerness. (p. 99)

The 'true English style' is here contrasted with the false, sentimental German (as it had been in *Mansfield Park*), and there is a touch of the mock-heroic in the way it is done. The undemonstrativeness of the English brothers, though admired, is lightly mocked by a hint of exaggeration, and their exemplary interest in the improvement of the estate is made a little bathetic through the blunt references to the drain, the fence and the turnips.

Mr Knightley's role is a curious one, for he is *both* a portrait of an English gentleman, as Jane Austen thought he ought to be, *and* a mock-heroic 'parfit gentil knight'. In so far as he shows a preference for what accords with Reason and Nature, as he does in his own open nature and manners, and in his valuing them in women as well as in men, he is the Enlightenment feminist's ideal of a man of sense. In his tactful kindness to the Bateses and Harriet Smith, he shows a consideration for women which must gladden a feminist's heart, for the half-blind old clergyman's widow, her old-maid daughter and the 'natural' daughter of the respectable tradesman who cannot give his girl a name, are truly in need of the protection which his acts of 'courtesy' give them in a society where the clerisy is represented by Mr and Mrs Elton. But, in his preference for the company of his solid bourgeois neighbours, the Coles, Mr Perry and even Mrs Goddard, rather than anything 'higher', his regard and respect for his quite unfashionable brother with his London legal practice, and his sense of John Martin's 'superiority', he is associated with such characters as belong to 'low life' – at least in a long tradition of literary association.

Mr Knightley wears the 'thick leather gaiters' of a working-farmer (p. 289), and, although he is the owner of Donwell Abbey, he is plain *Mr* George Knightley, not *Sir* George Knightley, Bart. If he is, as his name and his character suggest, a sort of *Saint* George, he is designed by his author to mock latter-day romantic notions of the chivalric tradition, and latter-day aristocrats with their aversion to work of any kind, and their incurable habits of flattery and deception in sexual relationships.

In *Mansfield Park*, Fanny allowed herself to fantasise about the name 'Edmund' as proper to a hero of the age of chivalry. Her romantic vision of her cousin as a knight in shining armour is mocked by his quite humdrum concern with the economic realities of the world in which he lives. In the same chapter, he insists that he aims at nothing better than 'honesty . . . in the middle state of worldly circumstances'. Edmund Bertram has disappointed some readers and most critics on account of his *unenthusiastic* (in the eighteenth-century sense) evaluation of the responsibilities he must accept in following a younger son's profession as a clergyman. Mr Knightley, to those who think he is supposed to represent, without the mock-heroic tinge, an ideal English gentleman, also appears wanting. R. W. Chapman, for example, missed the point when he compared George Knightley with Trollope's Plantagenet Palliser, Duke of Omnium, and found him 'not nearly so great an achieve-ment of creation'.[1] But, of course, Austen's point in making Mr Knightley wear thick leather gaiters, bother about drains, and treat old Mrs Bates and her daughter with respect and kindness, is that, in his mock-heroic role, he functions as a critic not only of snobbery, disguised as romantic feeling as in Mrs Elton and sometimes in Emma, but of that extensive class of literature which makes gods of Baronets and Dukes – Grandison being an example known to Austen, Omnium yet to come.

We can see very clearly Jane Austen's subtle extension of the mock-heroic if we consider her use of material drawn from Eaton Stannard Barrett's *The Heroine*, the second work to which allusion is made in *Emma*. We know that she read it in March 1814 soon after beginning work on the new novel. During June and July she visited relations in Surrey, and it appears that the name 'Knightley', as well as 'Randalls', was brought into the novel after a visit to Leatherhead. It would seem, therefore, that Jane Austen began working on the material derived from Kotzebue and *The Watsons* before she had formed an idea of the Harriet Smith sub-plot and of other elements connected with it, for this part of *Emma* seems pretty clearly to have resulted from reading Barrett.

The Heroine, or Adventures of Cherubina

The Heroine, published in 1813, is a burlesque on the sentimental novel, of a kind much in vogue at an earlier period, though the vein was not yet exhausted, Peacock returning to it a few years later. Jane Austen shows that she was excited by reading it, saying that she has 'torn through the third volume', and describing it as 'a delightful burlesque, particularly of the Radcliffe style' (*Letters*, p. 377).

It concerns Cherry Wilkinson, the daughter of a respectable and affectionate, though undistinguished, father who, guided by her romantic governess, turns against him, imagines herself into the role of Heroine, and embarks on a series of absurd adventures in which she narrowly escapes ending up in prison. Cherry's father wishes her to marry Bob Stuart, his former ward, who has been her childhood friend and playmate, but she, almost deranged by her reading of Mrs Radcliffe and other romantic authors, has persuaded herself that Wilkinson is not her father. Adopting the name of Cherubina de Willoughby, and supposing herself to be the natural child of an Italian Count, she will have nothing to do with Bob. Illegitimacy becomes, for her, an essential mark of superiority. Writing to her governess, who has run off with the wine-loving butler, she says:

Here is another precious project against my peace. I am to be forced into a marriage, am I? And with whom? A man whose legitimacy is unimpeached, and whose friends would certainly consent. His name Robert too: – master

Bobby, as the servants used to call him . . . Now indeed my wretchedness is complete. An orphan, or at least an outcast; robbed of my birthright, immured in a farmhouse – threatened with a husband of decent birth, parentage and education – my governess gone, my novels burnt, what is left to me but flight?[2]

Fleeing from such degradation, Cherry gets herself into innumerable scrapes and causes all kinds of distress to other people – ending up by having her father immured in a lunatic asylum – before Bob Stuart rescues her, preaches her a few sermons, puts all right with her father, and marries her. Among the incidents which bear on *Emma* are Cherry's visit to a poor, sick, cottage woman, and her mischief-making in the love affair of Mary, a village girl, and her honest swain William, which includes her contriving to come between them. Cherry invents a William of her own, persuades Mary to be her amanuensis in writing him a letter of rejection, and then sends it to the real William.

As will be clear from this partial summary, *The Heroine* is a broad, improbable burlesque, attacking the most favoured targets of this genre: ignorant governesses, silly girls, romantic novels, and a host of villains who, affecting the pose of Men of Feeling, exploit Cherry for their own advantage. Dedicated to George Canning, it opposes the *status quo* of conservative England to the violence, hypocrisy and danger of the romantic imagination. Its heroine is safe only when she accepts the tutelage of Bob Stuart, who assures her that, once her father is released from the asylum, 'past follies shall be forgotten, past pleasures renewed; you shall return home, and Cherry Wilkinson shall again be the daughter of an honest squire'. The title-page includes this quotation: 'L'Histoire d'une femme est toujours un Roman', and women in it are shown always as in need of the guidance and protection of honest men of sense. The novel is ostensibly written in a series of letters from Cherry to her ex-governess, Biddy, though this is used simply as a burlesque device, the character of the governess, as that of an idiot, being established at the outset, and her use thereafter restricted to her role as the recipient of Cherry's outpourings. Jane Austen's letters show that she enjoyed *The Heroine*, but her use of themes and characters taken from it shows quite a different point of view from Barrett's. In *Northanger Abbey*, she had already modified the burlesque schema of an ignorant heroine misled by romantic reading. Stimulated by Barrett's revival of the form she went further, finding ways of correcting the burlesque stereotype, as well as mocking romantic delusions. Broadly speaking, what Austen does is to restrict her heroine's delusions to relatively minor matters, leaving her, with all her youthful faults, essentially right in her judgements and feelings on a great many important matters. In this way, while giving us in Miss Woodhouse anything but a 'picture of perfection', she manages to portray a heroine whose qualities fit her to become mistress of Donwell Abbey and to marry Mr Knightley not as a shrew or idiot, now reformed and subservient, but as one in whom he, rightly, recognises an equal, capable of becoming his partner in life – he, of course, being established as a man capable of open, unaffected and unpatronising relationships with women.

Jane Austen's feminist viewpoint is clearly responsible for her correction of Barrett on the following points: governesses, the natural imbecility of young women, illegitimacy and heroes as mentors.

In *The Heroine*, a crisis has been precipitated at the start of the novel by the governess's having eloped with the butler, upon which her sensible, if tactless, father discovers how much harm Biddy has already caused in her mishandling of his daughter's education. In *Emma*, Miss Taylor, the heroine's excellent governess, has just married Mr Weston when the novel opens. Mr Woodhouse's attitude to this marriage shows his inability to judge anything sensibly and emphasises his selfishness. The meaning of the relationships between father, daughter and governess could hardly be more different, though, as in Barrett, the heroine now starts on a new phase in her life.

In *The Heroine* Cherry's governess is an ignorant fool and not to be thought of as a lady. Her marriage to the butler places her where she belongs in Barrett's social structure – with the upper servants. As an educator she has proved a disastrous failure, having persuaded her pupil to read trashy novels and never having given her wise counsel or a sound piece of moral advice. In *Emma* there is, I suspect, just a relic of the burlesque schema – in Mr Weston's partiality to good wine – but Emma's former governess, who has 'run off' with him to Randalls at the start of the novel, is drawn in complete contrast to the burlesque stereotype. Not only is Mrs Weston shown throughout as a woman of true sense and sensibility, but her pupil's affectionate, and truly unsnobbish regard for her is one of the best proofs of her real superiority[Mr Knightley says: 'Nature gave you understanding: – Miss Taylor gave you principles. You must have done well.' Here he acknowledges that her true fitness to be the mistress of Donwell Abbey rests not on his 'interference' and 'lecturing', but on her own powers of mind and the sound moral education given her by

her governess) Perhaps it is in this adjustment and correction of
Barrett's schema that Jane Austen shows most clearly her feminist
convictions, for the low status of governesses and the humiliations
they endured were among the injustices which moved intelligent
women most throughout the eighteenth and nineteenth centuries.
Mary Woolstonecraft, who had herself experienced the role, speaks
bitterly of the unhappiness almost always associated with it. By
showing her heroine as a loyal and admiring friend of her former
governess, Jane Austen does much to show us that she is indeed,
whatever her faults, exceptionally sound in head and heart. Through
Jane Fairfax, and her feelings about being forced into becoming
governess in the family of one of Mrs Elton's friends, Mrs Small-
ridge, Jane Austen amplifies and stiffens her correction of Barrett's
notion of governesses, making the same analogy between the condition of the slave and the condition of the Englishwoman of the
middle class as she had implied in *Mansfield Park*.

Jane Fairfax in *Emma* is faced with the awful prospect of becoming
a governess, and the woman whose fortune has put her in a position
to play the part of patroness is a Bristolian. Before her marriage
'Bristol was her home, the very heart of Bristol'. No wonder she is
sensitive about the slave-trade, for the heart of Bristol at that period
was the wealth accumulated in the triangular trade whereby ships
took slaves to the West Indies and returned with sugar from the
plantations. Jane will not be hurried into a situation:

'When I am quite determined as to the time, I am not at all afraid of being
long unemployed. There are places in town, offices, where enquiry would
soon produce something – Offices for the sale – not quite of human flesh –
but of human intellect.'
    'Oh! my dear, human flesh! You quite shock me; if you mean a fling at the
slave-trade, I assure you Mr. Suckling [her brother-in-law] was always
rather a friend to the abolition.'

Jane is undeterred:

'I did not mean, I was not thinking of the slave-trade . . . governess trade
was all I had in view; widely different certainly as to the guilt of those who
carry it on; but as to the greater misery of the victims, I do not know where it
lies.' (pp. 300–1)

In *The Heroine* Bob Stuart, the hero, is 'a picture of perfection',
though his tendency to moralising might not recommend him to
everyone. At the start of the novel he is shown as sensible and as
sound in heart, and he does not deviate in any way from this
throughout, nor does he develop in any way, or learn anything new,
about himself or other people. Many critics have thought that Mr

Knightley is also 'a picture of perfection' – the idealised English gentleman, the only 'reliable narrator' among the fictional characters. This has led to the belief that *Emma* is a novel of education in which all the learning is done by the heroine, all the instruction provided by the hero. But *Emma* is not like Mrs Inchbald's *A Simple Story*, or like *Shirley* or *Daniel Deronda*, in reducing the relationship of hero and heroine to that of master and pupil. It corrects Barrett on this point. Mr Knightley is as ignorant as Emma about the state of his own feelings and, though many of his criticisms of her are just in themselves, he is often motivated by unconscious jealousy and envy of Frank Churchill. If Emma is unjust to Jane Fairfax, he is unjust to Churchill. If she is rude to Miss Bates when showing off with Frank, he is rude to her when roused by jealousy. In Volume II we read:

Mr. Knightley grew angry.
   'That fellow,' said he, indignantly, 'thinks of nothing but shewing off his own voice. This must not be.'
   And touching Miss Bates, who at that moment passed near – 'Miss Bates, are you mad, to let your niece sing herself hoarse in this manner? Go, and interfere. They have no mercy on her.' (p. 229)

Emma's fundamental soundness of mind and heart permit of a different relationship between them than that of master and pupil – a formula common to both burlesque novels, like *The Heroine*, and to many eighteenth- and nineteenth-century novels in which the romantic spirit overcomes the wish to show a heroine as a rational adult. When Mr Knightley says that he has blamed and lectured Emma, and that she has 'borne it as no other woman in England would have borne it', he is not simply indulging in a lover's exaggeration of his lady's virtues; there is some truth in his self-criticism.

If we miss, as much mid-twentieth-century criticism misses, the careful way in which Austen balances her heroine's faults and merits against those of the hero – his irritability and her snobbishness; his generosity and warm affections and her charitableness and loyalty to her governess – we are likely to make *Emma* a much less interesting novel than it really is and, of course, the extensive use of the interior monologue, through which the quality of Emma's mind is shown, even when her actions and judgements are mistaken, may appear divorced from the central purpose of the novel, instead of directly related to it.

In *The Heroine* Cherry Wilkinson thinks it would be splendidly romantic to be illegitimate, and persuades herself that she is, inventing an aristocratic father and giving herself the surname 'de Willoughby' instead of 'Wilkinson'. In *Emma* Harriet Smith really is illegitimate, and it is Emma who invents the aristocratic father, but Austen's handling of this is particularly careful. Emma's romanticising of bastardy in her protégée is given burlesque dismissal, but her sound moral judgement in refusing to accept that the child should be punished for the sins of the parents is not. Emma errs in her romanticisation of Miss Smith, but not in her objection to the general injustice done according to the laws and manners of the age towards 'natural children'. Her attitude here is not unlike Fielding's, and Austen, who shared with Wollstonecraft and Enlightenment feminist opinion the belief that 'unnatural distinctions in society' could not be morally justified, does not criticise her heroine's moral principles in this.

In Barrett, Cherry's behaviour towards the simple and sincere Mary, the rustic girl whom she abuses, is wholly wrong and irresponsible. In Austen, Emma's conduct towards Harriet is much more mixed. Mary is not illegitimate, Cherry only imagines she is. By making Harriet a genuine 'child of love', and showing the humiliations to which this exposes her at the hands of people like the Rev. Mr Elton and his wife, Austen de-romanticises illegitimacy and makes the attitudes of her characters towards it a sign of their ability, or inability, to judge in accordance with reason and nature. And here, as in much else, neither her hero nor her heroine sees absolutely clearly at first; though neither is capable of the vulgar cruelty of the parson and his wife. Cherry meddles in Mary's life in a malicious, tricksterish way. Deciding that William is not good enough for her, she invents a former lover of her own (also called William) and gets Mary to write, on her behalf, a letter of rejection to him. Then she sends it to the real William, thus bringing unhappiness upon the wholly innocent, though rather stupid, Mary. Austen transforms this, but keeps an allusion to it. Emma, convinced wrongly that Harriet is too good for Mr Martin, uses her powerful influence to persuade the rather stupid Harriet to act against her feelings and her interest and to write him a letter of rejection. When Emma and Mr Knightley discuss this action, a complex interplay of partly right and partly wrong attitudes is represented. Shocked and angered by Emma's telling him that Harriet has rejected John Martin, and that she knows this because she has seen Harriet's letter to him, he bursts out:

'You saw her answer! you wrote her answer too. Emma, this is your doing. You persuaded her to refuse him.' (p. 61)

In this he is right; Emma has indeed come close to Cherry at this point, but Austen now brings a new complexity to her treatment of this incident. Mr Knightley, in the heat of the moment, launches into an attack on Emma in which he points out John Martin's merits and Harriet's lack of them. Affected by anger, he goes too far, exclaiming: '"A degradation to illegitimacy and ignorance, to be married to a respectable, intelligent gentleman-farmer!"' (p. 62). Here he speaks with Barrett's voice, his unjust disparagement of Harriet matching Emma's high-faluting nonsense about her. Part of Emma's reply is just:

'As to the circumstances of her birth, though in a legal sense she may be called Nobody, it will not hold in common sense. She is not to pay for the offence of others, by being held below the level of those with whom she is brought up.' (p. 62)

Wrong in her estimation of Harriet and more wrong still in her estimation of John Martin, Emma is not wrong in the principle she puts here. We are reminded, or ought to be, of Mrs Weston's opinion that Emma has 'qualities which may be trusted . . . she will never lead any one really wrong . . . will make no lasting blunder' (p. 40).

As the novel develops, Emma is obliged to change her estimation of John Martin and of Harriet as a suitable wife for him, and Mr Knightley changes his mind about Harriet. Angered by the attitude of the Eltons to her, when Elton has snubbed both Harriet and Mrs Weston who proposed her as a partner, Knightley asks her to dance. Later he tells Emma:

'And I am changed also; for I am now very willing to grant you all Harriet's good qualities . . . I am convinced of her being an artless, amiable girl, with very good notions, very seriously good principles, and placing her happiness in the affections and utility of domestic life. Much of this, I have no doubt, she may thank you for.' (p. 474)

Earlier, he had thought that Harriet's illegitimacy, in itself, made her an unsuitable wife for Elton; now he thinks she would have been better than the one he has chosen. Towards the end of the novel, Emma, disabused of her fantasies about Harriet's aristocratic father, sees that she has not taken a realistic view of the disadvantages of illegitimacy. At the same time, she sees the hypocrisy inherent in the romantic association of bastardy with 'noble' blood. Ironically she reflects that 'the stain of illegitimacy, unbleached by nobility and wealth, would have been a stain indeed' (p. 482).

The heroine of *Emma* is like Cherry Wilkinson in her situation. Cherry, in her first letter, laments that she is doomed to endure the security of a home, and the dullness of an unimpeached reputation. For me, there is no hope whatever of being reduced to despair. Alas, I must waste my health, bloom and youth, in a series of uninterrupted prosperity.

Barrett shows that she should have rejoiced in her good fortune. Austen, placing her heroine in comparable circumstances against which she does not rebel, shows that there are real dangers in the situation of a highly intelligent and energetic young woman, wholly protected from the need to make her way in the world and with nothing much to do in life but pamper her silly father and meddle in the lives of those she thinks she is assisting. Whereas Cherry goes wrong because she leaves the protection of her father, Emma's misdeeds are the result of her staying at home in an environment which makes it difficult for her to grow up; her errors of judgement about social relationships in general are the direct outcome of the infantile role which she plays as perfect daughter. Endowed by Nature, as Knightley says, with understanding and taught principles by Miss Taylor (p. 462), she is a proper subject of burlesque only in her minor romantic fantasies.

Her genuine understanding and her warm feeling, as well as her nonsense, are illustrated in her visit to the poor cottage woman in Volume I. This incident has provoked hostile critical response because, it has been said, it does not reveal an adequate understanding of class relationships on Jane Austen's part.[3] I think this partly misses the point. It is intended to show that Emma is capable of a little exaggeration about the extent to which her awareness of poverty and distress actually induces a pious melancholy. In this she is mocked, but the incident also establishes her merits as a compassionate, uncensorious friend of the poor. It is derived, I think, from Barrett, and a comparison of it with a comparable incident in *The Heroine* will show what I mean. Cherry Wilkinson, rather down on her luck, is accosted by a small beggar girl. She follows her back to her grandmother's cottage, where the old woman, a cripple, is discovered suffering from the direst poverty, and with several orphaned grandchildren to feed. Cherry imposes herself upon them for the night, eats the last food in the house, and sleeps on the children's pallet, leaving them to nestle 'among some musty straw'. Writing to Biddy of the experience, she says:

Famine had set its meagre finger on their faces. I wished to pity them, but their whining, their dirtiness, and their vulgarity, disgusted me more than interested me. I nauseated the brats, and abhorred the haggard hostess. How it happens I know not, but the misery that looks alluring on paper is almost always repulsive in real life.[4]

Barrett uses the incident to expose Cherry's lack of any compassion for the poor, her romantic dream of 'asylum in some poor cottage' being quickly dissolved by her first acquaintance with the reality of poverty.

In *Emma*, Jane Austen's heroine visits a poor cottage woman, and there is an element of burlesque in the treatment of the incident. Coming away from the cottage, whose squalor is not glossed over, Emma feels sure that thoughts of the poverty she has seen will preoccupy her mind for a considerable period:

'These are sights, Harriet, to do one good. How trifling they make everything else appear! – I feel now as if I could think of nothing but these poor creatures all the rest of the day; and yet who can say how soon it may all vanish from my mind?' (p. 87)

Within a few minutes the two girls see Mr Elton approaching, and Emma acknowledges 'a very sudden trial of our stability in good thoughts'. So far Austen's heroine, like Barrett's, is mocked, though she herself does the mocking. In every other respect, she is as unlike the burlesque stereotype as possible, and also unlike the rather patronising heroines of didactic women authors like Maria Edgeworth, Hannah More or Elizabeth Hamilton. The narrator tells us that Emma is truly sympathetic and sensitive to the wretchedness of the poor, and also that she has the strong negative merit of not being either romantic or moralistic about them:

They were now approaching the cottage, and all idle topics were superseded. Emma was very compassionate; and the distress of the poor was as sure of relief from her personal attention and kindness, her counsel and her patience, as from her purse. She understood their ways, could allow for their ignorance and their temptations, had no romantic expectations of extraordinary virtue from those for whom education had done so little; entered into their troubles with ready sympathy, and always gave her assistance with as much intelligence as good will. (p. 86)

This much is told, but we are also shown her benevolence. Hanging about in order to further the chances of Mr Elton as Harriet's lover, she is overtaken by a little girl from the cottage who, at Emma's direction, is going to fetch broth from Hartfield. To Emma it comes quite naturally (though on this occasion there is little design with regard to Harriet) 'to walk by the side of this child and talk to her and question her' (p. 88). Even as her errors about Mr Elton are being mocked by the author, her kindness and friendliness towards the cottage child are also established.

Emma's comment to Harriet, when she realises that she will not spend all day thinking about the wretchedness of the cottage and its inhabitants, is this:

'Well (smiling), I hope it may be allowed that if compassion has produced exertion and relief to the sufferers, it has done all that is truly important. If we feel for the wretched, enough to do all we can for them, the rest is empty sympathy, only distressing to ourselves.' (p. 87)

A sentimental heroine would have brooded longer, a true burlesque heroine would not have shown compassion or made herself useful. Emma's refusal to cultivate sympathetic gloom when it can serve no useful purpose has offended some critics, used to expecting finer sentiments from pretty heroines, but Austen's purpose is to show that this heroine, once she gets over a few whims and nonsense about Harriet, will match Mr Knightley in active, intelligent, non-moralistic concern for those in need.

In his review of *Emma*, Scott says, 'The plot is extricated with great simplicity' then, having outlined the story, treating it all on much the same level, he continues, 'Such is the simple plan of a story which we puruse with great pleasure, if not deep interest.' To readers familiar with the modern critical literature this is likely to provoke a smile. Scott responded to *Emma* as though it were a straightforward, unproblematic imitation of English domestic life in the country, and he was too sure of its being a minor form of literature to probe beneath its naturalistic surface. His blindness was, perhaps, not surprising in one who had begun his literary career as the translator of Bürger's *Lenore* and *Der Wilde Jaeger* and who had no interest in Enlightenment feminism. As we look beneath the surface now we see that, for all its apparent simplicity, *Emma* is an extraordinarily complex work in which, mainly through allusion, much larger ideas than those usually associated with domestic comedy are articulated.

In the mid-twentieth century criticism has recognised and elucidated this rich complexity but without sufficient attention to the author's feminist point of view, or to its bearing on the allusive frame of reference through which it is expressed. *Emma*, as a novel of education, and as a novel about a heroine who, as Lionel Trilling says, 'has a moral life, as a man has a moral life', embodies the essential convictions of Enlightenment feminism, and a criticism of contemporary literature, in so far as it denied them. No wonder Jane Austen says wryly (though mistakenly) that no one but herself would like her heroine. As the novel unfolds, the education of hero and heroine, about themselves and one another as moral equals, is shown in a way which subverts the stereotype in which a heroine is educated by a Hero-Guardian. Emma, for all her faults, belongs with the Guardians of England as it ought to be – represented by Donwell Abbey, rather than Highbury – and Mr Knightley – no Abbot Samson or Egremont – is a hero who earns, or ought to earn, the respect of intelligent but far from perfect women, for he has the ability, seldom found in Great Men or Heroes, to treat them on the level. Austen's image of the Donwell estate as an ideal of England, ironically half-perceived by Emma (p. 360), shows that Austen, like Cobbett, responded to the turn of the century interest in the medieval as shedding light on what 'society' and 'culture' ought to mean but, unlike others then or later in the nineteenth century (with the partial exception of Morris), her ideal (founded on 'Nature', 'Reason' and 'warm affections') comprehended women as co-inheritors and improvers. Emma's moral development is largely one in which she learns, with the help of the hero, what her adult responsibilities are towards her own sex. As the drains and fences and vegetable crops are improved on the Donwell estate, and tenant farmers and honest servants given encouragement, so the education of daughters and the interests of poor spinsters are to be properly attended to – and will be where men and women, for all their imperfections, have such good heads and sound hearts as Mr and Mrs Knightley.

A Gradual Performance

According to Cassandra Austen's memorandum, *Emma* was begun on 21 January 1814 and finished on 8 August 1815. It was published early in 1816. There is, however, evidence that ideas which eventually came together in *Emma* were thought about and worked on at a much earlier stage. This novel was, perhaps, of longer gestation than any other, illustrating Henry Austen's remark that 'some of these novels had been the gradual performance of her previous life'.[5] Q. D. Leavis showed that material worked on in *The Watsons* was later recast and used in *Emma*, the relationship of a promising daughter with an invalid father being an important element in both.[6] The date at which *The Watsons* was written is disputed, but R. W. Chapman's belief that it must have been close to the watermark date of the paper used – 1803 – seems likely to be correct.[7] It thus belongs to the period when Jane Austen was in Bath, hoping to publish soon and susceptible to the influence of the Bath Theatre.

We know from her letters that she read the Bath newspapers, and there is a curious concentration of names used in *Emma* and some of the other novels in the 'Arrived Here' columns of the *Bath Journal* in the winter of 1801–2. Each week a list of the more notable arrivals was given: members of the Austen family, including Jane and Cassandra, were from time to time included as, of course, were well-known literary people. Between 9 November 1801 and 3 January 1802, the 'Arrived Here' list included some of Jane Austen's relations, Southey and his wife, and a number of names familiar to us from the novels. The list for 9 November 1801 included: Sir John and Lady Knightley, Dr Campbell and Mr Coles; 16 November: Mr and Mrs Southey, Mr and Mrs Perry and Mrs and Miss Dalrymple; 30 November: Colonel and Mrs Campbell, Mr and Mrs Leigh Perrott, Mr Ferrers and Mrs Austen; 21 December: Sir John and Lady Palmer and Dr and Mrs Grant; 3 January 1802: Miss Carterets and Mr Dalrymple. On 3 December, the *Bath Journal* carried an obituary of the actress, Mrs Crawford.

A search in later issues reveals no such clusters of Austen fictional names, and their presence here seems unlikely to be purely a matter of chance, though one cannot be sure. Perhaps, during her first full season in Bath, Jane Austen took a particular interest in who was there and some of these names stuck in her memory, or she may have used them at the time in 'scraps' which were later incorporated into the revision of early or the first writing of new work. I think this curiosity gives slight support to the belief that these years were important in the germination of novels to be published later, even if nothing substantial were written at this time. There is a further name to be noted, as of interest in the later novels; it is that of the heroine of Kotzebue's play, *Die Versöhnung*, translated into English as *The Birthday*, Emma Bertram. This play, which I believe provided the schema adapted and corrected in *Emma*, was performed at the Bath Theatre Royal on 21 May 1803 and it was probably then, close to the period when *The Watsons* was written, that Jane Austen became interested in Kotzebue's treatment of a daughter who could not marry because of her devotion to an invalid father, and the behaviour of brothers estranged about a garden. However, if she did see the 1803 performance, it was not the first time she had seen this play, for we know from her letters that she attended its first performance in Bath in 1799. Perhaps it stirred her imagination then. If my suggestion that *The Birthday* is as important to *Emma* as *Lovers' Vows* is to *Mansfield Park* is correct, we must suppose that the origins of this novel go back either to the period when *Northanger Abbey* was first written (1798–9) or to the period when it was revised for publication (1803).

One major element in the novel, the contrast between Emma and Jane Fairfax and their difficult relationship, certainly goes back to *The Watsons* and to Jane Austen's interest in contrasting pairs of heroines, the one representing Sense, the other Sensibility. I have argued that, after revising *Sense and Sensibility*, she became aware of the dangers of this dichotomy as likely to dehumanise both heroines and make it impossible for either to sustain the central role of discriminating moral consciousness. But she did not altogether abandon it. Instead, she sought in the revised *Pride and Prejudice*, *Mansfield Park* and *Emma* to modify it. In *Pride and Prejudice*, the central heroine is given both a good head and a warm heart; Jane Bennet, in whom heart is stronger than head, being pushed away from the centre, though without being censured. In *Mansfield Park*, Fanny's incongruously strong head, surmounting an all too vulnerable heart, is treated ironically, with Mary Crawford's head and heart being shown as culpably corrupt. In *Emma*, Jane Austen's command of narrative technique enables her to distance Jane Fairfax from the reader's attention and sympathy without the need either to censure or mock her, but leaving Emma, with her good but faulty head and heart, at the centre of the fiction and its moral concerns.

Further, this distancing of Jane allows the author to censure the man who, taking advantage of her vulnerability, makes her 'an object of pity, bordering on contempt', rather than Miss Fairfax herself. Emma's unconscious complicity in this is condemned, but it is made clear that both young women are shamelessly used by Frank Churchill in a speculative love-game where their blunders are innocent compared with his deliberate exploitation of power over them. Eventually, Emma and Jane come to understand and respect one another, each acknowledging errors of conduct and attitude. The major distinction is transferred to the hero and anti-hero – Mr Knightley's open, equal relationships with women being contrasted with the gallantry and trickery of 'Frank' Churchill. As in earlier novels, the use of the word 'angel' of a young woman pinpoints right or mistaken attitudes in men. In Volume I, at the end of a losing argument with Mrs Weston about Emma's relationship with Harriet Smith, Mr Knightley gives in with good and ironic grace: '"Very well; I will not plague you any more. Emma shall be an angel, and I will keep my spleen to myself"' (p. 40). In Volume III, after his engagement to Jane Fairfax is announced, Frank Churchill, having made his peace with Emma, reveals the shallowness of his regard for his future wife:

'She is a complete angel. Look at her. Is not she an angel in every gesture? Observe the turn of her throat. Observe her eyes as she is looking up at my father. – You will be glad to hear' (inclining his head, and whispering seriously) 'that my uncle means to give her all my aunt's jewels. They are to be new set. I am resolved to have some ornament for the head. Will not it be beautiful in her dark hair?'

'Very beautiful, indeed,' replied Emma: and she spoke so kindly that he gratefully burst out,

'How delighted I am to see you again! and to see you in such excellent looks!' (p. 479)

Not only does he commit the unpardonable mistake of calling Jane an angel, but he makes clear that he values her as a beautiful object. The ornament is to be for 'the' not 'her' head, and its decoration is the subject of 'serious' whispering. When Emma makes a kind, though reserved, reply, he at once compliments her on her appearance.

Critics eager to see Jane Austen's moral purposes expressed in her treatment of women in relation to men have not, perhaps, paid enough attention to chapters 12 and 16 of Volume III, where the most sensitive and sensible women in the novel examine what has passed, and make judgements about it. In Chapter 12, it is Mrs Weston who censures Jane – 'One natural consequence of the evil she had involved herself in . . . was that of being *unreasonable*' (p. 419, Austen's italics), Emma who excuses her. In Chapter 16, the warmth with which Emma and Jane forgive each other and blame only themselves contains an important part of the meaning of this novel, in which the moral status and capacities of women play so important a part. Mr Wildman's wish to think well of all young ladies would, no doubt, have prevented him from taking these chapters very seriously, but enlightened, asexist critics outght not to follow him.

It was Q. D. Leavis who first showed how Emma Watson, the heroine of *The Watsons*, had been split in two in the making of *Emma*, her role as a devoted daughter of an invalid father going to Miss Woodhouse, her vulnerable position, as a well-educated but penniless girl, threatened with the horrors of governessing and obliged to endure the patronage of a vulgar, overbearing young matron, going to Miss Fairfax. Their eventual *rapprochement* is an important aspect of the total meaning of *Emma*, as it deals with rich and poor young women of the middle class, and with the profession of the governess, who in *Emma* is a woman of education, sense and sensibility, deprived except as her rich, female pupils accord it her, of the status of Guardian. Emma's chief claim to heroism is that, whatever her faults, she does always give 'poor Miss Taylor' this status and comes to respect poor Miss Fairfax too, once all is made plain, 'decided and open'.

19 *Persuasion* and *Sanditon*

Jane Austen wrote 'finis' after the revised last chapters of *Persuasion* in July 1816. Her sister recorded that it was completed in August, but *Persuasion* is not a finished novel in the same sense as *Mansfield Park* and *Emma*, for there was not time for the 'gradual performance' to be fully achieved. As it stands, the novel includes some of Jane Austen's most accomplished writing but there is also a good deal which calls for further revision. I think that the final adjustment and correction of some characters, notably Lady Russell and Mrs Musgrove, could not be made until a proper allusive-ironic focus for the novel had been found, for this is what *Persuasion* lacks, and what accounts for its uneven tone and truncated length. No further work was done on *Persuasion* after August 1816, but Austen took no steps to secure its publication as she had done as soon as *Mansfield Park* and *Emma* were finished. Instead, she left it on one side and, in the few remaining months in which she was well enough to write, she began sketching out in *Sanditon* an apparently quite unrelated burlesque, highly contemporary in its social setting, but going back to Richardsonian grass-roots in its satire. It is almost as though, in the absence of such a stimulus as *The Heroine* provided to the final form of *Emma*, Jane Austen set about writing her own burlesque before finishing *Persuasion*. Whether *Sanditon* would have been used only as a 'scrap' to fertilise the author's comic imagination, or whether it would have become the germ of a new novel it is impossible to tell, but it is clear that her interest in feminist questions had not fallen off, and that she still felt the need of ironic literary allusion to enable her to deal with them adequately in a finished work of art. If we consider the two works together, we can see that Austen was extending the range of female character and experience with which she could deal, bringing it more fully into the second decade of the nineteenth century and, at the same time, giving further consideration to the whole tradition of sentimental fiction, starting with Richardson, in its anti-feminist aspect.

Both works are anti-Grandisonian in that they portray baronets incapable of securing for their womenfolk a proper place in society; in both women are shown as real and imaginary invalids; in both the role of women as nurses, or ministers to sickness, are considered. In *Persuasion* there is some satire on the self-indulgence of the rich at a fashionable, if by now declining, spa. In *Sanditon* the avarice and pretentiousness of a minor seaside resort, aping the Prince Regent's Brighton, is satirised. In both strictures are made, or implied, on the most fashionable Romantic authors, Lord Byron and Scott. In both, the burlesque stereotype of a young woman deluded by romantic reading and corrected by a hero of sense is reversed. Anne Elliot advises the self-dramatising Captain Benwick to read less poetry, Charlotte Heywood begins to think Sir Edward Denham deranged when she hears the way he talks about Wordsworth, James Montgomery, Burns and Scott.

Persuasion starts in the reversal of the schema used in *First Impressions*, and already greatly modified in *Pride and Prejudice*. This reversal gives the heroine a more authoritative moral position from the outset of the novel, for Anne's judgement, even as a young girl, was sound. Further, the roles played by Mr and Mrs Bennet in entering upon marriage are also reversed in Sir Walter and Lady Elliott. Mr Bennet had married a foolish wife, ensnared by what appeared to be her 'softness, and sweet attractive grace', living to find pleasure in very little about her, except making jokes at her expense. In *Persuasion*, Lady Elliot, 'an excellent woman, sensible and amiable', made a comparable mistake. Her 'judgement and conduct' were admirable, apart from 'the youthful infatuation which made her Lady Elliot'. Too sensitive to find pleasure in laughing at her husband, she had spent seventeen years hiding, or attempting to prevent, the effects of his foolishness and had died early, knowing that she must leave her three daughters to 'the authority and guidance of a conceited, silly father'. The first chapters of *Persuasion* expose relentlessly the unfittedness of Sir Walter Elliot to govern himself, and therefore to govern anyone else. What Mary Wollstonecraft had said about fashionable women as incapable of the one task allotted to them, the management of children, is here applied to a vain baronet, who cares more about his mirrors than his estate or his daughters. Anne's likeness to her mother, both in appearance and in character, is made clear through Lady Russell, the friend of the late Lady Elliot and the substitute mother to her daughter.

In *Persuasion* too Jane Austen comes close to completely reversing the role of the heroine as pupil–improver and of the hero as guardian–guide. At the end of the novel Anne still considers that her conduct at nineteen was right, though the advice given was wrong. It is Wentworth who is called on to accept the lion's share of the blame:

'I did not understand you. I shut my eyes, and would not do you justice. This is a recollection which ought to make me forgive every one sooner than myself. Six years of separation and suffering might have been spared. It is a sort of pain, too, which is new to me. I have been used to the gratification of believing myself to earn every blessing that I enjoyed. I have valued myself on honourable toils and just rewards.' (p. 247)

As he admits that his notion of 'honourable toils and just rewards' has been a little superficial, that he has not quite seen how Anne, in her much more restricted life, has also attempted to deserve happiness, Jane Austen reaches a new point in her treatment of men and women as moral equals, no matter how different their lives and their opportunity of independent action. The passage ends with a delightfully humane and comic note, Captain Wentworth, for all his masculine achievement in his naval career admitting that, when it comes to understanding and assessing women, he has not quite played the hero's part, and must thank Providence, or his author, for his present happiness:

'Like other great men under reverses,' he added with a smile, 'I must endeavour to subdue my mind to my fortune. I must brook being happier than I deserve.' (p. 247)

Here Austen shows both her reliance on Butlerian ethics, with their foundation in the 'rewards and punishments' notion of the natural moral order, and her warm, comic sense of how seldom the system actually operates justly when it comes to the examples which pass under our own observation. For all her rationality about morals, Austen brings into her comedy a strong sense that chance, luck or maybe grace, are factors which even the most rational of beings depend upon and must be grateful for, when exercised in their favour. There is, in the last part of chapter 11, Volume II, a strong sense of joy and gratitude which goes beyond deserts and rewards.

Anne, at the end of this chapter, experiences something of the elation felt by Portia on seeing Bassanio reject 'thou gaudy gold,/ Hard food for Midas' in favour of the leaden casket, and this mood is led up to from the moment when it crosses Charles Musgrove's mind that he could still get to the gunsmith's if he could hand his sister-in-law over to Wentworth. '"Are you going as high as Belmont?" he asks, "Are you going near Camden-place?"' Thus begins the walk up the Lansdown slope, with 'smiles reined in and spirits dancing in private rapture'. Portia, seeing her hopes about to be fulfilled, says:

> O love, be moderate; allay thy ecstasy;
> In measure rain thy joy; scant this excess!
> I feel too much thy blessing: make it less,
> For fear I surfeit! (III (ii), 111–14)

Jane Austen shows Anne in a similar, though lower-keyed, state of mind. The 'indirect free style' is used to convey that same joy, moderated by reflection and gratitude, which Portia had expressed:

she re-entered the house so happy as to be obliged to find an alloy in some momentary apprehensions of its being impossible to last. An interval of meditation, serious and grateful, was the best corrective of every thing dangerous in such high-wrought felicity; and she went to her room, and grew steadfast and fearless in the thankfulness of her enjoyment. (p. 245)

Jane Austen's language here suggests at least a half-consciousness of the casket scene in *The Merchant of Venice*, and she intends to show that she is far from unable to comprehend and value such 'high-wrought felicity' as her heroine now experiences, in a love returned and to be enjoyed, but she does not forget to insist that Anne, through the operation of her own powers of mind, improves at this very point in steadfastness and fearlessness.

Jane Austen spoke of the heroine of *Persuasion* as almost too good for her, and she makes her so gentle and sympathetic a character that it would be hard, even for a bigot, to see anything of the 'unsexed female' in her. Yet Anne, in her conversation with Captain Harville on the subject of constancy, puts a feminist point of view, making use of a point to be found in *Vindication* when she says: 'Man is more robust than woman, but he is not longer-lived' (p. 236). Her phrasing is not like Wollstonecraft's: 'Men cannot, however, claim any natural superiority from the grandeur of longevity; for in this respect nature has not distinguished the male.' But her argument is the same. She goes on to make a direct attack on male bias in literature:

'Yes, yes, if you please, no reference to examples in books. Men have had every advantage of us in telling their own story. Education has been theirs in so much higher a degree; the pen has been in their hands. I will not allow books to prove anything.' (p. 234)

No other Austen heroine is shown as putting a feminist viewpoint so plainly, and she does it not within the confines of a family, to a brother or sister, but conversing as a friendly equal with one of Wentworth's brother-officers. Anne is allowed to act as adviser to the romantic Captain Benwick on his reading, recommending him to read less of Scott and Byron, more of 'our best moralists', and such biographies as 'rouse and fortify the mind by the highest precepts'. Having done so, she indulges in a little ironic self-mockery, comparable with Wentworth's thoughts about 'other great men':

nor could she help fearing, on more serious reflection, that like other great moralists and preachers she had been eloquent on a point in which her own conduct would ill bear examination. (p. 101)

Thus Austen guards Anne against self-complacency, while making it clear that she endorses her point of view. At the end of the novel, Anne argues the case for the defence of her former actions, carefully distinguishing between the wrongness of Lady Russell's advice, and her own obligation, at nineteen, to accept it. She makes no mention of any obligation to accept her father's direction, for his character and conduct have not given him the claims of an affectionate parent.

Anne's gentleness of manner, together with her maturity, disarm criticism of her strength of character and her confidence in her own judgement, and I think they were designed to do so, for one of the central themes of the novel is the duty owed by children to their parents in the choice of a marriage partner, a question taken seriously by feminists, and about which Austen makes some fine distinctions. In Chapter II of *Vindication* ('Duty to Parents'), Wollstonecraft attacks parental tyranny, but insists that, where a parent has endeavoured to 'form the heart and enlarge the understanding' of a child, he (or she, presumably) 'acquires all the rights of the most sacred friendship, and his advice, even when the child is advanced in life, demands serious consideration'. She goes so far as to lay it down for *sons* that:

With respect to marriage, though after one-and-twenty a parent seems to have no right to withold his consent on any account, yet twenty years of solicitude call for a return, and the son ought not to marry for two or three years, should the object of his choice not entirely meet with the approbation of his first friend. (*Vindication*, p. 268)

In *Persuasion*, the heroine's father is a completely worthless character, but Lady Russell, her quasi-mother, is Anne's 'first friend' and her acceptance of Lady Russell's advice, when she was an inexperienced girl of nineteen, is intended to show both her rationally authenticated prudence and her sense of affectionate obligation. At the end of the novel, though she says that she would never give such advice herself, Anne defends her former acceptance of it as a matter of 'duty'. It is implied that, once past twenty-one and having allowed two years to elapse, she would no longer have felt obliged to accept Lady Russell's guidance. Thus Austen establishes her heroine's behaviour as in accordance with what Wollstonecraft had laid down as proper in a dutiful child of a 'solicitous' and affectionate, even though mistaken, parent.

To a modern reader it must seem so tame and moderate a view as to bear no tinge of reformist feminism, but one contemporary review of *Persuasion* shows how far from the truth this was in 1818. An unsigned review of *Northanger Abbey* and *Persuasion*, which appeared in the *British Critic* in March 1818, praises *Northanger Abbey* as an amusing, conventional burlesque, but has this to say of *Persuasion*:

With respect to the second of the novels, which the present publication contains, it will be necessary to say but little. It is in every respect a much less fortunate performance than that which we have been considering. It is manifestly the work of the same mind, and contains parts of very great merit; among them, however, we certainly should not number its *moral*, which appears to be that young people should always marry according to their own inclinations and upon their own judgement; for that if in consequence of listening to grave counsels, they defer their marriage, till they have wherewithal to live upon, they will be laying the foundation of years of misery, such as only the heroes and heroines of novels can reasonably hope ever to see and end of.[1]

By dismissing Sir Walter Elliot's claims to filial respect, and transferring them to Lady Russell, Jane Austen both emphasises that such claims rest on a gratitude associated with affection and not on parental rights *per se*, and makes the mother (though in this case no more than a surrogate) superior in her claim to the natural father, whose conduct is unnatural. Sir Walter Elliot is treated more harshly than any other Austen patriarch. In *Pride and Prejudice* the sympathetic character of Mr Bennet, and his warm affection for his second daughter, had made the morally independent role of Elizabeth all too easy. Having mocked Sir Thomas Bertram in *Mansfield Park* and reduced Mr Woodhouse in *Emma* to a condition not unlike that of Lady Bertram, Austen created in Sir Walter Elliot a *pater familias* whose character closely resembles that of the smart society woman of uncertain age, much despised in eighteenth- and nineteenth-century literature:

Vanity was the beginning and the end of Sir Walter Elliot's character; vanity of person and of situation. He had been remarkably handsome in his youth; and at fifty-four was still a handsome man. Few women could think more of their personal appearance than he did; nor could the valet of any new-made lord be more delighted with the place he held in society. He considered the blessing of beauty as inferior only to the blessing of a baronetcy; and Sir Walter Elliot, who united these gifts, was the object of his warmest respect and devotion. (p. 4)

Such is the man upon whom the laws and customs of England confer the control and protection of wives and daughters. Through this baronet, even more clearly than through Sir Thomas Bertram, Jane Austen shows that Richardson's solution of 'the woman question' in *Sir Charles Grandison* will not do. 'Good Men' being in such short supply, especially among the baronetcy, women do well to achieve respectability of themselves.

In *Persuasion*, although Anne is denied the support or concern of her two sisters, other female bonds are shown as strong and important. Apart from Lady Russell, her relationships with Mrs Smith and Mrs Croft are treated seriously, and they are perhaps more important because they illustrate an extended 'sisterhood', not based on 'blood' but on extra-familial ties between women. Anne is the only Austen heroine who has been sent away to school, and her relationship with a former school-friend, now fallen on hard times, represents an enlargement of Austen's treatment of female obligation and friendship. It is through her refusal to give up this friendship, in which she is supported by Lady Russell, and despite her father's disapproval, that Anne learns something of the character of Nurse Rooke, a woman of lower social status than any other female character treated sympathetically in the Austen novels. We do not see her at first-hand but through the eyes of Mrs Smith, who speaks of her as 'a shrewd, intelligent, sensible woman', superior in 'good sense and observation' to many who have received an expensive education. Mrs Smith later speaks of her as 'my friend, Nurse Rooke' (p. 197) and, in doing so, breaks down the barriers common between a woman of her gentility and an 'uneducated nurse'. Anne, the baronet's daughter, whose father thinks it disgraceful that she should visit Mrs Smith despite having been at school with her, says:

Women of that class have great opportunities, and if they are intelligent may be well worth listening to. Such varieties of human nature as they are in the habit of witnessing! . . . And it is not merely in its follies that they are well read. (p. 156)

Here the preference for an education which will teach women to think takes a new turn, for it leads two sensible women of higher social status to give a new value to the lowly, but intelligent and informed, Nurse Rooke. It is worth comparing with Wollstonecraft's treatment of Jemima in *Mary*, for, though more realistic and more tentative, it fulfils a similar function, showing the common interests of intelligent women, whatever their social status. Nurse Rooke also provides an antidote to the sentimental ideal of woman as 'ministering angel'.

It is clear that, in her conception of the character of the heroine of *Persuasion*, Jane Austen went further than in any previous novel to ensure that she should be seen unmistakably as the central moral intelligence of the novel. Anne's finely discriminating sensibility and warmth of heart is matched with a sound head; the reader is to understand that, in general, her view of things is better to be relied on that that of any other character. By making her father so plainly worthless and denying to the hero any semblance of a guardian-guide's role, Austen ensures that Anne's moral independence is both dearly bought and wholly necessary. In this novel, too, a development already plain in *Emma* is continued: the heroine's status as 'a moral being' is revealed and defined as much through her relationships outside the family as within it, and especially through her relationships with other women. In both novels the influence of father and sisters is harmful, in Emma's case encouraging pride and self-importance, in Anne's amounting to a destructive and insidious denial that she has any value as an individual at all. In both novels the heroine grows, or demonstrates her maturity, through the development of relationships with women outside her family. Despite her gentleness and tact, Anne puts loyalty to a former school-friend above respect for her father's wishes; she admires the 'unfeminine' Mrs Croft, and defends the respect she feels for Lady Russell, even though she is not uncritical of her. Anne's relationships with other women cannot be seen as belonging to a wayward phase of girlhood, to be set aside once she has a husband to direct her. Captain Wentworth takes her view of Mrs Smith not Sir Walter's, and, having heard Anne's defence of Lady Russell, whom he has regarded as an enemy, he allows that he may forgive even her in time: 'I trust to being in charity with her soon.'

In all these ways Jane Austen may be seen as doing rather more than 'adjusting and correcting' the burlesque schema in which a romantic heroine learns sense and comes to adopt the viewpoint of her pastors and masters, for she effectively reverses it completely. Her emphasis upon Anne's female friends, however, posed difficult problems, especially in the case of Lady Russell whose role and character are particularly important in defining a daughter's filial obligation. She must be seen to have been mistaken in her advice, and yet to have so many claims to the heroine's affection and respect as to make her having accepted it justifiable. Such a character, a woman past fifty who is neither exemplary, ridiculous nor vicious, presented great problems for there were virtually no models to assist in her creation. She had to be developed out of the stock figure of a worldly society woman, like Lady Freelove in *The Jealous Wife*, and Mrs Stanhope and Lady Delacour in *Belinda*, and at times she appears too close to them. For example, when she is absorbed in looking out for some 'drawing-room window-curtains' in Pulteney Street, which her friends, 'Lady Alicia and Mrs Frankland' had admired the night before (p. 279). Further refinement of Lady Russell's character was needed so that she might appear more credibly as both 'generally speaking, rational and consistent', despite her 'prejudices on the side of ancestry' (p. 11), and warm-hearted. As it is, she is not quite convincing. We see that she is fond of Anne, and that her carriage, to Sir Walter Elliot's disgust, conveys her to the lowly Westgate Buildings to visit Mrs Smith, yet her dislike of Uppercross in the school holidays, her love of Bath, and her failure to see through Mr William Elliot, the heir to Kellynch, are felt a little too forcibly. In the end, we are not quite so sure as we ought to be that Anne's regard for her was wholly justified.

In the revisions made to chapter X of Volume II we can see Austen at work in adjusting and correcting her drawing of Admiral Croft. He, like Lady Russell, originates in a stock character of stage and fiction. He has many of the characteristics of 'the benevolent tar' who, as C. V. Clinton-Baddeley shows, became after 1800 the 'tar without reproach'.[2] The Admiral's good heart and salty language belong to the stereotype but, since he must also be seen as Mrs Croft's respected partner in life, he must not be shown as exhibiting too much of the bluff insensitivity which also belongs to the stereotype. In the cancelled chapter of *Persuasion* he does; in the revised version this is avoided, as B. .C. Southam demonstrates.[3] Similar revision was needed to make Lady Russell more appropriate to the complexities of the role she has to play.

Revision was also required in the handling of Mrs Musgrove, especially with regard to her ne'er-do-well son, Dick. Many critics have found her 'large fat sighings' over 'poor Richard', 'whom alive nobody had cared for' (p. 68), unfeeling and incongruous, the intrusion of the narrator clumsy, and the tone uncertain. The difficulty here is again one of incomplete adjustment and correction of a schema, for Mrs Musgrove originates in a farcical fat lady, such as Cherry Wilkinson encounters in a stage coach in *The Heroine*. In such a character insincerity and self-delusion do not come amiss. But, for the greater part of the novel, we see a much more finely differentiated Mrs Musgrove – a kindly, good-hearted and perfectly sincere example of commonplace motherliness – much to be preferred to the cold-hearted pretentiousness of Sir Walter Elliot and two of his daughters, though inferior to the greater discernment of Anne, Wentworth and Mrs Croft. The differentiated Mrs Musgrove would have felt genuine affection for her son, however hopeless, and is not therefore a proper target for quite such crude burlsque as attaches to her whenever 'poor Richard' is mentioned. It all seems to have had something to do with Jane Austen's finding the name 'Richard' irresistibly comic, but I think it would have been changed had *Persuasion* been 'finished' for publication by its author.

In Mrs Croft, who is destined to become the true sister that Anne has lacked, we may also see the adjustment and correction of a crude stereotype, but here it is more than adequately achieved. Mrs Croft corrects the caricature of the 'unsexed female', the woman who does not fit the sentimental ideal of femininity created by Richard Polwhele and the anti-feminists at the end of the eighteenth century, and drawn on by Maria Edgeworth in *Belinda*, where Mrs Freke, the mannish advocate of female rights, is made ridiculous and contrasted unfavourably with Lady Anne Percival. Mrs Croft, with her 'excellent health', her 'reddened weather-beaten complexion', her 'keen, intelligent looks' and her ability to take the reins of their gig, whenever 'my dear Admiral' is in danger of hitting a post or 'running foul' of a dung-cart, is not a feminine woman as Rousseau had defined femininity, and her energy and intelligence make nonsense of the limitations of the role to which women had been confined in *Emile*. She is the exact opposite of Sir Walter Elliot, whose house she and her husband occupy after he has made himself all but bankrupt. But Mrs Croft, unlike Mrs Freke, is no man-bater, though she hates to hear her brother talk of women as though they were 'fine ladies' rather than 'rational creatures'. She is the constant and affectionate companion of a husband who feels deprived when he has to do without her company. Nina Auerbach sees Mrs Croft as a new kind of woman in the Austen novels,[4] and this is so, but she is not drawn only from the life. It is no accident, but a nice bit of irony, that gives her the Christian name 'Sophy', for she is designed to represent a more robust, feminist ideal of womanhood than Rousseau's 'Sophie'. Past thirty, with a complexion that speaks of her active participation in life, and a blister 'the size of a three-shilling piece', acquired through tramping round Bath all day with the Admiral, she is nevertheless represented as a woman to be admired and, moreover, one much loved.

In *Persuasion*, Jane Austen enlarged the scope of her fiction by creating a heroine who is strictly too old and too wise to play the part in what is still conceived as a comedy. That she left *Persuasion* aside in a state which she evidently did not regard as ripe for publication, and went on to write *Sanditon*, shows that she still believed comedy to be her proper genre and suggests that, had she lived longer, she might have found the right allusive-ironic frame within which Anne Elliot could appear, without endangering the comic form of the novel quite so markedly. At all events, *Sanditon* shows a continued interest in some of the same themes as appear in *Persuasion*, though the tone is much more like that of the 'poor Dick' passages than the elevated tone of the penultimate chapter, or the melancholy tone of some of the earlier parts of the novel.

In *Sanditon*, through Sir Edward Denham, Jane Austen makes her most outright attack on Richardson, creating a burlesque hero who models himself on Lovelace. Instead of the giddy heroine of Beckford or Barrett we have a light-brained baronet, unhinged by romantic reading. Charlotte Heywood, 'sober-minded as she was', discovers the disordered state of his mind and syntax as he raves about Wordsworth, James Montgomery, Burns and Scott. By the time she had heard him out, 'she began to think him downright silly'. Charlotte censures Burns for his faithless treatment of women which interferes with her enjoyment of his poems, but Scott is the chief target of Austen's irony. Sir Edward appears unable to remember anything much about Scott's poems except a passage from *The Lady of the Lake* in which parental affection is treated as having a supernatural or divine aura, and another from *Marmion* in which Woman is praised. According to Sir Edward, Scott's 'Soul was the Altar in which lovely Woman sat enshrined, his Spirit truly breathed the immortal Innocence which is her Due' (p. 297). Here Austen parodies the dubious language Scott had used in the last paragraph of his review of *Emma*, and makes her anti-hero quote the first line of the following extract from *Marmion:*

> O Woman! in our hours of ease,
> Uncertain, coy, and hard to please,
> And variable as the shade
> By the light quivering aspen made;
> When pain and anguish wring the brow,
> A ministering angel thou! (canto VI, part XXX)

– lines which pointedly reveal Scott as a Rousseauist, and which we may be sure Austen thought open to objection.

In chapter 8 of *Sanditon*, Sir Edward's admiration of *Pamela* and *Clarissa* is used to mock him and to criticise Richardson:

> His fancy had been early caught by all the impassioned, & most exception-able parts of Richardson's; & such Authors as have since appeared to tread in Richardson's footsteps, so far as Man's determined pursuit of Woman in defiance of every opposition of feeling and convenience is concerned . . . With a perversity of Judgement, which must be attributed to his not having by Nature a very strong head, the Graces, the Spirit, the Sagacity, & the Perseverance, of the Villain of the Story outweighed all his absurdities & all his Atrocities with Sir Edward. With him, such Conduct was Genius, Fire & Feeling. – It interested him & inflamed him; and he was always more anxious for its Success & mourned over its Discomfitures with more Tenderness than co. ever have been contemplated by the Authors. (p. 404)

I take it that the last sentence, about authorial intention, is ironic, and that irony is also present in the subsequent passage in which Sir Edward's education is said to have been completed by his reading of modern authors. Through her treatment of him, Austen casts doubt on the moral principles, as well as the style, of 'our most approved Authors' – presumably including those criticised in the Northanger Defence of the novel:

> Though he owed many of his ideas to this sort of reading, it were unjust to say that he read nothing else, or that his Language were not formed on a more general Knowledge of modern Literature. – He read all the Essays, Letters, Tours & Criticisms of the day – & with the same ill-luck which made him derive only false Principles from Lessons of Morality, & incen-tives to Vice from the History of its Overthrow, he fathered only hard words & involved sentences from the style of our most approved Writers. (pp. 404–5)

At the end of the chapter Sir Edward's longing to ape Lovelace is treated in a strongly satirical way; his lack of money, plus perhaps a little meanness, is used to deflate his villainous-heroic ambition:

> He knew his Business. – Already he had had many Musings on the Subject. . . . If he were to strike out something new, to exceed those who had gone before him – and he felt a strange curiosity to ascertain whether the Neighbourhood of Tombuctoo might not afford some solitary House adapted for Clara's reception; – but the Expence alas! of Measures in that masterly style was ill-suited to his Purse, & Prudence obliged him to prefer the quietest sort of ruin & disgrace for the object of his Affections, to the more renowned. (pp. 405–6)

Angus Wilson, missing the feminist point of Jane Austen's satire of Richardson, supposes that she shut her eyes to the dangers 'middle-class girls', as well as 'shopkeepers' daughters, landladies' daughters, farmers' daughters' stood in, 'from the arrogant sexual designs of their aristocratic social superiors in Regency times, let alone in the days of *Evelina* or, more still, of *Clarissa*'. He continues: 'It was hardly necessary in 1860, let alone 1810, to go to Tombuctoo to find brothers, complaisent Sinclairs, and the possibilities of sexual violence'.[5] There is no need to suppose that Jane Austen did not know this. Her satire does not imply that she was unaware of the reality of wickedness and vice, but it does show that she was contemptuous of the belief that glamourised accounts of it did anything to improve morals, especially in the male sex. By making Sir Edward Denham a ridiculous Lovelace she mocks the treatment of sexual violence and degradation in sentimental literature. By making her heroine of sense, Charlotte Heywood, see through this so easily she makes the valid point that women are likely to be protected from such seducers as this, if capable of critical laughter. My guess is that Clara Brereton would have turned out to be a little sly, as well as having the proper air of a heroine of sensibility, and that she might well have displayed the cunning Rousseau thought proper to her sex, to Sir Edward's disadvantage. Jane Austen mocks what was truly absurd in Richardson's general characterisation of Man as Hunter, Woman as Prey, and perhaps, even more, those clerics and critics who took it more seriously than it deserved, using a fantasy with no more than a partial truth about it to encourage girls to behave like quarry when, with the exercise of a little wit and a good deal of common sense, they might avoid such obvious traps – without being driven to become trappers themselves either. This would seem to be a valid point of view, more especially in an author who always makes it clear that she writes under the inspiration of the comic muse.

Sanditon itself is mock-Brighton and, whereas Brighton was clearly associated with Regency wickedness, especially when there was a military camp nearby as in *Pride and Prejudice*, Sanditon is inhabited by lesser villains and a considerable number of fools. Here in a pretentious seaside resort Mr Parker, Mrs Griffiths, Lady Denham and Sir Edward attempt to cash in on the imaginary invalids and doubtful heiresses who can't afford Brighton prices. It is shown as a hot-bed of petty and probably ill-fated commercial/sexual intrigue, where the 'capture' of the supposedly rich 'Miss Lambe', with her putative need of 'goats milk' is to further the social ambitions of the Parker family, fill the pockets of the local trades people, and increase the value of Lady Denham's property.

How it might all have worked out, how *Charlotte* Heywood and *Clara* Denham were to figure, had the fragment been continued, must remain uncertain, though the first names of these two tell us that a heroine of Sense and a heroine of Sensibility, related to German literature at the end of the eighteenth century, were under consideration. Perhaps 'Charlotte', whose name was already well Anglicised as an appropriate name for a heroine of sense, was to become the central intelligence, with *Clara*, unprotected by a solid English Christian name, such as 'Jane' Fairfax's, reduced to unequivocal hypocrisy. Perhaps not. Most likely the fragment would have been abandoned as incapable of further development, for it is no more than an exercise towards what might have been created had not Jane Austen died in the summer of 1817. As it is, the critic who tries to understand Austen's thought and art is left with some pretty clear indications about how *Sanditon* connects with and continues the moral preoccupation of extant published work.

It is fairly clear that, in the creation of poor young Mr Arthur Parker, Austen continues the reversal of male/female stereotypes. Arthur Parker, at one-and-twenty, with nothing apparently wrong with him except what exercise, occupation and absence from his foolish sisters would cure, has adopted a role and style of life which parodies that of Mary Musgrove and other female hypochondriacs whose real disease is indolence and lack of purpose in life. Austen, I think, uses him to show that the characteristic female disease of hypochondria is not a gender-determined malaise, but a common human attribute of laziness and pampering. Poor Arthur is less important than his more dominant older sister, Diana, who is clearly conceived as a figure of satire. Miss Diana Parker has 'a spirit of activity' which rivals that of Aunt Norris, and she is equally lacking in rational, self-critical powers of mind. Herself the prey of imaginary illnesses, she believes that she is strong-minded, and in this she prefigures a long line of Victorian women, both historical and fictional, who cast themselves in the role of 'ministering-angelscum-social-workers'. Diana Parker, like so many 'strong-minded' women of the later nineteenth century, brings the idea of the rational female mind into disrepute by equating 'strong mindedness' with insensitive interference in other people's lives, rather than with any ability to think. Given to such aphoristic utterances as

'But, my dear Miss Heywood, we are sent into this World to be as extensively useful as possible, & where some degree of Strength of Mind is given, it is not a feeble body which will excuse us – or incline us to excuse ourselves. The World is pretty much divided between the Weak of Mind &

the Strong – between those who can act & those who cannot, & it is the bounden Duty of the Capable to let no opportunity of being useful escape them.' (p. 410)

she is an uncanny forerunner of W. H. Auden's Social Worker, whose aphorism runs: 'We are here to help others. What the others are here for, I do not know.' Miss Diana Parker, despite all the contrary evidence, believes herself to be an invalid and, when she is not annoying other people by inflicting her dubious medicines and remedies upon them, takes to her bed-chamber for a satisfying bout of self-doctoring. Unfinished and undeveloped though this sketch is, it shows us how quickly and critically Austen responded to the changing times. Women like Miss Parker were, throughout the nineteenth-century and beyond, to latch on to a simplistic notion of female 'usefulness', in which 'mind' in the sense that Wollstonecraft and Austen valued it played no part. This caricature, contrasted with the apparently more delicate Anne Elliot's superior powers of reasoning, as well as her intelligent interpretation of 'duty' and 'usefulness', suggests how well Jane Austen was equipped to withstand the Victorian form of Rousseauist restriction of women into apparently enlarged 'usefulness', but where 'usefulness' became for so many synonymous with petty, ill-directed benevolence, combined with tacit support of male authoritarianism and self-aggrandisement.

One other 'scrap', probably written in 1816 – the 'Plan of a Novel, according to hints from various quarters' – confirms that Jane Austen was still, at the time *Persuasion* was written, much influenced by burlesque, both for the pleasure she took in it and as a mode in which she could clarify her own ideas and the means by which they might be embodied in comedy of more scope than burlesque. The 'Plan' gives a burlesque account of a sentimental novel in which the heroine is to be:

a faultless character herself, perfectly good, with much tenderness & sentiment, & not the least Wit – very highly accomplished, understanding modern Languages & (generally speaking) everything that the most accomplished young Women learn, but particularly excellent in Music – her favourite pursuit – & playing equally well on the Piano Forte & Harp – singing in the first style. Her person quite beautiful – dark eyes and plump cheeks.

This faultless creature is to be the devoted daughter of an excellent father, 'without the smallest drawback or peculiarity to prevent his being the most delightful companion to his Daughter from one year's end to the other'. She is to be 'often carried away by the anti-hero, but always rescued by her Father or the Hero', who is 'all perfection of course'. Her friendship is to be sought by 'a young Woman in the same Neighbourhood, of Talents & Shrewdness, with light eyes & a fair skin, but having a considerable degree of Wit, Heroine shall shrink from the acquaintance' (*Minor Works*, pp. 428–30).

We have only to read this to see how it bears on the conception and presentation of Anne Elliot. True, she seems almost too perfect for an Austen heroine, but careful distinctions, separating her from the sentimental ideal, are made. Although she is not witty in the striking way that Elizabeth Bennet and Emma are, there are nice moments when she shows a quick, critical mind and sharpness of language. For instance, when Mr Elliot asks her to translate a song from the Italian, she says:

'This is nearly the sense, or rather the meaning of the words, for certainly the sense of an Italian love-song must not be talked of, – but it is as nearly the meaning as I can give; for I do not pretend to understand the language. I am a very poor Italian scholar.' (p. 186)

Mr Elliot makes this the excuse for gallant over-praise of her Italian, to which she replies with a critical self-appraisal that ought to shame him into a more honest style: 'I will not oppose such kind politeness; but I should be sorry to be examined by a real proficient.' Although Anne enjoys listening to music she does not play, and shows the same freedom from real or affected musicality which characterises all the Austen heroines, 'she had never liked a concert better, at least during the first act'. The second 'hour of pleasure or of penance . . . was to give delight or the gapes, as real or affected taste for it prevailed. To Anne it chiefly wore the prospect of agitation.' This is because she can't concentrate on the music, being too concerned about speaking to Captain Wentworth. She shifts herself down the bench to make herself more accessible, reflecting that her conduct bears comparison with the inimitable (and ridiculous) Miss Larolles in Fanny Burney's *Cecilia*. Without denying musical taste or appreciation to her, Austen has managed to distance her from the ideal heroine of sensibility, both by the ease with which she is distracted from music when something more pressing is in view, and by her self-conscious awareness that her own small attempt at engineering contact with Wentworth is not entirely becoming – or would not be in a true heroine of sensibility.

Anne's father, far from being an excellent man and a satisfying companion, is a snobbish fool. Wentworth's conduct and constancy fall far short of perfection. The anti-hero, Mr Elliot, although oily and faulty, is not a straightforward picture of unlightened wicked-ness and, although Anne has no light-skinned, blue-eyed female friend, she values the company and regard of Lady Russell, Mrs Smith and Mrs Croft, all of whom are capable of sharp, intelligent utterance, not to mention Nurse Rooke, whose shrewdness is seen as a recommendation.

A number of critics have seen in Anne Elliot a heroine close enough to the sentimental model to feel that Jane Austen had changed fundamentally in her view of Romanticism. But the truth is that she had learned to make more subtle distinctions, enabling her to submit the aspects of Romanticism which she disliked most to a stronger, more penetrating criticism.[6]

Postscript: Jane Austen and the Critical Tradition

If it is true that Jane Austen's 'moral interest' – which F. R. Leavis spoke of as 'the principle of organisation and the principle of development in her work' – was that of a feminist of a particular historical period, and of a particular phase in the development of English fiction, how has it come about that so little attention has been paid to it?

In the first place, the history of feminist ideas and their relation to literature and politics before the late nineteenth century, when women's suffrage became an active political issue, has yet to be written. Indeed, until 1980, when Susan Moller Okin published *Women in Western Political Thought*, it was not possible to refer students to a clear modern account of Rousseau's ideas about women and their education, or the political implication of these ideas. Until the advent of women's publishing houses and the growth of women's studies, the history of ideas and the history of literature were not written in such a way as to reveal the connection between feminist thinkers and the feminist tradition of fiction in the eighteenth century. Lacking a proper history of eighteenth-century feminist thought, it has not been easy to see why those women who set the greatest store upon the equality of the two sexes were alienated, in whole or in part, from the Romantic Movement. Jane Austen's anti-Romanticism, which is a mark of her clear understanding of contemporary conflict on the feminist issue, is frequently set down as evidence of her disengagement from the important and controversial currents of thought and literature in her time.

Besides this general difficulty, there is also the particular difficulty associated with the period at which the Austen novels were first published. They appeared, belatedly, in the aftermath of the anti-feminist reaction which followed Mary Wollstonecraft's death, a time when open discussion of feminist ideas, however unexceptionable they might seem to modern readers, was almost impossible. Jane Austen's use of irony, which some critics have seen as personally defensive, should be seen in this context for, while it protected her from personal attack, it also enabled her to say what was unsayable in public otherwise. In *Northanger Abbey* she had openly criticised sexist bias in literary works and in reviewers, and the novel had been suppressed by the publishing house to which she had sold it. The avoidance thereafter of any open statement of a similar kind is not surprising. Jane Austen learned to tell the truth though a riddling irony which 'dull elves' might misread, but which she hoped readers of sense and ingenuity would not. However, as it turned out, she soon began to acquire something of a literary reputation among those who either did not understand, or did not think it right to show too much understanding of, the moral riddles posed in her works.

It is one of the ironies of literary history that it should have been Scott who became Jane Austen's presenter to later generations, for, despite his praise of the 'spirit and originality' of her sketches from common life, he was, by the time he wrote the review of *Emma*, the most influential British novelist of the school to which she was opposed. The review, with its failure to mention *Mansfield Park* (though not *Sense and Sensibility* and *Pride and Prejudice*), and its trivialising remarks about the rejection of 'Cupid, king of gods and men' and 'authors of moral fiction who couple Cupid indivisibly with calculating prudence', not only fails to do justice to the Austen novels, but shows Scott's hostility to the moral point of view which they embody. Yet what, after all, could Scott have said about Austen's treatment of Kotzebue, without discussing the character of her objection to him and perhaps referring to Mary Wollstonecraft? Perhaps his avoiding mentioning it at all was tactful, for John Murray, the publisher who had asked him to 'dash off' a review of *Emma*, saying that it 'wants incident and romance', would have been likely to have pointed out that it was to be dedicated to the Prince Regent, and that any direct mention of the feminist nature of the author's anti-Romanticism, or her strictures on the double standard of sexual morality, would be inopportune.

Whatever Scott's motives were in ignoring *Mansfield Park*, it is clear that his doing so rankled with its author, who would hardly have chosen Scott to introduce her work to posterity. But such is Scott's prestige that, whenever a modern critic seeks to show that Austen's merits did not pass quite unnoticed in her lifetime, it is his review that is first called in evidence. This would not matter if the underlying hostility between Scott and Austen with regard to feminism and the Romantic Movement were better understood but, as it is, Scott's assessment of Austen is usually treated as more disinterested and sympathetic than it really is.

Richard Whately who, as a young man of twenty-four, wrote the only other important contemporary essay on Austen, is seen by B. C. Southam as following in Scott's footsteps, but there are important differences between them. Whately understood and sympathised with the moral interest he perceived in the six novels, saw how *Mansfield Park* belonged with the rest, and placed a high valuation upon it. He shows that he understood Austen's point of view as a feminist moralist and did not regard it as incompatible with enlightened Christian faith. As Southam says: 'Whately's Jane Austen is fundamentally a serious writer whose morality and values are communicated implicitly, wholly in terms of her fiction.' His estimation of her work is higher than Scott's and more intelligent, yet it is often assimilated to his as though there were no significant distinctions.

The belief that Scott was an unbiased admirer of Austen and the assumption that she was an uncritical admirer of his – an assumption not borne out by her letters, nor her association of him with Lord Byron in *Persuasion* – has done much to obscure the polemical character of her anti-Romanticism and its feminist point. Scott enjoyed a European reputation in the nineteenth century and, in the twentieth, has been seen by Lukacs as bringing a new, historicised awareness to the writing of fiction. Beside him, Jane Austen appears in the European account of literary history as a minor, provincial figure, of no particular importance in the development of political ideas or politicised consciousness through fiction. Scott's historicised, essentially Romantic, treatment of nationalism has been sympathetically understood by Marxist critics, but Jane Austen's bourgeois feminism has not. Marxist-feminist criticism has tended to take its literary history from the European account and, alienated by Austen's concentration upon women of the middle class and not connecting it with Wollstonecraft's similar concentration in *Vindication*, has not seen enough about its historical importance. Romanticism has too often been seen as inherently revolutionary, its tendency to anti-feminism and to the assimilation of the artist to the heroic aristocrat insufficiently considered. Auden's perception of what is radical in her work and in her stance as novelist deserves to be remembered:

> You could not shock her more than she shocks me;
>   Beside her Joyce seems innocent as grass.
> It makes me uncomfortable to see
>   An English spinster of the middle-class
>   Describe the amorous effects of 'brass',

Reveal so frankly and with such sobriety
The economic basis of society. (*Letter to Lord Byron*, 1936)

The European account of literary history places Scott as the most important British novelist, and Madame de Staël as the major woman writer of the time. Madame de Staël has not only the advantage of belonging with the Romantic Movement, but also of having supported the French Revolution. Like Scott, she enjoyed a European reputation in her lifetime and remains an important historical figure even though she is no longer regarded as a major novelist. Madame de Staël was much admired by English and American women writers of the mid-nineteenth century. As Cora Kaplan shows, *Corinne* was of great importance to both Elizabeth Barrett Browning and to Emily Dickinson.[1] As Ellen Moers shows, it exerted a powerful influence upon literary women from Felicia Hemans to George Eliot, from Harriet Beecher Stowe and Margaret Fuller to Kate Chopin.[2] Since American feminist critics have tended to take the mid-nineteenth century as the focal point of their account of women's literary history, they have paid more attention to the Victorian admiration of de Staël than to the criticism made of her by contemporary Englishwomen, particularly Mary Wollstonecraft. It has been assumed that Jane Austen admired *Corinne*, but the assumption is without foundation and, since her attitude was, in fact, much closer to Wollstonecraft's than to Elizabeth Barrett Browning's, and since this disagreement is important to a proper understanding of a major difference between Austen and the mid-century women novelists, it needs detailed examination.

As the author of *De l'Allemagne* (published in the year Jane Austen finished *Mansfield Park*) Madame de Staël was much admired by Romantic Germanists, as well as for *Corinne*. A great divide opened up between those literary women who knew and understood with sympathy why Mary Wollstonecraft had attacked de Staël and those who did not. To a later generation Corinne was an inspirational figure; to an earlier, she and her author were among those who had 'rendered women objects of pity, bordering on contempt'.

Germaine de Staël was seven years younger than Mary Wollstonecraft, nine years older than Jane Austen. Like Wollstonecraft, she was on the revolutionary side in France, but she was not a feminist. Unlike Wollstonecraft, she did not advocate the enfranchisement of women under the revolutionary constitution, and she accepted Rousseau's beliefs about what was natural and proper to the two sexes as neither Wollstonecraft nor Austen did. G. E. Gwynne says that de Staël abandoned the cause of women in general in favour of the special emancipation of 'women of genius':

De plus en plus, Madame de Staël s'occupe de la position des 'femmes de génie' dans la société, et abandonne la cause des femmes en général. Ce thème est traité surtout dans ses deux romans *Delphine* et *Corinne*. Mme. de Staël se plaint amèrement du sort des 'femmes supérieures', détestées par les hommes, calomniées par le public, et incapables de se justifier.[3]

In *Corinne*, Madame de Staël had projected herself into fiction. As Ellen Moers points out

For her contemporaries, the single name denoted them both, for after the publication of the novel in 1807 Mme. de Staël was everywhere known as Corinne.[4]

Corinne, when she appears in public to deliver her 'improvisations', is 'an inspired priestess consecrating herself with joy to the worship of genius'. She receives in ample measure the applause of distinguished literary men, a concourse of 'Roman poets' assembling to read aloud sonnets and odes in her honour. We are told that 'all praised her to the skies' and that this praise, authenticated by literary men of genius, was couched in such terms as might apply to all women 'conspicuous for literary gifts from the time of Sappho to our own days', containing 'a pretty blending of images and allusions to goddesses'.[5]

But in Jane Austen's time the myth of Corinne did not take hold of women who believed that an improvement in the status of their sex depended primarily upon their being shown to possess rational powers of mind. To Mary Wollstonecraft, Madame de Staël's acceptance of Rousseau's view that men and women were different in their moral nature and function made her an enemy of female improvement and emancipation. Calling her 'a rhapsodist', Wollstonecraft objected to the idea that it did not matter if Man's reason 'disputes with them [women], the empire, when his heart is so devotedly theirs'. She is firm: 'It is not empire – but equality, that they should contend for.' To Jane Austen, *Corinne* must have raised, and in a new and more objectionable form, the old, sexist aspects of the 'Sense and Sensibility' question. The 'femme de génie', revelling (however improbably) in an assemblage of Italian poets praising her as a 'goddess', was but the pretty middle-class girl's being flattered as 'an angel' writ large. Neither did women of sense any good at all. To Austen, who resolutely refused to put the most extraordinary side of herself – the ability to write novels – into her heroines, it cannot have been pleasant to see *Corinne* and its author made the Queen of

Romantic fiction. It is recorded that when one of Austen's novels (probably *Pride and Prejudice*) was drawn to Madame de Staël's notice in 1813, she pronounced it 'vulgaire'.[6] We need not, I think, doubt that Austen thought *Corinne* inflated and self-indulgent, bearing, like Sir Samuel Egerton Brydges' *Fitz-Albini*, too much 'internal evidence of its author'.[7]

What, then, is the evidence that Jane Austen admired Madame de Staël? It is based on two references, one in a letter written in 1808, the other in Henry Austen's revised *Biographical Notice* of 1833. To take the latter first: Henry Austen added to his earlier (1818) account of his sister a report of her refusal to meet Madame de Staël in 1813. He adduces it in proof of his statement that 'in public she turned away from any allusion to her character of an authoress', following on his assurance that 'in the bosom of her family' she was 'thankful for praise, open to remark, and submissive of criticism'. This then follows:

In proof of this, the following circumstance, *otherwise unimportant*, is stated. Miss Austen was on a visit to London soon after the publication of *Mansfield Park*: a nobleman, personally unknown to her, but who had good reasons for considering her to be the authoress of that work, was desirous of her joining a literary circle at his house. He communicated his wish in the politest manner, adding what his Lordship doubtless thought would be an irresistible inducement, that the celebrated Madame de Staël would be of the party. Miss Austen immediately declined the invitation. To her truly delicate mind such a display would have given pain instead of pleasure. (my italics)

In the surviving letters there is but one reference to Madame de Staël – an allusion to *Corinne* – which Ellen Moers thought it difficult to interpret as it is clearly ironic. This letter was written in 1808, the year after *Corinne* was published. Jane Austen was in Southampton with her mother and had spent an evening at 'the boarding-house' where she had met an assortment of new acquaintances, including a stone-deaf elderly gentleman called Mr Fitzhugh. She tells Cassandra:

He has lived in that house more than twenty years, and poor man! is so totally deaf that they say he could not hear a cannon, were it fired close to him; having no cannon at hand to make the experiment, I took it for granted, and talked to him a little with my fingers, which was funny enough. I recommend him to read *Corinna*. (*Letters*, p. 242)

We may, I think, be sure that, whatever this means, it does not mean that Jane Austen actually recommended the poor gentleman to read *Corinne* for, even if her knowledge of finger-language were equal to such a recommendation, it is inconceivable that she should have teased the old man in such a way. The allusion was clearly designed to convey some sort of joke to her sister, and it is not too difficult to see what it was. In Book the fifteenth, chapter VII, Corinne, in Venice with her lover Lord Oswald Nelvil (sic), receives a premonition of her parting from him, and perhaps from this world altogether, when she hears a cannon fired thrice across the lagoon. A gondolier explains to her that the firing of the cannon signifies:

the moment when a religieuse takes the veil in one of our convents in the midst of the sea. Our custom is for a girl, at the moment she pronounces her sacred vows, to cast behind her the bouquet of flowers that she has carried during the ceremony, as a sign that she renounces the world, and a cannon is fired to announce the sacred moment.

Jane Austen, we need not doubt, conveyed to Mr Fitzhugh only such things as kindness and compassion, limited by the difficulty of communicating with him at all, made proper. To Cassandra, however, she allows herself to make a joke about *Corinne*, evidently knowing that her sister will connect Mr Fitzhugh's inability to hear 'a cannon fired close to him' with a passage in Madame de Staël which it seems likely had provoked irreverent laughter in both sisters.

On this evidence alone, and there is no other, it is clear that the idea that Jane Austen admired Madame de Staël and *Corinne* is baseless, and it is hard not to convict Henry Austen of a little sleight-of-hand in using his sister's refusal to meet her as confirmation of her retiring, feminine character. Had he been able to say that she had refused to meet Fanny Burney, Maria Edgeworth or Crabbe, this might indeed have suggested that she was too timid to meet literary notables whom she admired, but her declining an invitation to appear in the wake of Madame de Staël carries no such clear significance.

In 1813, the twenty year old Mary Russell Mitford also recorded her reaction to the progress of 'Corinne'. Mary Mitford was twelve years younger than Jane Austen (nearly twenty years younger than de Staël) and, at this time, when literary London (including the well established and by now conservative Romantic poets, like Southey, Coleridge and Scott) was flocking to do honour to the author of *De l'Allemagne,* she had not yet published anything. But young Miss Mitford already had literary ambitions which were to be fulfilled in the now much neglected *Our Village*. Her youthful gossip (which she admits to be unreliable) about Jane Austen has often been quoted,[8] but her praise of *Pride and Prejudice* as 'a precious gem' and her later defence of Mary Wollstonecraft as one who, 'married or not married wrote like a modest woman – was a modest woman', is less well quoted.[9] Mary Mitford came from the same social milieu as Jane Austen and was educated at the same rather remarkable school in Reading; her remarks on *Corinne* and Madame de Staël's London triumph are, therefore, worth attention. She too received an invitation to attend a literary gathering in her honour, and she too declined. Writing to her friend, Sir William Elford, she says

to tell the truth I am not very much her [Madame de Staël's] admirer. Her learned works are too deep and too shallow; her morality seems to me of a nature to *demoralise* the world; and her novels want that likeness to nature in which the beauty of fiction consists. To counterbalance all this, she has nothing but eloquence – the eloquence both of passion and of style; and of this she has certainly a great deal, almost as much perhaps as Rousseau, whom she greatly resembles in talents and singularity.[10]

In the same letter she censures *Corinne*, and tells a disparaging anecdote about it which bears a faint resemblance to Austen's Fitzhugh joke, since it is about an out-of-touch, elderly gentleman who made an amusing *faux pas* about 'Corinne's' sexual morals, in the belief that a reference had been made to Corinna, the Greek poet, and not to Madame de Staël. The young Miss Mitford would clearly have understood more than later literary women did about Jane Austen's attitudes and 'moral interest', for she was old enough to know how the battle-lines of the Feminist Controversy of her childhood had been drawn up, and she was still capable of defending them thirty years later when she contrasted de Staël's 'miserable bombast' in French with Mary Wollstonecraft's 'pure and perfect style' in English.[11]

The unfounded belief that Jane Austen admired Madame de Staël, yet refused to meet her, has proved misleading in more ways than one. It helped to lend substance to the idea of Austen as exceptionally retiring; it obscured her active interest in an important literary conflict of her own time; and it made it more difficult to understand the estrangement of the mid-century women novelists, particularly Charlotte Brontë and George Eliot, from her work. To a generation which admired Madame de Staël and saw her as the predecessor of George Sand, Jane Austen's pointed avoidance of 'genius', both in her presentation of herself as narrator and in her heroines, could not be sympathetic. And, since by the 1840s Mary Wollstonecraft's works had become difficult to obtain – George Eliot seems not to have known that she had written novels[12] – it was no longer intelligible as a mark of feminist anti-Romanticism. The most gifted women novelists of the mid-century – Emily and Charlotte Brontë and George Eliot – were all, in different ways, critical of the romanticisation of sexual relationships, and of heroines, but they had come to see themselves as 'femmes de génie' and this, in itself, made a barrier between them and Jane Austen, who did not. Henry Austen's 1833 treatment of his sister's declining to meet Madame de Staël, together with his unplaced, and therefore misleading, quotation of the 'little bit of ivory' letter,[13] can only have added to the alienation of the later English women novelists from the predecessor to whom, despite their coolness about her, they owed much.[14] Women as literary artists had become detached from feminism as a political issue, and, whereas the odd Miss Harriet Martineau, born in 1802, re-read all the Austen novels before starting on *Deerbrook* (1839) and recorded that she had done so,[15] the major women novelists acknowledged no important debt to '*Pride and Prejudice* &'. But Harriet Martineau had no pretensions as a woman of genius and she, at the age of sixty-four, supported J. S. Mill's 1866 petition for female suffrage, whereas George Eliot, born in 1819, did not.

The difficult problem of how the woman literary artist ought to see herself as novelist and literary critic, and as feminist, re-emerged in the early twentieth century with Virginia Woolf. And, among the many tensions which she tried to resolve in thinking about her own position and that of the women novelists of earlier times, Woolf was well aware of conflicts between her conception of herself as an androgynous artist and her feeling that, as a woman, she could not avoid some degree of commitment to the Women's Movement, as a political cause primarily concerned not with women of literary genius, but with ordinary women in their quotidian life. Woolf, with her own Modernist conception of the literary artist, and her understandable ignorance of former feminist controversy, made Austen her chief exemplar of the individual female talent untrammelled by the difficulties which she herself experienced.

In *A Room of One's Own*, which rightly takes the status of a classic critical essay for feminist criticism, Virginia Woolf sees Austen as the well nigh miraculous example of the female artist of androgynous mind, whose art transcends such irritations as the author, as a woman, must have experienced. This may not be so far wrong, but it ignores everything which connects Jane Austen with the feminist thinking of the Enlightenment, and with her awareness of the novel itself as a species of writing in which moral and religious questions, germane to the feminism of her time, had to be resolved in the art of a self-conscious female novelist. Virginia Woolf seeing, as the mid-nineteenth-century women novelists could not, that Austen is a major novelist, could still not relate her literary achievement to the growth in the eighteenth century of the novel as a form in which the women novelist addressed herself to women and men, while the poet was 'a man speaking to men'. In *A Room of One's Own*, Woolf's treatment of Austen is completely unpatronising, although she gives more credence than is deserved to the family biography which represented the author of '*Pride and Prejudice* &' as for ever hiding her manuscripts under bits of blotting paper, or on the *qui vive* for a creaking door. But, by making her something of a miracle, she effectively isolates her from her real roots, and in the earlier *Common Reader* essay of 1922, more often quoted in the modern critical literature, she made a serious blunder, possibly connected with the de Staël story. She speculated with a Bloomsburyite confidence in London dinner parties, as a means of enlarging the mind, upon how Jane Austen might have developed had she, after 1813, 'dined out, met famous people, made new friends, read, travelled, and carried back to the quiet country cottage a hoard of observations to feast upon at leisure'.[16] This is important not so much for what Woolf herself said, though it shows ignorance of Austen's involvement in the literary and political currents of her time, but for what later critics have made of it. Virginia Woolf avoids all mention of Madame de Staël in relation to Austen, but her *Common Reader* essay allowed Angus Wilson to raise the old spectre again, and to give it a new erroneous meaning.

Wilson, in his 'Neighbourhood of Tombuctoo' essay, convicts Jane Austen of a characteristically English, middle-class philistinism, which he associates with Virginia Woolf's speculations about how she might have developed had she lived long enough to enjoy her literary success. He tells us that: 'Her refusal to meet Madame de Staël is perhaps insufficient evidence to tell us how she would have reacted to further overtures from literary society, but it is not promising.'[17] However, Wilson takes no notice at all of the 'said he' or 'said she' of the Austen novels, and dismisses the central moral issue of *Emma* – the relationship between the young 'handsome, clever and rich' heroine, and the middle-aged, not handsome, not clever and not rich Miss Bates, the daughter of a former incumbent of the Highbury rectory, now occupied by Mr Elton and the former Miss Augusta Hawkins with her probably ill-gotten Bristol fortune. Treating Emma as an 'honorary man', as Madame de Staël treated Corinne, he finds Austen's insistence that Emma is unfit for adult social responsibilities until she learns to estimate her obligations to Miss Bates aright 'a depressing compromise'. But then he sees Miss

Bates only as 'a foolish spinster in straightened circumstances', whereas Austen represents her as both absurd and worthy of loving respect, the neighbour through whom her heroine's capacity for right judgement and decent social response is tested and in the end found not far from the true.

Jane Austen's high standing in trans-Atlantic criticism was established in the late 1940s and 1950s, a period in which feminist criticism was unknown and when no one connected Jane Austen, as a moralist, with Mary Woolstonecraft. It is a period which is now seen, both by feminists and others, as markedly conservative in temper, and the fact that Austen was elevated to the status of major novelist at this time has invited suspicion on the part of critics of the Left. As early as 1963, Ian Watt, in the Introduction to his influential Twentieth Century Views' *Collection of Critical Essays* on Jane Austen, spoke of the contrast between 'the slightness of the matter and the authority of the manner' as constituting the 'enduring problem of Jane Austen criticism'.[18] Seeing her social and moral attitudes as 'traditional', and observing that it was in 'the new literary and political conservatism of the post war world' that she had been discovered to be a major novelist, he implied doubt about the value of her work and the inflation of her critical reputation. The belief that Jane Austen's moral outlook was uncritically orthodox alienated her both from the new feminist critics of the 1970s and from others who refused to accept a total divorce between critical and political judgement. In 1975 Marilyn Butler argued a new case: Jane Austen's acceptance of the 'orthodox' views of the English moralists was not neutral; it was a sign of her commitment to Burke and political reaction.[19] I believe this view to be mistaken because it fails to take account of the extent to which Wollstonecraft in *Vindication*, and the whole line of English feminism from Astell to Austen, relies upon rationalist eighteenth-century argument about ethics, and uses it to promote the idea that women are accountable beings of the same kind as men. Marilyn Butler's view not only ignores this but, having done so, runs into intractable difficulties about Jane Austen's command of her art as a novelist. The three-volume structure of *Mansfield Park* and *Emma*, which it must be supposed Austen authorised, becomes unintelligible and, more seriously, Jane Austen's most important innovation in control of narrative technique appears unconnected with her moral interest.

According to Butler, having discovered how to use the 'indirect free style', Austen found it an embarrassment because it did not fit the moral purpose attributed to her. She says of *Emma*:

Although so much of the action takes place in the inner life, the theme of the novel is scepticism about the qualities that make it up – intuition, imagination, original insight.[20]

Thus, the argument runs, Austen developed the means of presenting the non-rational aspects of the inner life of individuals but, because she distrusted them, she found she had invented a technique she did not want. If this were true it would be quite extraordinary, for it can seldom be the case that a major artist wastes his, or her, time on the difficult development of new ways of representation, without believing that they are necessary to the overall intention of the art in question. I do not believe it was so in Jane Austen's case. The difficulty arises because rational reflection is here excluded from the inner life, although that aspect of a woman's inner life was of particular interest to Austen. Dr Butler says that, in Jane Austen's day:

the very form of the novel prompted an enquiry of central importance and urgency: what was the moral nature of *the individual*, and what was *his* true role in society. The *novelist* who evaded, or simply did not notice that *he* was called upon to put the question was the true artistic cripple. (my italics)[21]

Here the customary use of the generic 'his' and 'he' obscures the argument, for it obliterates the sex of 'the novelist' in question and of 'the individuals' in whose moral nature and social role *she* was primarily interested. Austen is found to belong to a class of 'artistic cripples' because her female identity and her concern with the moral status of individual women is not given enough attention. Thus the most forward-looking element in her social morality remains obscure, while her art is estranged from her moral ideas.

Jane Austen was distrustful of 'imagination and original insight', especially when they came into conflict with her clear, rational and materialistic view of society, and even more when women were made, or made themselves, peculiarly their representatives, while men appropriated to themselves the sovereignty of reason. Since she took a comic artist's delight in mortal absurdity and self-delusion, no matter in which sex it appeared, and since she did not seek to make her heroines pictures of perfection, she does not make them entirely rational. On the contrary, they are often deceived by their own self-interested or self-aggrandising fantasies and, where their arguments are valid, the premises upon which they are based are often false. Austen often uses the 'indirect free style' to show us such things, laying bare to us the inner consciousness of her heroines when they are most in error, but she also uses it to show us that, for all their mistakes, they have the capacity for stringent rational reflection and it is through the exercise of this capacity that they learn to judge aright of their own conduct and that of other people, including those in higher places, carrying greater authority than themselves.

Through the 'indirect free style' a novelist may reveal the private thoughts of his or her characters and seek to engage the reader's sympathies with them, however greatly they offend public taste and public opinion. Austen uses it to show not only the intimate personal feelings of her heroines but their argumentative, hard-headed minds, and she needed such a technique because, in the age in which she lived, a young woman's ability to think rationally, to test general moral principles in the light of personal experience, and to apply them impartially to conduct and character within her own domestic circle, was likely to be the most private – because least acceptable – aspect of her mental life. A young woman's capacity for rational thought was not only suspect in itself but liable to be hedged about by all kinds of unstatable personal considerations. Confined as middle-class women were to a sphere in which 'personal relations' became their occupation in life, they were seldom free to draw general inferences from their own experience without, as Anne Elliot puts it, 'betraying a confidence, or in some respect saying what should not be said' (*Persuasion*, p. 234). Whereas a man's judgement of character and motive, as it affected individual conduct in 'public life', might be openly expressed and yet held free of personal animus or bias, this could rarely apply to women, whose sphere was so much more limited as scarcely to admit the possibility of the exercise of rational, principled, moral judgement, independent of personal interest. Anne Elliot, with the wisdom of comparative maturity, is able to define the problem with which women are faced, but Austen shows it also in her less mature heroines. For example, in *Mansfield Park*, Fanny Price's inability to communicate to her uncle her perfectly clear, well thought out objections to Crawford as a husband rests on clear, rational principles but remains incommunicable because she cannot make an open statement of the evidence on which she has formed her view of him:

Her ill opinion of him was founded chiefly on observations, which, for her cousins' sake, she could scarcely dare mention to their father. Maria and Julia – and especially Maria, were so closely implicated in Mr. Crawford's misconduct, that she could not give his character, such as she believed it, without betraying them. (p. 318)

Marilyn Butler's *Jane Austen and the War of Ideas* remains a most stimulating and informative contextual study, but her conception of *the* war does not make sufficient allowance for the many and varied battles which made it up. In a later book she has discussed the complex relationship between Romanticism in literature and revolutionary politics, showing that the two did not always cohere in the revolutionary and Napoleonic decades.[22] The Feminist Controversy was one skirmish in which this was particularly true and it is essential to appreciate it in considering the form and meaning of the Austen novels. It is also important, in considering the nineteenth-century reception of Austen, to bear in mind that this battle was lost and not re-fought for half a century.

F. R. Leavis's placing Jane Austen as inaugurator of *the* great tradition of nineteenth-century fiction of moral (social) concern also needs further consideration, for there are marked differences between her and those thought of by Leavis as her successors. Her moral interest was a feminist one, not shared by George Eliot, Henry James or Conrad. Her view of English society was not influenced by Carlyle, since she was dead before he had begun to exercise an influence, but there is reason to think that, unlike the later novelists whom Leavis thought of as seriously concerned with individual and social morals in the nineteenth century, she would not have admired Carlyle as they did. She would not have sympathised with his early Germanism, let alone the form it took later and, while she might have enjoyed some of his blasts against the more absurd features of 'Benthamism', her own ethics were essentially secular and utilitarian. She disliked the cash nexus as the basis for marriage and abhorred the financial calculations which set a dowry of so-many-thousand pounds as the purchasing price of a husband and an 'establishment', but she supposes that moral principles are reached through careful observation and through sensitive reflection in which head and heart co-operate. Morals are learnt, not given in flashes of inspired revelation, especially not from Great Men and hero-worshippers. Leavis thought that Jane Austen

in her indebtedness to others, provides an exceptionally illuminating study of the nature of originality, and she exemplifies beautifully the relations of 'the individual talent' to tradition . . . She not only makes tradition for those coming after, but her achievement has for us a retroactive effect.

Perhaps that is true, but how critical a point of view she brought to bear upon 'tradition' is only apparent if we consider her 'individual talent' in its collective, feminist context.

Notes

Page references to the novels of Jane Austen are to R. W. Chapman's *The Novels of Jane Austen*, Oxford, 1926, and to his *Minor Works*, Oxford, 1954. Page references to the letters are to *Jane Austen's Letters*, ed. R. W. Chapman, Oxford, 1952. Page references to Mary Wollstonecraft's *A Vindication of the Rights of Woman* are to the Penguin edition, ed. Miriam Kramnick, 1975.

Introduction

1. Mary Astell, Preface to *The Travels of an English Lady in Europe, Asia and Africa*, 1724; reproduced in *The Complete Letters of Lady Mary Wortley Montagu*, ed. Robert Halsband, Oxford, 1965, vol. 1, p. 466.
2. Ian Watt, *Jane Austen: A Collection of Critical Essays*, Englewood Cliffs, New Jersey, 1963, p. 2.
3. Marilyn Butler, *Jane Austen and the War of Ideas*, Oxford, 1975, p. 298.
4. ibid., p. 45.
5. Mary Wollstonecraft, *A Vindication of the Rights of Woman*, ch. 5, *passim*. See also, Susan Moller Okin, *Women in Western Political Thought*, part 3, 'Rousseau', London, 1980, *passim*.
6. Gilbert Ryle, 'Jane Austen and the Moralists', *Critical Essays on Jane Austen*, ed. B. C. Southam, London, 1968, p. 107.
7. *The Feminist Controversy in England, 1788–1810*, a collection of works in facsimile, ed. Gina Luria, New York, 1974.
8. ibid., Introduction.
9. *Vindication*, ch. 5, pp. 191–6.
10. 'Mansfield Park', from *The Opposing Self*, reprinted in *Jane Austen: A Collection of Critical Essays*, ed. Ian Watts, New Jersey, 1963, p. 125.
11. 'Emma and the Legend of Jane Austen', Introduction to the Riverside edn. of *Emma*, reproduced in *Emma: A Casebook*, ed. David Lodge, London, 1968, p. 154.

Part One

Introduction
1. *Oxford English Dictionary*, Supplement of 1972, ed. R. W. Birchfield,

gives the first instance of 'feminism' in the sense of 'Advocacy of the rights of woman (based on the theory of the equality of the sexes)', as of 1895, 'feminist' 1894.

Chapter 2

3. Doris Stenton, *The English Woman in History*, London 1957, pp. 220–1.
4. ibid., p. 234.
5. Elizabeth Carter was unmarried. 'Mrs' was a courtesy title sometimes given to mature spinsters of distinction.
6. Montagu Pennington, *Memoirs of the Life of Mrs. Elizabeth Carter*, London, 1807, pp. 20–1.
7. ibid., p. 303.
8. See note 20 below.
9. Claire Tomalin, *The Life and Death of Mary Wollstonecraft*, London, 1974, p. 57.
10. Ray Strachey, *The Cause*, 1928, reprinted Virago, London, 1978, p. 13.
11. Annette Meakin, *Hannah More: A Biographical Study*, London, 1911, pp. 312, 323–4.
12. Stenton, op. cit., pp. 308–9.
13. *History of England*, London, 1763, vol. 1, p. vii.

Chapter 3

14. William Roberts, *Memoirs of the Life and Correspondence of Mrs. Hannah More*, London, 1835, vol. 1, p. 169.
15. John A. Dussinger, *The Discourse of Mind in Eighteenth-Century Fiction*, The Hague, 1974, p. 131.
16. ibid., p. 133.
17. *Lives of the Poets*, Oxford Paperback Texts, 1971, ed. J. P. Hardy, p. 91.
18. T. C. Duncan Eaves and Ben D. Kimpel, *Samuel Richardson. A Biography*, Oxford, 1971, p. 121.
19. Bernard Harrison, *Henry Fielding's 'Tom Jones'. The Novelist as Moral Philosopher*, Sussex, 1975, p. 122.
20. *A Series of Letters between Mrs. Elizabeth Carter and Miss Catherine Talbot*, ed. Montagu Pennington, London, 1809, vol. 1, p. 161.
21. ibid., p. 297.
22. ibid., p. 298.
23. *Vindication*, p. 108.
24. *The Analogy of Religion*, 1736, ch. 5., Religious Tract Society edn, ed. Joseph Angus, p. 108.
25. Eaves and Kimpel, op. cit., p. 286.
26. ibid., pp. 294–5.
27. ibid., p. 233.
28. *Letters between Mrs. Elizabeth Carter and Miss Catherine Talbot*, vol. 1, p. 206.
29. Eaves and Kimpel, op. cit., p. 200.
30. ibid., p. 174.

31. ibid., p. 288.
32. ibid., p. 353.

Chapter 4

33. *The George Eliot Letters*, ed. Gordon S. Haight, New Haven, 1954–5, vol. I, p. 240.
34. ibid., vol. II, p. 65.
35. Eaves and Kimpel, op. cit., p. 371.
36. *Letters between Mrs. Elizabeth Carter and Miss Catherine Talbot*, vol. 1, p. 291.
37. ibid., pp. 246–7.
38. Brian Southam, Introduction to 'Sir Charles Grandison' by Jane Austen, Oxford, 1980, p. 22.
39. Introduction to *Sir Charles Grandison*, Oxford, 1972, p. xvlii.
40. C. Griffin-Wolff, *Samuel Richardson and the Eighteenth-Century Puritan Character*, Anchor, 1972, p. 191.
41. ibid., p. 191.
42. *Letters of Jane Austen*, ed. R. W. Chapman, Oxford, 1932, pp. 322, 344.
43. *Jane Austen's 'Sir Charles Grandison'*, ed. Brian Sontham, Oxford 1980, pp. 56, 149n.

Chapter 5

44. Frank W. Bradbrook, *Jane Austen and her Predecessors*, 1966, p. 90.
45. 'Jane Austen and the Feminist Tradition', *N.C.F..*, vol. XXVIII, 1973, p. 321.
46. ibid., Lloyd Brown, p. 338.
47. R. Brimley Johnson, *The Women Novelists*, London, 1918, p. 12.
48. *Mary and the Wrongs of Women*, eds James Kinsley and Gary Kelly, Oxford, 1976, p. 73.
49. *Letters for Literary Ladies*, London, 1795, pp. 53–4.
50. James Boaden, *Memoirs of Mrs. Inchbald*, London, 1833, vol. 2, p. 237.

Chapter 6

51. Claire Tomalin, *Life and Death of Mary Wollstonecraft*, p. 131.
52. *Letters on Education*, p. 210, quoted by Stenton, op. cit., p. 314.
53. *Carter-Talbot Letters*, vol. 2, pp. 260–1; Stenton, op. cit., p. 307.
54. J. M. Todd, Introduction to *An Historical and Moral View of the Origin and Progress of the French Revolution*, by Mary Wollstonecraft, Scholars Facsimiles and Reprints, New York, 1975.
55. *Women in Western Political Thought*, London, 1980, pp. 99–100.

Chapter 7

56. Tomalin, op. cit., p. 290.
57. Austen calls her 'good Mrs. West' (*Letters*, p. 466), but with a facetious

reference to her having 'collected so many hard words'. In another letter about contemporary novelists she says: 'I think I can be stout against anything written by Mrs. West. (*Letters*, p. 405.)

Part Two

Chapter 8

1. R. W. Chapman, *Jane Austen: Facts and Problems*, Oxford, 1948, p. 43.
2. See W. and R. A. Austen-Leigh, *Jane Austen, Her Life and Letters*, London, 1913, p. 98.
3. Jane Aiken Hodge, *The Double Life of Jane Austen*, London, 1972, p. 11.
4. Chapman, op. cit., p. 140.
5. *Northanger Abbey and Persuasion*, Oxford edn, p. 8.
6. The 'ivory' reference, known to every reader of Austen after 1818, occurs in a letter written on Jane Austen's fortieth birthday to her schoolboy nephew. Read in context it does not have the significance it is given in the Postscript to the *Biographical Notice*.
7. *A Defence of the Character and Conduct of the Late Mary Wollstonecraft Godwin, founded on the Principles of Nature and Reason as Applied to the Peculiar Circumstances of Her Case in a Series of Letters to a Lady*, London, James Wallis, 46 Paternoster Row, 1803, p. 148.
8. 'A Critical Theory of Jane Austen's Writings' (I), *Scrutiny*, 1944, reprinted in *A Selection from Scrutiny*, Cambridge, 1968, vol. 2, p. 67.
9. *The Common Reader*, 1925, reprinted in *A Collection of Critical Essays*, ed. Ian Watts, 1963, p. 23.

Chapter 9

10. V. J. Kite, *Libraries in Bath, 1618–1969* (thesis for Fellowship of the Library Association), 1949.

Chapter 10

11. See below, Part Three, p. 179.
12. See B. C. Southam, *Jane Austen's Literary Manuscripts*, Oxford, 1964, p. 53.
13. Ch. 23.

Chapter 11

14. See *Jane Austen: The Critical Heritage*, ed. B. C. Southam, London, 1968, pp. 68–9.

Part Three

Chapter 12

1. Eric Auerbach, *Mimesis*, Princeton, 1953, p. 489.
2. Lloyd W. Brown, 'The Comic Conclusions of Jane Austen's Novels', *P.M.L.A.*, no. 84, 1969, *passim*.
3. '*Emma* and the Legend of Jane Austen', Introduction to the Riverside edn of *Emma*, reprinted in *Emma: A Casebook*, ed. David Lodge, London, 1968, p. 154.
4. 'Regulated Hatred: An Aspect of the Work of Jane Austen', *Scrutiny*, VIII, 1940.
5. Wollstonecraft, *Vindication*, p. 139.
6. 'Jane Austen and the Moralists', *Critical Essays*, p. 117.
7. E. H. Gombrich, *Art and Illusion*, London, 1960, p. 29.
8. ibid., p. 155.

Chapter 16

9. Introduction to *Neue Schauspiele*, quoted by L. F. Thompson, *Kotzebue, A Survey of His Progress in England and France*, Paris, 1928, p. 47.
10. ibid., p. 55.
11. Quoted by William Reitzel, '*Mansfield Park* and *Lovers' Vows*', *R.E.S.*, vol. 9, no. 36, October 1933, p. 453.
12. Thompson, op. cit., p. 103.
13. *Bath Herald and Register*, 29 June 1799, quoted by Jean Freeman, *Jane Austen in Bath*, 1969, p. 15.

Part Four

Chapter 17

1. '*Mansfield Park*', Watts, p. 125.
2. *The Parish Register: Marriages*.
3. *Critical Heritage*, ed. B. C. Southam, p. 138.
4. '*Mansfield Park* and Kotzebue's *Lovers' Vows*', *M.L.R.*, XXVIII, 1933, p. 326.
5. ibid., p. 454.
6. *Lectures*, 1818.
7. See George Odell, *Shakespeare from Betterton to Irving*, New York, 1920, I, pp. 425–7.
8. Final chapter.
9. ibid.
10. *Life of Johnson*, ed. J. W. Croker, London, 1876, p. 562.
11. 'The Subjection of Women' in *John Stuart Mill: Three Essays*, ed. R. Wollheim, p. 541.
12. C. Griffin-Wolff, *Samuel Richardson and the Eighteenth-Century Puritan Character*, Anchor, 1972, p. 191.

Chapter 18
1. R. W. Chapman, *Jane Austen*: Oxford, 1948, p. 201.
2. *The Heroine*, ed. Michael Sadleir, London, 1927, p. 40.
3. See Arnold Kettle, 'Jane Austen: *Emma*' in *An Introduction to the English Novel*, reprinted in *Emma: A Casebook*, ed. David Lodge, pp. 100–2.
4. *The Heroine*, p. 228.
5. *Biographical Notice*.
6. 'A Critical Theory of Jane Austen's Writings' (I), *Scrutiny*, vol. X, 1941.
7. Chapman, op. cit., p. 49.

Chapter 19
1. See *Critical Heritage*, p. 84.
2. C. V. Clinton-Baddeley, *The Burlesque Tradition in the English Theatre after 1660*, London, 1952, p. 98.
3. *Jane Austen's Literary Manuscripts*, Oxford, 1964, pp. 86–99.
4. 'O Brave New World: Evolution and Revolution in *Persuasion*', *E.L.H.*, 39, 1972, pp. 122–4.
5. 'The Neighbourhood of Tombuctoo: Conflict in Jane Austen's Novels', in *Critical Essays*, ed. B. C. Southam, p. 196.
6. See Nina Auerbach, 'Jane Austen and Romantic Imprisonments' in *Jane Austen in a Social Context*, ed. David Monaghan, London, 1981.

Postscript

1. Introduction to *Aurora Leigh*, p. 11.
2. Ellen Moers, *Literary Women*, London, 1978, p. 176.
3. *Madame de Staël et la revolution française*, pp. 178–9. 'Madame de Staël is increasingly concerned with the position of 'women of genius' in society, and abandons the cause of women in general. This theme is explored especially in two novels, *Delphine* and *Corinne*. Mme de Staël complains bitterly of the fate of 'superior women', hated by men, ridiculed by the public, and unable to vindicate themselves.'
4. *Literary Women*, p. 177.
5. Wollstonecraft, *Vindication*, ch. 5, section IV.
6. *Memoirs of Sir James Mackintosh*, 1835, quoted in B. C. Southam, *The Critical Heritage*, p. 110.
7. *Letters*, p. 322.
8. *Life and Letters of Mary Russell Mitford*, ed. A. G. l'Estrange, London, 1870, vol. I, pp. 305–6.
9. ibid., vol. III, p. 294.
10. ibid., vol. I, p. 235.
11. ibid., vol. III, p. 294.
12. Leader article on 'Margaret Fuller and Mary Wollstonecraft', October 1855, Haight, *Essays*, p. 201.
13. See note 6, Part Two, chapter 8, above.
14. See *Critical Heritage*, pp. 20–8, 160–1, 140.

15. R. K. Webb, *Harriet Martineau: A Radical Victorian*, London, 1960, p. 184.
16. *The Common Reader*, reprinted in Ian Watts' *Collection of Critical Essays*, p. 23.
17. *Critical Essays*, ed. B. C. Southam, 1968, p. 184.
18. Ian Watts, Introduction, *Collection of Critical Essays*, p. 12.
19. Marilyn Butler, *Jane Austen and the War of Ideas*, Oxford, 1975, *passim*.
20. ibid., p. 273.
21. ibid., p. 298.
22. *Romantics, Rebels and Reaction: English Literature and its Background*, Oxford, 1981.

Index